HER VOICE WILL BE ON THE SIDE OF RIGHT

AMERICAN ABOLITIONISM AND ANTISLAVERY
John David Smith, series editor

The Imperfect Revolution: Anthony Burns and the Landscape of Race in Antebellum America
GORDON S. BARKER

A Self-Evident Lie: Southern Slavery and the Threat to American Freedom
JEREMY J. TEWELL

Denmark Vesey's Revolt: The Slave Plot That Lit a Fuse to Fort Sumter
JOHN LOFTON   NEW INTRODUCTION BY PETER C. HOFFER

To Plead Our Own Cause: African Americans in Massachusetts and the Making of the Antislavery Movement
CHRISTOPHER CAMERON

African Canadians in Union Blue: Volunteering for the Cause in the Civil War
RICHARD M. REID

One Nation Divided by Slavery: Remembering the American Revolution While Marching toward the Civil War
MICHAEL F. CONLIN

Her Voice Will Be on the Side of Right: Gender and Power in Women's Antebellum Antislavery Fiction
HOLLY M. KENT

Her Voice Will Be on the Side of Right

Gender and Power in Women's Antebellum Antislavery Fiction

HOLLY M. KENT

THE KENT STATE UNIVERSITY PRESS
Kent, Ohio

© 2017 by The Kent State University Press, Kent, Ohio 44242
ALL RIGHTS RESERVED
Library of Congress Catalog Card Number 2017016131
ISBN 978-1-60635-317-2
Manufactured in the United States of America

LIBRARY OF CONGRESS CATALOGING-IN-PUBLICATION DATA
Names: Kent, Holly M., 1981- author.
Title: Her voice will be on the side of right : gender and power in women's antebellum antislavery fiction / Holly M. Kent.
Description: Kent, Ohio : The Kent State University Press, 2017. | Series: American abolitionism and antislavery | Includes bibliographical references and index.
Identifiers: LCCN 2017016131 | ISBN 9781606353172 (hardcover : alk. paper) | ISBN 9781631012778 (epdf)
Subjects: LCSH: American fiction--Women authors--History and criticism. | American fiction--19th century--History and criticism. | Antislavery movements in literature. | Slavery in literature. | Power (Social sciences) in literature. | Sex role in literature.
Classification: LCC PS374.W6 K55 2017 | DDC 813/.3093552--dc23
LC record available at https://lccn.loc.gov/2017016131

21 20 19 18 17   5 4 3 2 1

To my parents,

NANCY KENT *and* DOUGLAS KENT

who always knew that I could

Contents

Acknowledgments ix

Introduction: "How a Woman Touches the World's Heart": Women and Antislavery Fiction in the Antebellum Era 1

1 "Her Heart Was Touched with the Wrongs of the Injured Ones": The Emergence of Women's Antislavery Fiction, 1821-1832 17

2 "An Influence Comparatively Silent, but Deep, and Strong, and Irresistible": Women's Literature and the Rise of Radical Abolitionism, 1831-1839 41

3 "They Did Not Relinquish Freedom without a Struggle": Violence, Empowerment, and Moral Suasion, 1839-1851 75

4 "We Women Will Set All Things Right": Moral Suasion and Political Empowerment, 1851-1861 113

Conclusion: "The Duty of Woman in Aiding in Extending This Influence of Letters" 147

Notes 155

Bibliography 181

Index 197

Acknowledgments

When I was a junior in college, I had the remarkable (and totally inadvertent) good fortune to sign up for two classes that changed my life dramatically and permanently, on U.S. women's history and antebellum America. These courses not only gave me my life's work (sparking my desire to become a historian of women) but also planted the seeds for this project, as they introduced me to *Uncle Tom's Cabin* and the messy, complicated visions of freedom, femininity, and race that novel contains. Reading that book inspired me to learn more about how fiction shaped public dialogue about slavery in antebellum America—and lead me to the difficult, complex, and compelling texts this monograph examines.

This project's path from undergraduate term paper to master's thesis to dissertation to book has been a long and lively one, and it would be impossible to thank all of the people and institutions that helped guide and steady me through that process. Daniel W. Crofts and Ann Marie Nicolosi, my undergraduate mentors at The College of New Jersey, offered boundless support to an aspiring historian finding her way into the field, and the members of my dissertation committee at Lehigh University—my committee chair, Monica Najar, and my committee members, Gail Cooper, Dawn Keetley, and Jean Soderlund—were instrumental mentoring me through the research and writing process and teaching me to hold my work to the highest possible scholarly standards. Colleagues at the University of Illinois-Springfield kindly went to brown bag talks and offered comments on my book proposal, as my erstwhile dissertation started its journey into print. I am also deeply grateful to the College of Liberal Arts and Sciences at UIS for providing me with two incredibly valuable course releases as I worked on editing my manuscript. My students at Lehigh University and The College of New Jersey (past) and at UIS (past, present, and, I have no doubt, future) have been and are not just a delight to teach, but also a constant inspiration to ask more complicated questions, steadfastly refuse easy answers, and recognize the tremendous importance of the stories that we tell about the past and the ways we tell them.

Several archives and libraries also made the research for this project possible (and so much fun to conduct, to boot). While working on my dissertation, I had the great good fortune to delve into collections at the Boston Public Library and the Ohio Historical Society, where the archivists could not have been kinder or more helpful. I was also honored to receive a Travel to Collections Award to the Sophia Smith Collection at Smith College in Northampton, Massachusetts, and to be a short-term Andrew W. Mellon Fellow at the Massachusetts Historical Society in Boston, while undertaking my research. The impact of those archives, and of the wonderful scholars I got to work with and know at these institutions, on this project and on my work as a scholar overall is incalculable.

Presenting on this research as it evolved at the conferences of Historians Against Slavery, the Pennsylvania Historical Association, the Society for the Study of American Women Writers, and the Southern Association of Women Historians was also invaluable as I continued to fine-tune my arguments and ideas. I am also deeply grateful to director of Hastings College Press Patricia Oman for the chance to write an introduction for HCP's beautiful edition of *Madge Vertner* (which, even as I try not to play favorites, I will confess is totally my favorite antebellum abolitionist novel), and to Thomas Dublin and Kathryn Kish Sklar for the opportunity to create a document project centered on antislavery women writers for the wonderful *Women and Social Movements* database. Reflecting on women's fiction in these venues was greatly beneficial for me as I worked on this book, and was also a fantastic opportunity to bring these dynamic, complicated texts to a wider audience.

The anonymous reviewers for the Kent State University Press also offered incredibly insightful, detailed feedback about how to tighten my prose, sharpen my thinking, and generally make this book richer and more thoughtful. All of the editorial board and staff at KSUP have been unfailingly encouraging, inspiring, and helpful throughout the process of moving my project from a manuscript (e-mailed off with hope and crossed fingers), to a real, live, actual book. I couldn't ask for *Her Voice Will Be on the Side of Right* to have a better home or to be in better company, as it joins the American Abolitionism and Antislavery series.

Friends who will listen to you talk about a "damned mob of scribbling women" for more than a decade are dear and precious friends, indeed, and I am very grateful for each of them. This project was in its infancy (and it sometimes feels like we were, too) when I met Christina Gillim, Kelly Holland, Colleen Martell, Kelli Oliver, and Melissa Yingling, and I am so very grateful for their many years of asking about the thesis / the dissertation / the book. Since becoming a midwesterner, I have been blessed to find not only remarkable colleagues but also wise and wonderful friends in Kathy Petitte Novak, Shannon O'Brien, and Julie Perino—women who care passionately about the academy and the vital, transformative work we can do here but who also know the value of stepping outside of this dear ivory tower of ours every now and again. I had the great good fortune of starting my career at UIS the same semester as Meagan Cass, and without her friendship, generous willingness to concoct beautiful gin cocktails on request, and wise encouragement to sometimes exchange staring at the computer for going thrift store shopping, that career (and this book) would surely not have been possible (or nearly as much fun). My sister and brother-in-law, April Kent and Brandon Kempner, have also been sources of unending support and wise counsel, as I sought to learn how to manage this whole "academic" thing (process still ongoing and doubtless to be lifelong.) Christianne Gadd made getting our masters' actually doable, getting our PhDs actually enjoyable, attending conferences together reliable intellectual and culinary adventures, and every year I've had the great privilege of being her friend immeasurably better and brighter.

And finally, this book is dedicated to my parents, Nancy Kent and Douglas Kent. When I was a girl, I said I thought wanted to write a book one day, and they told me that of course I could, and that they were sure I would.

And so I did.

INTRODUCTION

"How a Woman Touches the World's Heart"

Women and Antislavery Fiction in the Antebellum Era

In 1853, abolitionist and women's rights advocate Theodore Parker delivered an address to an animated crowd in Boston on the contentious subject of "The Public Function of Woman." Parker informed his audience that women would be instrumental in making the nineteenth century one of true gender and racial equality. In working for such radical social change, he insisted that women could not allow themselves to be limited by conventional notions of women's "proper sphere." They needed to be willing to petition their government, support political parties, and even make public speeches in order to rid their nation of the tremendous evils of racial and gender injustice.

A staunch advocate of women's involvement in a diverse assortment of reform activities, Parker singled out one specific form of female activism as particularly significant: women's authorship of reform-oriented fiction. "The literature of women in this century is juster, more philanthropic, more religious, than that of men," he declared to his audience. "How a woman touches the world's heart!—because she speaks justice, speaks piety, speaks love."[1] Defining women's fiction as more focused on social reform and more infused with moral principles than men's literature, Parker argued that emotionally potent fiction written by activist women had the power to "touch the world's heart" as no other medium could. Female authors, he contended, had a gender-specific capacity to write literature that would shock the reading public out of its complacency and force it to recognize the many injustices that lay at the heart of the American nation.

This monograph considers the issues Parker raised in his speech, analyzing the ways fiction provided antislavery women writers with a significant public site to voice their ideas about slavery and abolition.[2] Living in a culture that discouraged white, middle-class women from public commentary on political subjects and female lecturing, female antislavery authors turned to fiction as an appropriately "feminine" means of discussing abolitionism. Insisting that their work as writers was essentially private, these authors nonetheless wrote fiction in the hopes of influencing public policy and mobilizing female readers against slavery. Writers contended that richly imaginative, profoundly emotional stories would be far more effective in reaching the female American public than more "rational" appeals could be. In making this argument, authors simultaneously sought to reclaim women's imaginations and feelings (all too often represented as dangerous liabilities for serious thinkers and citizens in antebellum American culture) as positive attributes, even as they worried about the capacity that (ostensibly more frivolous and easily swayed) female readers had to become truly invested in the antislavery cause.

This study also argues that white antislavery women writers' fiction offered a problematic, but significant, challenge to the racial and gender order of the antebellum United States. Representing enslaved female characters as virtuous citizens and faithful antislavery advocates, authors questioned social hierarchies that unrelentingly subordinated morally pure women to (consistently morally inferior) white men. Despite these positive representations, however, white antislavery female authors also raised questions about enslaved women's ability to conform to antebellum ideals of feminine respectability and morality. Their depictions of enslaved female characters contained an uneasy undercurrent of concern about enslaved women's failure to conform to middle-class standards of modesty and their capacity for violent action. However, white antislavery authors also insisted that enslaved women shared with white women an innate desire for sexual purity, a deep dedication to their families, and an unerring, innate moral astuteness. By so doing, they invested their fiction with significant subversive potential. Emphasizing that both enslaved African American and white women shared the same moral purity (which men in these narratives conspicuously lack), these stories indicated that gender was a more significant category than race in American society. These narratives thus questioned a social and political order in which white men wielded considerable power over the white and African American women who were their undoubted moral superiors.

This project also contends that antislavery women writers developed a unique form of difference feminism, insisting that morally clear-sighted women's, not morally unsound men's, ideals ought to shape public policies and political decisions about slavery. At the same time, writers remained uncomfortable with the idea of women becoming involved with the (in their eyes, hopelessly corrupt) public, political sphere of men. Antislavery female authors represented emotional, domestic moral influence as the most desirable, gender-appropriate form of activism for women. But as the antebellum era advanced, writers expressed increasingly grave doubts about this approach's efficacy. Ever more dubious about men's willingness to be influenced by women's moral ideals and deeply aware of men's greater social, political, and legal power, antislavery women writers expressed growing unease about the future of the abolitionist cause.[3] If men at once refused to heed women's moral guidance and remained the leaders of both households and the government, prospects for the antislavery movement looked grim. Rejecting women's rights activists' calls for the direct political empowerment of women, female antislavery authors created contradictory visions of how women could best participate in abolitionism.[4] Their literature indicated that American society would have to be radically reordered so that women's pure morality, rather than corrupt, male-dominated political systems, would determine the future of slavery. How, exactly, this could be achieved without forcing women into unnatural, unwelcome positions of political authority, writers were not sure. But for antislavery authors, the idea that the success of abolitionism lay in the hands and the hearts of women was never in doubt.

This study contributes to the dynamic historiography about women and abolition, in part through its sustained focus on a significant cross-section of women's antislavery fiction (much of which was written by still obscure, understudied authors) and that fiction's depictions of female characters' activism. There have been excellent studies of the fiction of well-known, influential writers such as Lydia Maria Child and Harriet Beecher Stowe, which consider these specific authors' contributions to antislavery literary culture.[5] Scholars such as Eve Allegra Raimon, Karen Sánchez-Eppler, Deborah C. DeRosa, and Sarah N. Roth have also done important work analyzing white women's abolitionist fiction. Sánchez-Eppler's pioneering scholarship details the ways white writers wrote about enslaved women's bodies as a means of voicing anxieties about their own sexual autonomy, and Raimon's work analyzes how white writers created mixed-race "mulatta" characters to explore changing conceptions of race and American identity during an era of increased white migration west and shifting national boundaries. DeRosa's study examines antislavery children's literature, arguing that through this genre of fiction, white female authors crafted public personas as "mother-educators" and claimed maternal authority to educate the American public about the evils of slavery. Roth's monograph traces how depictions of African American masculinity evolved in white women's literature from the 1830s through the Civil War. Her work skillfully documents how white female authors expressed anxieties about black male autonomy and violent resistance to slavery, by increasingly depicting African American men as feminized, passive martyrs.[6] My study contributes to this rich, complex scholarship, considering how female antislavery authors depicted white and enslaved women in their literature, and their efforts to access public power and shape the abolitionist movement during the antebellum era.

This project also enters into the extensive historiography about white, middle-class women's literary work in the antebellum United States. Pioneering studies of women's literature centered on questions about whether the sentimental fiction white women wrote during this era was fundamentally conservative or was subversive of existing notions of gender. In her groundbreaking work about this fiction, Ann Douglas argues that sentimental women's literature cheapened the tone of American public discourse in the nineteenth century and encouraged Americans to eschew deep thought in favor of easy tears. Nina Baym and Cathy Davidson, by contrast, maintain that women's fiction had subversive potential for both its female readers and its female authors. Baym contends that white antebellum female authors infused their works with a subtle emphasis on female independence, and Davidson demonstrates that fictional narratives offered their female readers valuable lessons about how to successfully navigate an oppressive patriarchal society.[7] This study builds on such arguments of scholars about the subversive possibilities of women's fiction. The medium of fiction, I argue, gave antislavery women unique scope to imagine new worlds, in which women's principles mattered more than the color of their skin and in which women's moral visions predominated in American society. Yet white antislavery authors' fiction revealed the limitations as well as the possibilities of their antislavery thought, demonstrating their inability to fully transcend racial prejudice or to imagine a world of true gender egalitarianism.

Scholarship on white women's literary work has also devoted significant attention to questions of female authorship, asking in what ways antebellum white, middle-class women were (and were not) able to successfully blend their identities as public authors and domestic women. Mary Kelley's groundbreaking study *Private Woman, Public Stage: Literary Domesticity in Nineteenth-Century America* skillfully traces the considerable anxieties that many white female authors experienced in seeking to reconcile what they believed were deeply contradictory roles. Susan Coultrap-McQuin's monograph *Doing Literary Business: American Women Writers in the Nineteenth Century* continues in this vein, noting the difficulties that antebellum women authors had in reconciling their status as "private" women with their involvement in the public, commercial business of fiction.[8]

More recent scholarship on white women and authorship in the nineteenth century has complicated this vision of white women writers' anxiety about assuming the public role of authorship. Martha Cutter's study on women writers and public identity, Melissa Homestead's work on female authors' negotiation of copyright law, Lora Romero's scholarship on female authors' grappling with ideologies of domesticity, and Elizabeth Young's monograph about women writers entering Civil War politics stress the ways white women embraced, claimed, and asserted their right to act on the public stage of authorship without necessarily engaging in significant justification of their status as public authors. As these studies demonstrate, the rigidity of the ideology of separate spheres did not necessarily engender deep anxieties in all white female authors about the potentially transgressive nature of their literary work.[9]

Valuable as this scholarship is, my work stresses the importance of not losing sight of the power ideologies of domesticity had on the ways white, middle-class female authors conceptualized their work. This study brings our attention back to the persistent anxieties about female authorship that appeared in white, middle-class women's literature during the antebellum era. Female antislavery authors felt the need to justify their literary work as essentially private and domestic. In writers' frequent protests that fiction was a decidedly noncontroversial arena for women to enter, we see the ways anxieties about the propriety of feminine authorship continued to permeate women's literary work in the decades before the Civil War.

This project also contributes to literature focused on white, middle-class women's activism. Several historians of women have vividly demonstrated the negative consequences of white, middle-class women's deploying the rhetoric of feminine difference in their work as reformers and activists. Christine Stansell's study of white, working-class women in antebellum New York finds that white, middle-class female reformers' imposition of their ideas about domesticity compromised working-class women's physical safety and increased their risk of sexual assault. In his monograph about white female moral reformers in the mid-nineteenth century, Daniel Wright locates similar trends in middle-class reformers' efforts to eradicate prostitution, with their notions about female "passionlessness" having negative impacts on the lives of female sex workers. Peggy Pascoe, in her history of white female activists in the home mission movement in the late nineteenth- and early twentieth-century West, notes the ways white women's use of rhetoric about gender difference empowered them, at the cost of silencing Asian American women.[10]

My work adds to and complicates these arguments, analyzing the complex ways white female authors deployed the rhetoric of feminine difference in their fiction. In some respects, white antislavery writers constructed exclusionary arguments about female difference that defined the category of "woman" in ways that conformed to white, middle-class models of femininity. In other ways, however, authors' discussions of innate gender difference were far more expansive, with female antislavery authors insisting that gender, and not race or class, was the primary dividing line in American society. As such, their literary works contained considerable subversive potential, suggesting ideologies of feminine difference had the potential to include as well as exclude—to unite as well as divide—women of different races and classes.

In evaluating a medium that at once asserted the primacy of the domestic arena and claimed public space for women, this monograph also contributes to scholarship concerning gender and notions of the public and the private during the antebellum era. Considerations of the ideology of separate spheres have permeated studies of white, middle-class women since the 1960s. In pioneering works published during these decades, scholars such as Nancy Cott, Mary Ryan, and Barbara Welter argue that this ideology was an oppressive one, in the case of Welter, and that it contained significant potential to destabilize the gender hierarchies it ostensibly worked to uphold, in the cases of Cott and Ryan.[11] More recent scholarship has complicated these discussions of the ideology of separate spheres. Cathy Davidson and Jessamyn Hatcher, Alison Piepmeier, and Joan W. Scott and Debra Keates pay particular attention to the ways race, class, religion, and region have shaped how various communities of American women formulated, disseminated, and interpreted the ideology of separate spheres.[12]

In recent years, several historians have offered valuable reassessments of the ways the ideology of separate spheres operated in the lives of white, middle-class women during the early republic and antebellum eras. Catherine Allgor's work on theaters, Susan Branson's on salons, Catherine Kelly's on New England marketplaces, and Cynthia Kierner's on southern sites of sociability have all provided insights into how white, middle-class women's lives consistently slipped outside of the tidy confines of a narrowly defined "public" and "private."[13] Through their scholarship, these authors demonstrate that the ideology of separate spheres was not a rigid straitjacket that confined white, middle-class women to the private sphere. To the contrary, this seemingly narrow ideology often proved a surprisingly supple, imprecise one that operated in complex ways in women's day-to-day lives.

My study refocuses scholarly attention from women's lived experiences to the realm of ideology and imagination. Important as scholarship about how women utilized separate spheres ideology in their daily lives is, it is of equal importance to analyze how women reified this ideology through their imaginative literary work. Antislavery women writers at once placed a strong emphasis on the desirability of women engaging in domestic forms of activism and the need for women not to be bound by restrictive notions of the public and the private in the fight against slavery. This unresolved contradiction was one that female antislavery writers uneasily grappled with throughout their literary work.

By discussing female authors of antislavery literature, this project also engages with the considerable historiography concerning women and abolitionism. Numerous scholars have ably written about the different ways female abolitionists participated in the antislavery movement during the early republic and antebellum eras. Julie Roy Jeffrey's and Beth Salerno's work on women's participation in female antislavery societies, Debra Gold

Hansen's and Deborah Bingham Van Broekhaven's on women's involvement in antislavery fairs, Michael D. Pierson's on female abolitionists and antislavery politics, and Alisse Portnoy's and Susan Zaeske's on antislavery women's petition campaigns have greatly enriched historians' knowledge concerning women's work in abolitionism and the ways it reshaped their lives. Participation in these diverse forms of abolitionist activity had the potential to foster a sense of sisterhood among female antislavery activists, strengthen their commitment to building egalitarian marriages, and increase their sense of themselves as full American citizens.[14]

Valuable as these scholars' insights are, this study argues that it is important to examine not only what antislavery women actually *did* but also what antislavery women *imagined*. This project refocuses our attention from how female abolitionists acted and how these actions affected their lives, to what female abolitionists speculated and dreamed about—to what they feared and hoped for. By concentrating on women's imaginations rather than on their actions, this monograph provides insight into both the radical promise and the troubling limitations of white women's abolitionist thought. Female writers dared to imagine a world in which women played a central role not only in abolitionism but also in American society as a whole—a world in which feminine moral values were, quite literally, the law of the land. Yet their literature also reveals thinking that is at least as constrained as it is audacious. White female antislavery authors' works demonstrate their struggles to imagine a world in which female power was disconnected from female domesticity or in which African American women enjoyed full equality with white women.

The years in which white antislavery authors wrote their fiction were significant, transformative ones for the abolitionist movement, the women's rights movement, and American print culture. During the decades this project examines, a radical abolitionist movement mobilized, organized, and spread across the Northeast and the Midwest, an ideology of separate spheres and an independent women's rights movement developed and expanded, and technological innovations in transportation facilitated the growth of a truly national print culture. Female antislavery authors grappled with and reflected on all of these important developments.

The majority of the authors discussed in this study were both white and female. Since they lived in a culture that defined fiction-writing as a gender-appropriate pursuit for women (while also simultaneously discouraging women from other forms of activism, such as oratory), female writers were much more likely than their male counterparts to turn to fiction to express their antislavery ideas.[15] In the early republic and antebellum United States, fiction was also a distinctly gendered medium, with much of the public discussion about fiction gendering both its writers and readers as female. Virtually all of the authors in this study are white, because of the unfortunate reality that African American women had significantly less access than white women to literacy skills and white-dominated print culture during this era. In a culture in which access to education for enslaved and free African American women was illegal at worst and challenging at best, and even antislavery white periodicals and editors discriminated against free African American writers, African American women had significantly more difficulty in writing and publishing fictional works than white women did.

Despite white female antislavery authors' eagerness to reach a broad, popular audience, they had significant challenges in doing so during the 1821 to 1861 period.[16] Although they circulated throughout the Northeast and Midwest, most antislavery periodicals had relatively small numbers of subscribers, a large percentage of whom were already members of the abolitionist movement. Prior to the publication of Harriet Beecher Stowe's best-selling novel *Uncle Tom's Cabin*, most antislavery novels and short story collections were published by abolitionist presses, enjoyed only small distributions, and were reviewed almost exclusively in antislavery periodicals. In the wake of *Uncle Tom's Cabin*, the landscape changed, as the white American reading public became (temporarily) more interested in antislavery fiction. Despite this brief flair of popularity in the 1850s, for the most part, antislavery female authors could assume that their works would primarily be read by those already involved in the antislavery movement. Mindful of this, writers in part directed their literature toward antislavery advocates, discussing how they could best engage in activism, and sharing their thoughts on what the future direction of abolitionism ought to be.

Yet several factors suggest that the circulation of antislavery literature throughout the United States was more extensive than statistics alone indicate. The works of scholars such as Jacqueline Bacon and Elizabeth McHenry point to the existence of a flourishing antislavery literary culture that lay behind the relatively small number of readers purchasing antislavery books and subscribers paying for antislavery periodicals. In her study of the *Freedom's Journal* newspaper, Bacon demonstrates that free African Americans in the North made sustained efforts to circulate this periodical as extensively as possible, with subscribers sharing the paper with nonsubscribers, and the literate reading the newspaper to the illiterate. McHenry finds similar behaviors in African American women's literary societies during the antebellum era, with female members pooling financial resources and drawing on networks of friends and relatives to facilitate the circulation of antislavery literature throughout free African American communities.[17]

Antislavery literature even made some inroads in the South, despite white southerners' concerted efforts to prevent it from doing so. Peter Hinks, in his scholarship on African American abolitionist David Walker and his pioneering 1829 treatise *Appeal to the Coloured Citizens of the World*, demonstrates that, because of the efforts of African American sailors, the *Appeal* circulated quite widely in the South. During the early 1830s, anxieties about the *Appeal*, Nat Turner's slave rebellion, and abolitionists' aggressive campaign to blanket the South with printed materials resulted in southern states passing increasingly strict laws to prevent the circulation of antislavery literature. In her monograph *Closer to Freedom: Enslaved Women and Everyday Resistance in the Plantation South*, Stephanie M. H. Camp proves that these efforts were not entirely successful, as enslaved people managed to both obtain and retain works of antislavery literature.[18]

Although abolitionist women writers may have doubted their fiction's ability to successfully infiltrate the South, they certainly hoped their literature would pass through the largest possible number of hands. These aspirations shaped the particular types of literary forms through which they chose to convey their ideas. By electing to present their arguments in novels and stories, authors indicated a hope that their works would not only attract more purchasers but also be more likely to be shared with readers' friends and family members.[19] The publication of antislavery gift books indicated a similar hope: gift books were, after all, a medium explicitly intended to be displayed in their middle-class owners' parlors, hopefully catching the eyes of all visitors. Consequently, although the actual numbers are relatively small, it seems likely that antislavery literary works made their way to more readers than the data about their rates of publication and circulation suggest.

During the early republic and antebellum eras, abolitionists devoted significant time to reflecting on whether antislavery advocates ought to use fiction in the service of their cause. Always anxious about their ability to reach and convert an indifferent at best and hostile at worst white reading public, antislavery advocates eventually seized on fiction as a vital, if problematic, means of disseminating their ideas. Believing many white Americans would resist picking up an antislavery tract or listening to an antislavery speech, abolitionists hoped skeptical members of the white public might more successfully be lured into reading an engaging antislavery novel or short story.

As this study demonstrates, antislavery activists also maintained that fiction would speak to what they assumed would be one of the most difficult to reach demographics—women. Convinced female audiences were even less likely than male ones to willingly grapple with the painful and unpleasant issue of slavery, antislavery writers and editors believed women might well be converted through the use of fiction. Focusing as it did on such conventionally "feminine" matters as romance, family, and female friendships, fiction might capture female readers' attention and convince them of the evils of slavery where other, less dynamic and emotionally engaging types of media had failed.

This monograph analyzes women's antislavery fiction published in a diverse range of venues during the early republic and antebellum eras. It draws on short stories from six antislavery newspapers, six gift books, and three periodicals intended for child readers. All of these publications printed fiction on a regular basis, with the exact number of stories published varying by issue.[20] My work also considers twenty-seven antislavery novels written by twenty-two authors. To provide context for this literature, this study also draws on the papers of antislavery editors such as William Lloyd Garrison and Benjamin Lundy; antislavery authors including Elizabeth Margaret Chandler, Lydia Maria Child, Caroline W. Healey Dall, Eliza Lee Follen, and Catharine Maria Sedgwick; and female and juvenile antislavery societies such as the Boston Female Anti-Slavery Society and the Juvenile Anti-Slavery Society of Boston, which were actively involved in the consumption and production of antislavery literature.

To most vividly illuminate the dramatic changes that took place in female antislavery authors' thought, this monograph is arranged chronologically, with each chapter covering roughly a decade of the 1821 to 1861 period. In the beginning, antislavery women writers insisted that women's domestic activism alone would be successful in ensuring the success of the abolitionist cause. By the end of the antebellum era, by contrast, antislavery authors insisted that women's moral influence in the home could do little to secure the abolition of slavery.

Chapter 1 focuses on the 1820s and early 1830s, examining the literature women published during these formative years in antislavery print culture. I argue that white antislavery authors and editors represented the feminized medium of fiction as both a positive and negative part of their movement. On one hand, they insisted that fiction had a unique capacity to play on the emotions of its readers, which they believed would be of tremendous value in reaching a white female audience. On the other hand, though, praising both fiction's emotional power and white women's emotional capacity, editors and authors also suggested that emotionality might also be a sign of white women's unreliability as effective antislavery activists.

The literature of the 1820s and early 1830s also offered contradictory visions of enslaved women and the roles they ought to play in the fight against slavery. Enslaved women are scarcely present, with authors focusing almost exclusively on white women as antislavery actors. In the rare cases in which enslaved female characters do appear, they are at once morally admirable and, problematically, in need of guidance from white women. The vision of enslaved women that emerges from these years is therefore a conflicted one, in which enslaved female characters are at once morally wise yet also in profound need of white women's leadership. This fiction thus troublingly points to a postslavery world in which enslaved women would be free but in which the fundamental racial hierarchies of American society would nonetheless remain largely unchanged.

Finally, this chapter argues that white female authors defined white women as the heart of the antislavery movement: innately moral white women were the ideal antislavery advocates, and they made significant contributions to the antislavery cause by decorously persuading their loved ones of the evils of slavery in the private sphere of the home. Authors maintained that for white women, involvement in abolitionism was not a violation but rather a just extension of their proper roles as loving wives, mothers, and friends. Provided that white women confined their abolitionist activities to domestic, gender-appropriate forms of activism, writers argued, they would be successful in bringing their male relatives into the cause and greatly advance the interests of the antislavery movement.

Chapter 1 ends in 1832, when the influential author Elizabeth Margaret Chandler ceased publishing her fiction in the antislavery periodical the

Genius of Universal Emancipation. Chapter 2 commences in 1831, when William Lloyd Garrison began publishing his abolitionist newspaper the *Liberator,* and centers on the 1830s, the decade that witnessed the rise of the radical abolitionist movement and the attendant growth of antislavery literature. This chapter argues that during this decade authors and editors continued to represent fiction as a significant means of emotionally connecting with vitally important female readers, to praise the emotional potency of both fiction and women, and yet to remain uneasy that female readers' and writers' connection to abolitionism was more rooted in emotion and imagination than in reason. In the face of mounting public criticism about the "unfeminine" nature of abolitionist women's activism, authors and editors also became increasingly insistent that fiction writing and reading were not public but rather private acts, which in no way transgressed the "proper" boundaries of white, middle-class femininity.

White female authors further underlined the gendered respectability of female antislavery activism by making their white female characters not only dedicated abolitionists but also unfailingly decorous ladies and consistently selfless wives and mothers. And although virtuous white female characters are successful in persuading their husbands, fathers, and sons of slavery's evils, they nonetheless struggle to make morally fallible men recognize the need to value abolitionism more than worldly self-interest. These narratives are thus haunted by unease about the fact that morally unreliable white men are more socially, economically, and politically powerful than their ethically astute female counterparts.

This chapter also maintains that the fiction published during the 1830s offers complex visions of African American women's involvement in struggles for abolition and racial justice. The fiction published during this decade likely offers more in-depth, nuanced reflections about black women's roles in the antislavery movement as this was the decade in which the largest number of African American female authors published their antislavery literary work. Black women writers' works possessed both significant commonalities with and notable differences from the literature of white women. Both stressed the centrality of women in the fight against slavery and the unwavering, gender-specific nature of women's commitment to the antislavery cause. Unlike white female authors, however, black female authors also discussed the evils of racial prejudice, insisted on the need to fight for racial equality in both the North and the South, and debated the desirability of free African Americans remaining a part of the racist American nation or seeking to build a new, more egalitarian society in Africa. That these issues are absent from white women's literature is troubling, given that white women possessed more power in both the antislavery movement and American society overall. As such, white female writers' failure to incorporate free African American women's concerns into their own fiction signaled a problematic lack of interest in ensuring full racial equality within their movement or in a postemancipation world.

The tumultuous 1840s are the focus of chapter 3, which considers the evolution of antislavery female writers' thought as the abolitionist movement increasingly turned toward electoral politics and moved away from moral suasion. Eager to turn the growing popularity of sentimental fiction and gift books to their advantage, antislavery authors and editors also worried about the potential pitfalls of targeting antislavery literature toward a broad popular audience. Anxious to give the female-dominated reading public texts that would appeal to it, abolitionist writers nonetheless also expressed concerns that their message would be diluted if their works were forced to conform to the conventions of the popular literary marketplace. This tension further demonstrates that antislavery authors and editors saw female readers and writers as vital participants in abolitionism while still remaining uneasy about the intellectual and activist value of the "feminine" medium of fiction.

This chapter also maintains that the fiction of the 1840s deepened the tensions long present in white female authors' depictions of their enslaved female characters, who are, for the most part, models of "true womanhood"—centering their lives on their children, battling valiantly to maintain their sexual purity, and embracing Christian values to the point of being willing to die for them. By insisting that enslaved women shared the same ideals and had the same capacity for selfless love and self-sacrifice that white women (ostensibly) did, white women writers indicated that enslaved women would, if emancipated, be model citizens and "angels in the house."

This positive depiction was troubled, however, by white authors' concerns about how slavery had potentially corrupted enslaved women's feminine virtue, to the point of making enslaved women become violent. White female authors thus created a potentially radical, but also distinctly flawed, vision of enslaved women's future in the American republic. Indicating that if liberated they would enrich the nation through their work as virtuous wives and mothers, white antislavery writers also indicated that enslaved women might need to be closely supervised and carefully guided by whites, lest they erupt into uncontrolled, irrational violence.

Female antislavery authors' discussions of white women's roles in abolitionism during the 1840s were similarly contradictory. Writing during the years in which the first antislavery political parties developed, antislavery women writers expressed considerable uneasiness about where white women could fit into an increasingly politicized movement. White male characters reveal themselves to be decidedly misguided in their political decisions, leaving white female characters to persuade them to undo the damage their votes for unjust legislation have caused. White female authors demonstrated that they were deeply conscious of the pitfalls involved in morally unsound men possessing political power that morally pure women did not. Yet despite these concerns, white writers remained uncomfortable with the prospect of white women directly engaging in political activity. White female authors writing during the 1840s thus wished to retain a moral influence-centered model of activism that made white women and their moral values central, but in the face of the antislavery movement's ever-growing politicization, they increasingly regarded this model as untenable.

Chapter 4 turns to the literature that white female antislavery authors published in the decade before the Civil War. Faced with the dazzling success of Stowe's *Uncle Tom's Cabin* in 1852, antislavery authors and editors of the 1850s largely shelved their concerns about using emotional fiction as a means of disseminating the antislavery message. Instead, they expressed hope that other female authors would replicate Stowe's success and write powerful narratives that successfully used the tropes of sentimental fiction to attract new readers.

The enslaved female characters white writers created during these years possessed the same uneasy blend of innate female virtue and troubling potential to lose control that had been present in the literature of previous decades. Deeply damaged by the sufferings they endured in slavery, enslaved women nonetheless remained dynamic resistors of the institution. While enslaved women in these novels successfully rebelled against slavery, over the course of the 1850s white female characters failed (increasingly dramatically) to take any meaningful abolitionist action. Seeking to use moral influence in the service of abolitionism, white female characters found themselves less and less able to shape the principles of the brutal, morally bankrupt men by whom they were surrounded.

Creating fictional worlds in which white women failed and enslaved women succeeded in their efforts to resist slavery, white antislavery writers offered a potentially radical vision of the future of the antislavery movement, one that gave enslaved women a central role in bringing slavery to an end. Yet by expressing concerns about enslaved women's capacity for violence, white female authors also raised questions about the desirability of a future in which enslaved women were slavery's primary resistors. By presenting the failure of white women's moral influence as profoundly damaging to the abolitionist cause, white female antislavery authors indicated that the current social order was a decidedly undesirable one. Convinced that a social structure which empowered corrupt white men at the expense of virtuous women was not to be trusted, white female authors struggled to articulate the best way forward for abolitionism. Uncomfortable with the idea of women becoming directly politically empowered, these writers indicated their society's gendered division of power needed to change, without offering a clear sense of how that change might take place.

On the eve of the Civil War, female antislavery authors still saw women as the rightful moral leaders of the abolitionist movement. Convinced that by virtue of their gender African American and white women shared a common moral clarity and purity, they maintained that women's ideas about slavery and abolition, not men's, were the best and most useful ones for the American republic. However, by the 1860s, antislavery women writers had lost faith in the ability of feminine moral suasion to convert corrupt individual men, and male-dominated social systems, to abolitionism. Uncomfortable with the idea of women claiming political power in their own right but convinced that women were crucial to the fight to end slavery, female antislavery authors created uneasy visions of their nation and its future. Certain that if slavery were ever to be abolished women's moral ideals needed to infuse American government, white writers remained unable to see how this would be possible without women's rightful place in society being perilously compromised.

CHAPTER ONE

"Her Heart Was Touched with the Wrongs of the Injured Ones"

The Emergence of Women's Antislavery Fiction, 1821–1832

> But we have perhaps extended these remarks too far—our readers may remind us, that it is our craft to write for their amusement & to allow them to extract instruction for themselves if perchance so valuable an essence can be obtained from the light material of a tale.
> —CATHARINE MARIA SEDGWICK

In 1831, Elizabeth Margaret Chandler published her story "Tears of Woman: An Allegory" in the influential antislavery newspaper the *Genius of Universal Emancipation*. In the tale, an angel is dispatched from heaven to see if he can persuade the people of earth to abolish slavery. The angel approaches numerous men, pleading with them to end the peculiar institution. Without fail, the angel's appeals are rejected by his listeners, with man after man refusing to accept any moral responsibility for the sin of slavery or to feel any pity for enslaved people. Having found men consistently indifferent to the sufferings of the enslaved, the angel is about to return to heaven in failure and despair when he has an inspiration: he stops addressing men and begins speaking to women. And here, he finds all of the empathy for the enslaved that men had so conspicuously lacked. As soon as free women begin to shed tears over the enslaved, freedom ceases to be an impossible dream and becomes a concrete reality. Enslaved people's best hope for liberation thus resides, the angel discovers, not in the economic or political power of men but in the emotional power of women.[1]

This chapter analyzes how fictional narratives such as "Tears of Woman" discussed women's place in the antislavery struggle during the 1820s and 1830s and argues that writers defined the medium of fiction as a powerful, gender-appropriate space through which white, middle-class women could appropriately convey their antislavery convictions. Concerned about enslaved women's ability to effectively seek their own emancipation in gender-appropriate ways, authors insisted that white women were rightly the central force for antislavery change; they alone had both the moral clarity and the emotional power necessary to be effective antislavery advocates without transgressing the proper boundaries of bourgeois womanhood.

This chapter centers on the literary work of two central, pioneering authors who were writing during these formative years of the antislavery movement, Catharine Maria Sedgwick and Elizabeth Margaret Chandler. Sedgwick published 1824's *Redwood,* one of the first American novels to take slavery and abolition as its primary subject, and Chandler served as the editor of the *Genius of Universal Emancipation*'s Ladies' Department, publishing a considerable amount of her own fiction there. While Sedgwick has been the subject of scholarly consideration for several decades, much of this scholarship focuses on her most famous novel, *Hope Leslie,* and on the domestic fiction she published during the antebellum era.[2] Scholarship about Chandler is still not terribly extensive, despite Chandler's vital importance as an author and editor in the early years of the antislavery movement.[3]

The years during which Chandler and Sedgwick wrote their antislavery fiction, the 1820s and early 1830s, have likewise remained relatively marginalized in studies of early antislavery activism. Recent work by scholars including Christopher Cameron, Bruce Dorsey, and Alisse Portnoy has brought these "lost years" more fully back into understandings of abolitionism, providing new insights into the connections between struggles for Native American rights, colonizationist activism, and abolitionism, and the vital importance of free African Americans as leaders and central figures in antislavery organizing and movement building.[4] Jacqueline Bacon and Sarah N. Roth have also written monographs about the importance of print culture in the early antislavery movement, demonstrating the significance of African American newspapers to the development of independent African American abolitionism and of antislavery fiction as a site for debates about African American men's relationship to the state during the early republic and antebellum eras.⁵ This chapter contributes to this wider scholarship about the development of antislavery print culture, reflecting on the complex ways female writers used fiction as a site for antislavery advocacy.

Chandler, Sedgwick, and the Role of Fiction in Antislavery Print Culture

Before discussing the fiction Chandler and Sedgwick wrote in the 1820s and 1830s, it is worth considering each writer's relationship to the emerging antislavery movement. By the time Chandler began working as editor of the *Genius of Universal Emancipation's* Ladies' Department, she had already been involved in the antislavery cause for several years. Born in Delaware in 1807, at the age of nine Chandler moved to Philadelphia, where she joined the city's Quaker abolitionist community. She quickly became a staunch supporter of the free produce movement and began expressing her antislavery views through the poetry she published in local newspapers as a teenager.⁶ Although Chandler published her work anonymously, her identity was known to many in antislavery circles, including *Genius* editor Benjamin Lundy. Lundy began publishing her work in 1826, asking her to become editor of its Ladies' Department three years later. Even after she moved to the Michigan frontier in 1830, Chandler continued her involvement in antislavery activism. She became one of the cofounders of Michigan's Logan Female Anti-Slavery Society, continued to correspond with Lundy, and worked as editor of the *Genius's* Ladies' Department until her death at the age of twenty-seven in 1834.

Lundy had founded the *Genius* in 1821, hoping the newspaper would be "an active instrument in the attempt to abolish that cruel and disgraceful system in the American Republic."⁷ A longtime antislavery advocate, Lundy worked at several colonizationist periodicals prior to founding the *Genius*.⁸ Although contact with radical abolitionists such as Chandler pushed Lundy closer to advocating immediate abolition during the *Genius*'s eighteen-year run, he nonetheless retained strong ties with the colonizationist movement throughout his career. Colonizationists, who advocated the migration of enslaved people to Africa after their emancipation, were an active, vocal presence in debates about slavery, freedom, and civil rights during the early republic and antebellum eras. Organizations like the American Colonization Society, founded in 1817, insisted that colonization was the best answer to the slave question, since, they claimed, enslaved African

Americans could, even if emancipated, never hope to enjoy true equality in the American republic. That white members of organizations such as the ACS were uncomfortable with the idea of an America with a large, free African American population went largely unspoken but was nonetheless a powerful undercurrent in colonizationist ideology.

Unsurprisingly, the majority of free African Americans were fiercely anti-colonizationist, though the movement did have a few vocal African American supporters, including John Russwurm, cofounder of the first African American newspaper, *Freedom's Journal.* Yet while a small number of free African Americans expressed support for colonization, most African American activists focused on the need to both end slavery and advocate for full racial equality on American soil. Given this reality, and Lundy's ongoing affiliation with colonizationists, it is perhaps not unexpected that his *Genius* does not appear to have attracted a significant number of African American readers. In the pieces he published in the *Genius,* Lundy did not make a concerted effort to overcome this racial barrier, instead addressing himself to his anticipated audience of white readers.[9]

In her literary work, Sedgwick manifested similar unease about immediate abolition, while at the same time decrying the evils of slavery. Born in Massachusetts in 1789, Sedgwick was the sister of an abolitionist brother, Henry Sedgwick, and was part of antislavery circles in her native state. Despite these connections, she remained reluctant to wholeheartedly embrace immediate abolitionism. One antislavery friend, fellow author Eliza Lee Follen, frequently sought to pin her down on the slave question. "What dear are your views & feelings upon the subject?" Follen asked in an 1834 letter. "We [Follen and her husband, Charles Follen] are very anxious to know; as far as pity for the suffering is in question we do not ask we know you feel for all that live but the benevolent as well as the wise differ upon this subject & we are particularly desirous to know what you think about it."[10] Sedgwick's reply, though not the ringing endorsement of abolitionism Follen likely hoped for, was nonetheless encouraging. "I do indeed feel with you," Sedgwick reassured her friend. "& I would do something more than feel—It is a subject that has much occupied my thoughts."[11] With her novel *Redwood* and an unpublished antislavery text she wrote during the 1830s, Sedgwick did "something more than feel"; she used fiction to make the case against slavery and in favor of white women's involvement in antislavery work.

Sedgwick, Chandler, and Lundy all stressed the value of using fiction as a means of encouraging (they assumed, reluctant) white readers to consider the issue of slavery. Sedgwick's friend Louisa Minot wrote to her after Sedgwick had published *Redwood,* "I think the work invaluable because it will instill principles into those who would never receive them from any other source."[12] Sedgwick echoed this idea in her unpublished antislavery novel, noting that, since she had made antislavery arguments central to her text, "our readers may remind us, that it is our craft to write for their amusement & to allow them to extract instruction for themselves if perchance so valuable an essence can be obtained from the light material of a tale."[13] With this assertion, Sedgwick at once noted that her readers might chafe at encountering moral messages in the context of a "light tale" written for their "amusement" and raised the question of whether "valuable" moral principles could, indeed, truly be "extracted" from fiction. She indicated that they could and that readers of her novel would find "instruction for themselves," provided that she presented these moral messages sufficiently engagingly in her fiction.

Throughout his editorial work, Lundy likewise stressed fiction's value in conveying antislavery messages to resistant audiences. After Chandler's death, he compiled a collection of her literary work, writing a preface for the volume that highlighted the importance of her fiction to the antislavery movement: "Knowing the eagerness of many to peruse the tales of fancy, she occasionally wrote a piece of that character. . . . But she always took especial care to choose the subject, and present the narration, so as to leave a moral impression on the mind of the reader, favourable to the cause of humanity."[14] Lundy clearly indicated his awareness that fiction, while popular, was still looked on with suspicion by some readers. As Nina Baym and Cathy Davidson have detailed, anxieties about the moral dangers of fiction, specifically the negative impact fiction could have on the minds of impressionable female readers, circulated widely in early republic and antebellum America.[15] Given these concerns, Lundy hastened to reassure readers Chandler had only penned her "tales of fancy" occasionally, in response to explicit reader demand, and had been careful to make her fiction explicitly moral in its content. Provided they were cautious about how they did so, Lundy noted, writers like Chandler could capitalize on readers' hunger for fiction by writing compelling antislavery narratives, which would engagingly introduce them to antislavery ideas.

As scholars such as Mary Kelley have demonstrated, during the early and mid-nineteenth century, the medium of fiction was consistently associated with female readers.[16] In the pages of the *Genius,* Lundy and Chandler certainly emphasized the power of fiction to bring antislavery ideas to a female audience. It was especially important that antislavery advocates successfully reach women, Lundy argued, because "the virtuous matrons of our country will have an important part to perform in the great work of emancipation."[17] Chandler echoed this point in an 1830 editorial, noting to her female readers that she wrote stories because she believed works of fiction would be successful "in arresting your attention, and bending an hour of your serious thought" on slavery.[18] Lundy took this point a step further, stating that if it were not for fiction, he doubted that women would take any interest in debates about abolition. "It is not to be expected that the ladies, generally," he asserted in 1821, "would be willing to sit down to what would seem to them an uninteresting detail of political transaction unless they could calculate on finding something likewise lively and amusing." Lundy would therefore endeavor to attract and retain his female readers' attention by publishing entertaining fictional works and "'blending the useful with the sweet,' to make it as interesting to them as possible."[19] To counteract female readers' preconceptions of antislavery as a tedious political subject, "lively and amusing" fiction would abound in the *Genius's* Ladies' Department.

To interest women in abolition, authors needed not ask them to contemplate abstract moral concepts but rather appeal directly to their naturally potent imaginations and emotions. It might be effective to use logic and rationality to bring men into the movement, but when seeking to convert women, an approach centered on the heart, rather than on the head, was necessary. To bring women into the cause, writers needed to publish emotional works that, as Lundy declared, "cannot fail to excite the tear of virtuous sensibility."[20]

Lundy consistently argued that by using emotional appeals in their fiction, antislavery writers could effectively reach female readers in ways that would be impossible through drier forms of rhetoric. In his edition of Chandler's writings, Lundy noted, "Her appeals were tender, persuasive, heart-reaching; while the strength and cogency of her arguments rendered them incontrovertible."[21] He drew a clear distinction between two key aspects of Chandler's work: its emotional content and its argumentative power. He asserted that Chandler first sought to reach her female readers through "tender" emotional appeals, and once she had done so successfully, she provided clear arguments against the institution. Female authors were thus *capable* of making rational arguments against slavery; they simply cloaked such arguments in emotional rhetoric to draw in female readers who might otherwise turn away from discussions of slavery uninterested.

Affirming that women needed to be approached through their hearts rather than their minds in some respects echoed dominant nineteenth-century stereotypes about women's intellectual inferiority to men. Yet these arguments also bear a different interpretation. That women were more emotional than men might, Lundy and Chandler contended, actually be a positive quality, decidedly advantageous to the antislavery cause. Writing during an era in which sentimental culture was ascendant in the United States, authors' privileging of women's gendered capacity to feel could signify not weakness but rather strength. As Lori Merish, Laura Mielke, and Stephanie Shields have noted, sentimental culture had some potentially positive implications for middle-class women, given that the rhetoric of sentimentality praised feminine emotion as superior to masculine reason.[22] Using intensely emotional fictional narratives to speak to women was, as such, an approach based not solely in writers' distrust of women's intellects, but also in their faith in women's feelings.

Chandler's and Sedgwick's decision to express their antislavery ideas through fiction was also rooted in cultural norms surrounding women's public speech in the nineteenth century. Writing during an era in which the idea of a female lecturer inspired horror in most Americans, and women's involvement in any political movement was distinctly controversial, fiction was a more feminine medium through which women could express their ideas. Despite the frequent presence of women at political rallies and public meetings in the early republic and antebellum United States, the notion of respectable, middle-class women directly engaging in public discussion of contentious issues, as Glenna Matthews, Mary Ryan, and Susan Zaeske have discussed, nonetheless remained controversial.[23] Fiction could allow women to enter into public conversations about difficult subjects such as slavery, while at the same time being presented, as scholars including Barbara Bardes, Suzanne Gossett, and Caroline Levander have demonstrated, as a fundamentally private activity, with works of fiction being both written and read in the private sphere of the home.[24]

Both Lundy and Chandler expressed these ideas, arguing that reading antislavery fiction was a gender-appropriate activity for white, middle-class women. In the preface to his edition of Chandler's writings, Lundy noted, "We earnestly commend them to the perusal of all Ladies, to whom this cause seems a political one."[25] In the editorials she wrote for the *Genius*, Chandler likewise emphasized the compatibility of bourgeois feminine domesticity with participation in antislavery print culture. Her female reader could easily become involved in the antislavery movement, Chandler maintained in her 1829 editorial "Opinions," "without [being led] one step beyond her own proper sphere." She assured her female audience:

> We have not the least desire to see our own sex transformed into a race of politicians, but we do not think that in this case such consequences are in the least to be apprehended. To plead for the miserable to endeavor to alleviate the bitterness of their destiny, and to soften the stern bosoms of their oppressors into gentleness and mercy, can never be unfeminine or befitting the delicacy of woman. . . . She does not seek to direct, or share with men, the government of the state; but she entreats them to lift the iron foot of despotism from the neck of her sisterhood; and this we consider not only quite within the sphere of her privileges, but also of her positive duties.[26]

By reading and even writing about the antislavery movement, women need not fear violating the tenets of middle-class femininity or encroaching into the masculine sphere of politics. Female writers' antislavery work was, rather, a result of their feminine empathy with enslaved women, and as such, an extension of women's rightful roles as the moral guardians of American society. Women were thus political only to the extent that they sought to shape the morals of politically empowered men, an action that her white, middle-class female readers, Chandler maintained, ought to regard as their proper feminine duty.[27]

White Women and Antislavery Activism in Chandler's Fiction

Because Chandler believed white women had a tremendously important part to play in the fight against slavery, it is not surprising that white women are the central antislavery actors throughout her fiction. Chandler, notably, did not give enslaved women similarly crucial roles in undermining the peculiar institution in her stories; rather, when enslaved women appear at all in her fiction, they are shadowy abstractions for white heroines to feel sympathy for, cry over, and subsequently act in the name of. In considering this passivity, it is worth remembering that Chandler published during an era of considerable anxiety on the part of many whites about enslaved resistance, with Denmark Vesey's uprising in South Carolina having been thwarted in 1822 and David Walker's tract discussing violent slave resistance, *Appeal to the Coloured Citizens of the World,* having been published in 1829.[28]

During the 1820s and 1830s, fears about uprisings of enslaved people consequently circulated extensively, not only in mainstream white American culture but also among white antislavery activists. Like many white antislavery advocates of the era, Chandler downplayed the idea of enslaved people claiming their own freedom, focusing instead on white allies' actions on enslaved people's behalf. Writing for the *Genius*'s Ladies' Department and its white female readership, Chandler's work highlighted the activism of white women who contributed to the antislavery cause by sedately exerting moral influence on behalf of the enslaved, rather than on enslaved women, who struggled for their own emancipation.

Like other female reformers involved in movements for social change in the early republic era, Chandler was aware that even white women's peaceful, seemingly sedate antislavery activity could be perceived as a violation of the ideals of domestic, bourgeois femininity. As Anne Boylan, Barbara Epstein, and Lori Ginzberg have documented, even women who participated in relatively conservative social movements, such as benevolent organizations, maternal reform groups, and temperance advocacy still faced criticism and resistance if their activism appeared to transgress the boundaries of gendered propriety.[29] Given the inescapably radical nature of speaking out against the powerful, entrenched institution of slavery, antislavery activism was even more risky for women. Chandler was, as such, particularly careful to argue that white, middle-class women could seamlessly incorporate antislavery advocacy into the rituals of genteel feminine sociability, domestic work in their households, and their rightful roles as society's moral guardians. By arguing that antislavery activism fit comfortably into conservative definitions of white, middle-class femininity, she worked to mask the innate radicalism of asking women to join the political, controversial fight to abolish slavery.

One key, gender-appropriate way white women could participate in the antislavery movement, Chandler's fiction argued, was through involvement in the free produce movement. This movement first emerged in America during the late eighteenth century in Quaker communities in Philadelphia and Boston, subsequently becoming part of mainstream American antislavery activism in the early nineteenth century.[30] Free produce advocates sought to live without any goods produced through slave labor, either by finding alternatives or doing without such goods altogether. Women were often at the forefront of this movement, as they were typically the primary purchasers for their households. Participation in free produce was consequently attractive for activists like Chandler, since it did not, at least, on the surface, appear to challenge gendered expectations that middle-class women focus their energies on the domestic sphere.[31]

Through her discussions of women participating in the free produce movement, Chandler entered into not just a national but also a transatlantic dialogue about how women could best become involved in antislavery activism. Women often took the lead in British antislavery boycotts, at the forefront of significant campaigns urging British consumers to abstain from sugar during the 1790s and the mid- and late 1820s, just as Chandler was writing about these issues for the *Genius*. As scholars such as Julie Holcomb and Charlotte Sussman have documented, middle-class British and American women alike made boycotting sugar a key part of their performance of the genteel rituals of femininity, by purchasing, displaying, and using sugar bowls and tea sets featuring antislavery images and slogans in their parlors.[32]

By urging her female readers to engage in such protests, Chandler also participated in a dynamic transatlantic print culture that focused on the evils of sugar consumption. In 1824, prominent British abolitionist Elizabeth Heyrick published her tract *Immediate, Not Gradual Abolition,* which argued that women's boycotting of slave-produced goods could play a vital role in securing the end of the immoral institution of slavery.[33] Heyrick was not the only British female antislavery author who made the West Indian slave trade and the British consumption of sugar central to her writings during the 1820s and 1830s. In 1826, popular author Amelia Opie published her poem "The Black Man's Lament; or, How to Make Sugar," which detailed the many cruelties enslaved people endured to produce the sugar British consumers regularly, unthinkingly purchased. Mary Prince, who had been enslaved in the West Indies, published her account of her life in slavery, *The History of Mary Prince*, in 1831.[34] Authors such as Heyrick, Opie, and Prince condemned the evils of the sugar-focused slave economy and encouraged its boycott. Chandler built on and added to these conversations, insisting to her female American readers that they, too, could make important contributions to the global antislavery movement through their consumer choices.

Chandler asserted to female readers of the *Genius* that, as she wrote in one 1831 editorial, "Free Produce is a very easy, as well as feminine method of avowing your sentiments."[35] Indeed, abstaining from goods produced by slave labor could be a vital way not just to express antislavery ideas but also demonstrate that women possessed proper feminine sensibility. In her 1832 essay "On the Use of Free Produce," Chandler expressed incredulity that any deep-feeling woman could consume slave-produced sugar and "reconcile it to themselves that they, Christian wives and mothers and daughters, with all the kind and gentle sympathies of woman's nature playing about in their hearts, should be accessories in supporting one of the most heinous systems of oppression ever known in the world."[36]

Chandler even contended that for white female consumers, failing to boycott goods produced by slave labor was a moral crime on par with slaveholding itself. In the 1832 "Tea-Table Talk," Maria argues to her abolitionist friend Helen that it doesn't matter whether or not she takes sugar in her tea. Helen forcefully declares to Maria that if she continues to use slave-produced products such as sugar, "you are a slave-holder; or that you are doing worse, by paying another for the commission of a crime which you would not dare to commit yourself!" Helen continues that she does not know "how any female who has even a partial knowledge of the horrors of slavery, can be willing to support such a system, or can receive the least enjoyment from the indulgence in comforts and luxuries which are purchased by the sacrifice of so many lives."[37]

"Tea-Table Talk" thus invested women's household consumption decisions with tremendous importance, as Helen argues that women who economically support slavery through their consumer choices are as morally culpable for the sufferings of the enslaved as actual slave owners. Even as she insisted that involvement in free produce activism was suitably domestic, Chandler also demonstrated that buying (and abstaining from buying) slave-produced goods were fundamentally political acts. Women like Maria might wave off their teatime decisions as unimportant, but Chandler's narrative maintained that they actually had significant public implications for the lives of enslaved people and the future of the antislavery cause.

Chandler's tale also warned female readers that buying slave-produced goods confirmed the worst possible stereotypes about female consumers as frivolous and self-indulgent. As scholars such as T. H. Breen have demonstrated, post-Revolutionary American society was riddled with anxieties about the potential for luxury-loving women to destroy the moral fabric of the young republic through thoughtless, extravagant consumerism.[38] Chandler's story fit into this broader discourse, as she warned her female readers that their consumer decisions would either demonstrate virtuous restraint or prove that they valued comfort and luxury more than they did the fundamental well-being of others. Women's involvement in consumer culture did not necessarily demonstrate their lack of virtue, as many commentators feared it might. But it certainly had the potential to do so, Chandler argued, if free women callously purchased goods produced through enslaved labor for their own selfish pleasure.

By setting her story, as the tale's title highlights, at a tea table in a bourgeois woman's parlor, Chandler underlined the ways free produce activism fit into dominant ideals of white femininity. Chandler's decision to have her female characters discuss the fraught topic of slavery during the mannered rituals of tea-drinking firmly embedded these conversations in the genteel rituals of feminine sociability.[39] Yet in the story, Helen also dramatically violates the expectations of "tea-table talk," as she does not engage in pleasant, restrained discourse with her friend while sipping tea in her parlor. Instead, she bluntly condemns the immorality of Maria's decision to take sugar in her tea in direct, unambiguous terms. There is thus a fundamental tension at the heart of this narrative, with Chandler at once carefully setting her story in the seemingly apolitical, feminine space of the tea table, yet also making that space one of forceful confrontation. Chandler therefore at once reassured her female readers that free produce activism was a genteel activity, even as she indicated that its moral imperatives could push women outside the sphere of refined sociability.

Much as she did in "Tea-Table Talk," in her other fiction Chandler made involvement in antislavery activity a litmus test of white women's capacity for emotional refinement and sensitivity. Chandler critiqued women who, on learning of slavery's evils, felt compelled to "sit quietly down, and satisfy their delicate feelings—too sensitively refined to bear a description of the horrors of slavery."⁴⁰ In her 1829–30 series of epistolary stories, "Letters on Slavery, to Isabel," letter-writer Agnes is baffled that the titular Isabel is not yet involved in antislavery activity, given that she has "a heart so alive to the impulses of humanity, so full of tenderness."⁴¹ Chastising her usually deep-feeling friend for remaining indifferent to the plight of the enslaved, Agnes notes, the thought of suffering enslaved women "has haunted me, Isabel!"⁴² In "Letters on Slavery," Chandler thus indicated that ignoring the pain enslaved women suffered in slavery belied any claims free women might make to possessing genuine emotional sensitivity. Caring about slavery was thus a key barometer through which middle-class women could demonstrate, or notably fail to demonstrate, their feminine capacity for empathy.

In the fiction she published in the *Genius*, Chandler argued not just that female readers demonstrated their capacity for genuine feeling by expressing empathy with enslaved women but also that this empathy could have a transformative impact on the antislavery movement. In her stories, white women's sympathy for enslaved women is central in moving the antislavery cause forward. The heroine of her 1829 "The Harmans," Mary Harman, successfully persuades her husband to emancipate the enslaved people he owns, purely through the power of her visible emotion. Having told her husband that she pitied devoted, loving enslaved wives and mothers for not having the same stable family life that she enjoyed, "Mary raised her eyes—they were suffused with tears." Hereafter, she allows her silent tears, rather than her words, to speak to her husband on behalf of enslaved women. As her husband begins discussing gradually emancipating the enslaved people on their plantation, "he felt her hot tears raining upon [his hand]; but she did not speak nor lift her face till he had concluded." Mary notably does not speak to or even look at her husband as he talks, influencing him not with her words or even her glances but rather purely with her silent, fervent tears. Only after he has finally decided to move forward with his plan for emancipation does she raise her face, still silent, her cheeks "wet with the passion of grateful tears."⁴³

White women's tears are a similarly potent force for antislavery change in Chandler's aptly titled "Tears of Woman," in which an angel descends from heaven to bid hard-hearted men to end slavery. The angel finds that "his repeated entreaties were again and again answered by the same cold repulse." He is successful only after he stops appealing to men:

> He called on woman. He pointed to her sister—suffering—degraded—miserable—and stretching out her manacled hands to her for succor. The call was heard . . . woman approached him. Her heart was touched with the wrongs of the injured ones, but she felt her arm was weak and her strength powerless; and bowing down her head, she wept in pity and sorrow over the objects of her compassion. But her aid was not in vain. The tears shed rusted the chains on that they fell![44]

Chandler's fiction thus painted a complex, contradictory picture of the relationship between enslaved and white women. In some ways, it highlighted the commonalities uniting white, middle-class and enslaved women, since Chandler noted that the latter were driven by the same desire to be loving wives and devoted mothers white women were. This was certainly a significant argument for her to make in the early nineteenth century, given the prevalence of stereotypes that defined African American women as hypersexual, immoral, indifferent mothers, fundamentally incapable of living up to bourgeois standards of chaste, self-sacrificing femininity and maternity.[45]

Yet at the same time, Chandler's fiction created a sharp division between white and enslaved women, enslaved women being the mute, passive subjects of white women's sympathy. In Chandler's stories, enslaved women displayed no agency, instead waiting for white women to save them. As Eve Allegra Raimon and Karen Sánchez-Eppler have demonstrated, such tropes were pervasive in both print and visual antislavery cultures. Images abounded of passive, vulnerable enslaved women imploring their white female "sisters" to liberate them from the gendered horrors of slavery.[46]

And of course, in some ways, the vast power disparity represented in these works reflected the realities of white, middle-class and enslaved women's lives, with white women having access to economic and social power and, most fundamentally, to legal recognition of their very humanity, denied to enslaved women. Yet such representations erased *all* of enslaved women's agency and individuality, making them visible only as faceless, undifferentiated subjects of white female sympathy. This depiction had troubling real-world implications, as it pointed to a broader failure on the part of white antislavery authors to recognize enslaved women's full humanity or to acknowledge that enslaved women's ideas about emancipation might differ from their own.

Chandler's stories also offered a complicated vision of the role of female emotion in the antislavery movement. Writing as sentimental culture was on the rise in American society; Chandler's work nonetheless also appeared during an era in which ideas about female emotionality were by no means uniformly positive. As Nancy Isenberg and Shirley Samuels have demonstrated, anxieties about women's emotions as uncontrollable and destructive remained a significant part of arguments against full female participation in the public sphere during the early republic and antebellum eras.[47] In a society that continued to define the ability to be objective and rational as the cornerstones of American citizenship, Chandler made a powerful statement by celebrating female emotion as a positive agent of social change; feminine feeling was not to be feared but rather to be embraced as a morally potent force inherently superior to masculine logic. Yet the argument that white women could most effectively express their antislavery convictions through silent emotional advocacy nonetheless remained a problematic one. Herself writing and publishing to protest slavery, Chandler's fiction paradoxically suggested that white women could best contribute to abolitionism not by writing, petitioning, or speaking but rather through the silent tears of sympathy they shed over enslaved women, who were themselves silent and powerless.

Enslaved and White Women Protesting Slavery in Catharine Maria Sedgwick's Novels

The antislavery fiction Catharine Maria Sedgwick wrote during the 1820s and 1830s shared notable commonalities and differences from Chandler's work. While Sedgwick also made white women's moral influence a vital force in the antislavery fight, her fiction featured enslaved characters as active, individualized people in ways Chandler's stories did not. That Sedgwick created richer, more complex portraits of enslaved people in her fiction is striking, as Chandler was decidedly more radical in her antislavery ideas and more committed to immediate abolitionism than Sedgwick was. One possible reason for Sedgwick's creation of more dynamic enslaved characters is the longtime presence of a self-emancipated woman, Elizabeth Freeman, as a domestic worker in the Sedgwick household. Freeman was employed by the Sedgwicks for most of her adult life, and the children of the Sedgwick family often said they regarded Freeman as a quasi-maternal figure.⁴⁸ That Freeman's stories about her life within slavery made a strong impression on Sedgwick may help to account for why she depicted enslaved people as individuals in her stories.

Sedgwick represented her enslaved characters as both nobly committed to realizing the American dream of personal liberty and unsettlingly allied with violence and disorder. Her 1824 novel *Redwood* featured the enslaved character of Africk, a pious man who had endured physical abuse and separation from his beloved family during his years in slavery. Prior to converting to Christianity, he dreamed of violently revenging himself on his master for his years of suffering. While his Christian faith transformed Africk into a pacifist, he nonetheless continues to believe that violence will ultimately be necessary to end slavery. "Pray for your father's land, and your father's children," he ominously tells a white character. "Pray to be saved from the curse that is coming . . . oh, I hear the cry of revenge; I hear the wailings of your wives and your little ones; and I see your fair lands drenched with blood. Pray to God to save you in that day, for it will surely come."⁴⁹ Though Africk leaves the details of this impending bloodbath vague, the final outcome is not in doubt. If slavery continues, whites who support the institution will be violently punished. Although Sedgwick gave this vision to a morally admirable character, Africk's voice is nonetheless a discordant one in a novel that otherwise promoted peaceful, gradual emancipation. By making the text's primary enslaved character an unsettling soothsayer who foretells the nation's impending violent doom, Sedgwick drew a disquieting link between enslaved struggles for liberation and the eruption of violence in American society.

That Sedgwick chose an enslaved *man* to voice these sentiments is particularly significant. Although she published her novel several years before the widespread panic unleashed by Nat Turner's slave rebellion, her book nonetheless entered into a culture in which white concerns about the potential for enslaved male violence were already considerable.⁵⁰ By the time of *Redwood*'s publication in 1824, Gabriel Prosser's and Denmark Vesey's plans for large-scale slave uprisings had fueled many white Americans' anxieties about the possibility of organized enslaved violence. In some respects, Sedgwick's narrative played into these fears, giving her primary enslaved male character ominous words about the violence that awaited the American nation if slavery did not soon end. Partially diffusing these tensions by insisting on Africk's personal commitment to pacifism, Sedgwick nonetheless also drew uneasy connections between enslaved men and the potential for violence against whites.

In an unfinished, unpublished novel that Sedgwick worked on during the early 1830s, one of her heroines is an enslaved woman who consistently makes powerful protests against the cruelties of slavery. Although the reasons she chose not to finish or seek publication for this novel are not definitively known, it is suggestive that one of the few texts from the 1830s to offer a dynamic vision of a rebellious enslaved woman remained unpublished during its author's lifetime. It seems plausible that one reason Sedgwick abandoned her antislavery tale was discomfort with the inescapable radicalism of having a revolutionary enslaved woman as one of her novel's primary characters.

The historical context in which Sedgwick began, and subsequently stopped, writing her novel is also significant. Though scholars remain uncertain as to precisely when she worked on her book, it is most likely that Sedgwick wrote the text between 1830 and 1834.[51] These years were decidedly noteworthy ones in the history of slavery and abolition. In 1831, William Lloyd Garrison founded the radical abolitionist newspaper the *Liberator,* which generated instant controversy. Many white southerners and northerners feared that the paper's calls for immediate abolition would lead to bloody conflict between enslaved people and whites.[52] These prognostications seemed to some to have been realized in August 1831, when Nat Turner led a slave revolt in Virginia, in which fifty-five whites were killed. In its wake, many African Americans, who were entirely unconnected to the rebellion, were murdered by fearful whites; southern states passed punitive laws that severely restricted the rights of enslaved and free African Americans; and fear spread throughout the country about African American men's perceived propensity for violence.[53] After the Turner uprising, Sedgwick may have been reluctant to publish any work in which a defiant enslaved character so much as raised the possibility of future slave uprisings.

Because of the example of her fellow New England writer Lydia Maria Child, Sedgwick would also have been very much aware of the tremendous professional and personal risks of publishing antislavery literature during the 1830s. Like Sedgwick, Child began her literary career in the 1820s, with the publication of a novel about relations between Native American and white people in the colonial era (with Child's *Hobomok* appearing in 1824, and Sedgwick's *Hope Leslie* in 1827). After the publication of *Hobomok,* Child's star continued to rise, as she launched the wildly successful, pioneering American children's periodical the *Juvenile Miscellany* in 1826, and published successful guides to household management and child-rearing in 1829 and 1831.[54] And then, in 1833, Child published her radical abolitionist tract *An Appeal in Favor of That Class of Americans Called Africans,* and her previously flourishing career as a popular author and editor came to an immediate, dramatic end.

While Child had expressed sympathy for the enslaved and critiqued slavery prior to the *Appeal*'s publication, she had not previously articulated as extensively or unambiguously her support for immediate abolition and her advocacy for full racial equality. Child's *Appeal* remains one of the most radical documents of the antebellum era, boldly calling for the immediate emancipation of the enslaved, complete civil rights for all African Americans, and the legalization and social acceptance of interracial marriage. Unsurprisingly given its content, after the *Appeal*'s publication Child awoke to find herself both a social and literary pariah. Not only did she lose personal friendships, she also saw her work banned in southern bookshops and subscriptions to the *Juvenile Miscellany* drop precipitously. Child had become so controversial and unpopular that in 1834 she was compelled to abandon her editorship of the *Miscellany.* Though the radical abolitionist community warmly embraced the *Appeal,* the tract ruined Child's prospects of enjoying mainstream literary success for many years. This was no small sacrifice, as she was the primary earner for her household and had previously relied on her literary career to support both herself and her husband.

The extensive damage speaking out against slavery had done to Child may well have been another factor discouraging Sedgwick from publishing her own antislavery work in the 1830s. After all, Sedgwick did not share Child's radical abolitionist values, which likely further weakened her desire to risk publishing an even moderately antislavery novel. Writing at a time when the white American reading public was expressing strong hostility to antislavery literary work, Sedgwick kept her novel quietly tucked away amid her private papers, rather than risk exposing it and herself to a negative response from the white reading public.

Sedgwick's unpublished antislavery novel tells the story of two slave-owning families, the Cuthberts and the Fitzhughs. Throughout the text, one of the Cuthberts' slaves, Meta, actively challenges slavery's injustices.

Characterized by her "erect figure and firm step" and her consistent "resistance to tyranny," the strong-willed, independent-minded Meta refuses to accept her subordination within the slave system.[55] By using powerful language about her struggles against tyranny, Sedgwick infused her discussions of Meta with quasi-Revolutionary overtones. This is by no means coincidental, as Sedgwick seems to have based Meta on Freeman, the first enslaved woman in the state of Massachusetts to legally secure her freedom. After learning during the Revolution of the passage of a new constitution that ostensibly protected the rights of all Massachusetts citizens, Freeman sued for her freedom in court. In an essay Sedgwick wrote about this event, Freeman approaches Sedgwick's father, lawyer Theodore Sedgwick, declaring, "I heard that paper read yesterday that says 'all men are born equal—&, that every man has a right to freedom'—I am not a dumb *Critter,* wont the law give me my freedom?"[56] Sedgwick's essay firmly linked the causes of American independence and liberation for the enslaved, emphasizing Freeman's insistence that the language of freedom and revolution applied just as much to enslaved black Americans as it did to free white ones.

Likely inspired at least partly by Freeman's fierce commitment to liberty and her open resistance to slavery, throughout her novel Sedgwick presented Meta as a woman who fearlessly defies the authority of her owners and overseers. Without regarding her physical safety, Meta challenges the domination of the Cuthberts' brutal overseer, Agar, and her violent mistress, Mrs. Cuthbert. After listening to Agar's account of the cruelties he had inflicted on Meta's father, Meta boldly declares, "You have told what my father was, I will now tell what you are." She then denounces Agar for his unjust treatment of all of the Cuthberts' slaves. Similarly, when Mrs. Cuthbert threatens to hit Meta's daughter with a poker, Meta interposes herself between the two, telling her mistress, "'Strike on . . . but touch her at the peril of your life!'"[57] Threatened with violence, Meta refuses to become violent herself, accepting a blow from her mistress but notably not returning it. Instead, she demonstrates a selfless, maternal willingness to endure violence for her beloved daughter's sake.

Noble as Meta's resistance to slavery was, Sedgwick also represented it as a troubling violation of feminine standards of propriety, particularly in terms of how Meta publicly displays her wounded body as part of her antislavery protest. After Mrs. Cuthbert strikes her, Meta deliberately leaves her sleeves rolled up while working around the Cuthbert home, so that all members of and visitors to the household will see the wound her mistress's violence has left behind. The narrator informs the reader, "Meta never complained of her wound, nor spoke of it, but she left it, as has been told uncovered, & it did not require the gift of a seeer [sic] to perceive that there was a prophecy of evil to Mistress Cuthbert 'in its dumb mouth.'"[58] Meta's baring of her wounded flesh to the public gaze is a bold, physical form of antislavery protest, radically unlike the decorous, restrained antislavery activism that white female characters engaged in.

Of course, white female characters did not take part in similar forms of antislavery protest in large part because they did not face the same high risk or terrible reality of violence that enslaved female characters did. In fiction as in life, slavery was fundamentally about the denial of enslaved people's ability to make decisions about their mobility, labor, bodies, and, particularly significantly to enslaved women, sexual access to their bodies and control over their reproductive lives. Enslaved women's inability to claim the bodily integrity routinely afforded to white women was consistently demonstrated in the rituals of slavery. As Stephanie M. H. Camp and Walter Johnson have vividly detailed, at slave auctions enslaved women were systematically stripped, scrutinized, and subject to forcible gynecological examinations by prospective purchasers.[59] In Sedgwick's novel, Meta thus directly inverts the usual terms of how enslaved women's bodies were made visible in antebellum southern society: she consciously chooses to display her wounded body to white onlookers.

The differences in how Meta and white female characters use their bodies in their struggles against slavery are striking. In antislavery fiction, white women primarily make bodily appeals against slavery by shedding silent tears on behalf of enslaved women. In direct contrast, Meta exposes her injured body as her primary testimony against slavery. Given severe taboos about the visibility of female bodies in the nineteenth century— particularly in a genteel home like the Cuthberts'—Meta's revealing of her wounded flesh, however morally justified, violates standards concerning the regulation of women's bodies in the domestic space.[60] In her resistance to slavery, Meta thus demonstrates her willingness to transgress expectations of genteel womanhood to further the antislavery cause—something that white female characters in antislavery fiction, notably, do not do.

It is not only in how she uses her body that Meta's antislavery protests differ from those of white female characters. Meta is also much more confrontational than white women; she goes to her master to verbally denounce her mistress's violence. Meta's protests against slavery far more dramatically subvert the class, racial, and gender hierarchies of her society than did white women's, which were typically addressed to white men with whom they had romantic or familial relationships. In some ways admiring of this defiance of existing power structures, Sedgwick also expressed uneasiness about such subversive forms of protest on the part of an enslaved woman.

Sedgwick signaled this ambivalence by showing Meta's protests to be abject failures. In her novel, it is the decorous, gradualist antislavery advocacy of Augusta Cuthbert (the virtuous daughter of Meta's owners) that is ultimately successful. Augusta is staunchly antislavery in her beliefs and is the primary force in restraining Meta's more direct resistance to slavery. Immediately after Meta's mistress strikes her, Meta wants to go to her master to condemn this act of violence. She is delayed in doing so only because Augusta believes such a protest unwise and tries to persuade Meta to remain discreet about the abuse she has suffered. As the narrator notes, Meta would have immediately denounced her mistress to her master, but her "irresistible young lady kept her silent."[61]

The novel endorses Augusta's belief that such direct protests are ill-advised; it shows Meta's eventual efforts to convince her master of slavery's evils, undertaken in direct defiance of Augusta's advice, as entirely futile. After her master finally notices her wound, Meta pleads with him to recognize the cruelty of his wife and of the slave system overall. While her words initially move him, Mr. Cuthbert quickly regresses to callous indifference to enslaved people's sufferings. Meta, the narrator recounts,

> had touched his heart and conscience, but . . . enfeebled as they were by habits of selfishness . . . it would have been no less [than] a miracle to stimulate them to any effective efforts than to restore health to a mutilated & fatally diseased body—He wiped his spectacles—bit his nails for a few moments . . . pushed round the bottle & forgot—or tried to forget the abuses to which his indulgence had exposed his slaves.[62]

Meta's protests against slavery thus ultimately go nowhere, as she is unable to create any lasting antislavery feeling in her master. Unlike the moral appeals of white female characters, the verbal advocacy of enslaved women has no impact on slave-owning men's beliefs. The novel thus indicates that while Meta is very morally astute, she is not a truly effective agent for change.

Instead, Sedgwick placed the power to advance the antislavery cause in the hands of elite white women like Augusta. Rather than directly protest the evils of slavery to her corrupt parents, she instead quietly plans on marrying her equally antislavery fiancé and then liberating the enslaved people on both of their plantations after their marriage and their parents' deaths. The vision of emancipation that Sedgwick puts forward here is thus a decidedly gradual one, radically different from the immediate change sought by enslaved characters like Meta. As sympathetically as Sedgwick depicted Meta's desire to be free, her novel rejects immediate emancipation as both unlikely and undesirable.

Sedgwick further suggested that prior to their emancipation, enslaved women like Meta still had important lessons about femininity, decorum, and restraint to learn from their white mistresses. Throughout the novel, young Augusta plays the role of moral guide to Meta, who is old enough to be her mother. Augusta teaches Meta to be patient and to embrace cautious activism and gradual abolition. In this regard, Sedgwick's novel uneasily echoed the proslavery ideology of the antebellum era, which insisted that one of the primary benefits of slavery was that it allowed supposedly ignorant enslaved women to be educated by their benevolent mistresses.[63] Sedgwick invested Augusta with a quasi-maternal power over Meta, suggesting that, for all her courage and intelligence, Meta is in some ways still a child in need of guidance. The novel indicated that enslaved women needed more time to be educated in feminine restraint before they could be fully independent people, living without the guiding hand of wise white women.

Sedgwick's discussions of violence further underlined her uneasiness about enslaved women's capacity to be decorous, autonomous free women. Despairing about the deep entrenchment of slavery in American society and the persistent unwillingness of white southerners to confront its evils, Meta warns the Cuthberts' overseer that if slavery were not abolished, the day would soon arrive when the enslaved "shall be not monkeys, but lions and wolves."[64] Personally devoted to nonviolent resistance, Meta nonetheless foresees a future in which enslaved people will inevitably, violently seek their liberation. Stressing Meta's own willingness to endure violence without returning it, Sedgwick nonetheless indicated that Meta possessed a violent imagination. While she might not act violently herself, she still saw a future in which her fellow slaves would become violent.

The vision of enslaved women Sedgwick created in her fiction was thus a contradictory one. By indicating that, unlike white women, enslaved women had the potential to contemplate violence and were willing to defy gendered ideals of respectability in their protests against slavery, Sedgwick raised significant questions about enslaved women's ability to meet the standards of restrained femininity.

Yet even this limited vision of enslaved women's activism had some potentially positive aspects. Uncomfortable with Meta's actions, Sedgwick nonetheless expressed confidence in her innate morality and her status as a naturally virtuous mother. There is no doubt that Meta is a devoted parent and extremely morally perceptive woman who recognizes the evils of slavery, to which many of those around her are blind. She thus has a great deal in common with wise, moral white women like her young mistress. Contrary to stereotypes that predominated in nineteenth-century society, Sedgwick insisted that enslaved women were capable of both profound moral insight and deep devotion to their families. Arguing that enslaved women inherently possessed these qualities, her text offered some hope that, once emancipated, enslaved women had the potential to live lives as rooted in domestic affection and moral rectitude as their white counterparts did.

Chandler and Sedgwick's fiction at once offered profoundly radical and deeply conservative visions of the future of the antislavery cause. Making white women central to antislavery advocacy, these authors indicated that for their activism to be both gender-appropriate and effective, white women needed to carefully remain within existing definitions of respectable, bourgeois femininity. Both authors also deliberately marginalized enslaved women in their visions of antislavery change. Thus, the fiction that emerged from the 1820s and early 1830s powerfully challenged, even as it troublingly reinforced, the gender and racial hierarchies of the deeply patriarchal society in which its authors lived and wrote.

CHAPTER TWO

"An Influence Comparatively Silent, but Deep, and Strong, and Irresistible"

Women's Literature and the Rise of Radical Abolitionism, 1831–1839

> The fact is, there are few subjects of importance, now agitating the christian world, with which ladies have not something to do, on which they do not exert an immense influence—an influence comparatively silent, but deep, and strong, and irresistible. I will not adopt the insulting language of those, who, making women a mere creature of feeling, draw the boundary of their dominion and the heart.
> —"Philadelphia," "What Have the Ladies to Do with Anti-Slavery?" March 29, 1834

> High and beautiful lessons may be inculcated by a good story, and as a good a rule in morals deduced, as laid down.... We want works of imagination that shall do us honor and good at the same time; and these we can have.
> —*North American Review*, on Lydia Maria Child's *Juvenile Miscellany*, July 1833

In 1831, William Lloyd Garrison published the first issue of his radical abolitionist newspaper, the *Liberator*. From its very beginnings, the periodical sparked contentious debates both within and outside of the antislavery movement. With the pieces he published in the *Liberator*, Garrison consistently managed to provoke not only abolitionism-averse white southerners and northerners but also his fellow antislavery activists. For he and his contributors raised precisely the issues most likely to stir up controversy among even antislavery advocates, including the desirability of immediate abolition, the importance of seeking full civil rights for free African Americans, and the need to create more egalitarian roles for women in the antislavery movement.

The so-called woman question was a particularly sensitive, divisive one in antislavery circles. While few abolitionists would have denied that women needed to be involved in the fight to end slavery, consensus about how, exactly, they ought to participate was nonetheless extremely difficult to come by. As abolitionists formed new antislavery organizations during the 1830s, they struggled to define what women's roles in these institutions, and in the abolitionist movement overall, ought to be. And as female abolitionists such as Maria W. Stewart and Angelina and Sarah Grimké began, and ended, their controversial careers as antislavery orators during the 1830s, their fellow antislavery activists sought to decide whether the urgency of the antislavery cause justified such drastic violations of traditional notions of femininity. Female abolitionist authors who published during this decade actively engaged in these debates about gender, propriety, and the future course of the antislavery movement, endeavoring to define the most useful, appropriate place for women within it.

This chapter considers this transformative decade in the antislavery movement and print culture, analyzing how the literary works women published during these years engaged in discussions about women's roles in the antislavery struggle. The literature of the 1830s featured three notable changes within this print culture: an influx of free African American women's voices into antislavery periodicals, female authors' increasing willingness to openly critique the American government's culpability in upholding slavery, and the rise of antislavery literature explicitly intended for children. All of these developments had significant impacts on antislavery literary culture. The desire of editors like Garrison to seek out and publish works by black female writers opened important new public platforms from which African American women could speak. Female abolitionist authors' increasing willingness to openly condemn the actions of the American government signaled an expansion of the topics considered suitable for women to consider in antislavery literature. And abolitionists' desire to convert children to their cause opened up new spaces for female authors, as female writers were assumed to be naturally better at the maternal work of educating children than male activists were. Female authors argued that both white and African American women could make vital contributions to the abolitionist movement by carefully raising their children, particularly their sons, to embrace antislavery ideals and to implement those ideals in the public sphere. Yet as they also consistently represented female children as more innately, fiercely abolitionist than male ones, these writers expressed unease about less morally sound boys and men being the primary public actors against slavery.

By considering how antislavery fiction debated women's proper roles in activism, this chapter enters into the extensive historiography concerning the connections between abolitionism and feminism during the nineteenth century. In the 1960s and 1970s, the dominant narrative concerning antislavery women focused on how involvement in abolitionism was crucial in inspiring white women to become involved in organized struggles against gender oppression. In their monographs, scholars including Ellen Carol DuBois, Blanche Glassman Hersh, and Gerda Lerner argue that the more white female abolitionists reflected on the plight of enslaved women, the more thoroughly they recognized their own unequal position in American society. Similarly, the more thoroughly white women adopted the role of public antislavery activists, the more they chafed at conventional restrictions on free women's behavior and became interested and involved in feminist reforms.[1]

This narrative has considerable merit, rightly emphasizing the central role that involvement in abolitionism played in shaping the feminist ideals of several nineteenth-century woman's rights activists. However, as Julie Roy Jeffrey cogently argues in *The Great Silent Army of Abolitionism: Ordinary Women in the Antislavery Movement,* the connection between abolitionism and feminism has often been overstated and misrepresented, as the majority of female abolitionists did not become woman's rights activists. Involvement in abolitionism did not always, or even typically, lead women into the organized woman's rights movement. Yet, Jeffrey documents how involvement in abolitionism nonetheless did fundamentally transform women's thinking about what kinds of activism were appropriate for them to engage in—even those who least expected or desired it. Participating in the antislavery movement led even rather conservative women to engage in activities, such as petitioning and organizational leadership, they had never before thought suitable for women.[2]

This chapter refocuses scholarly attention from women's lived experiences as abolitionist and feminist activists to the ideas about gender, activism, and women's rights they expressed in antislavery fiction. An examination of women's antislavery literature provides useful insights into the development of feminist consciousness in antislavery women writers' thought. Firm believers in innate gender difference, antislavery female authors rooted women's right to become involved in abolitionism and to speak out against slavery in their inborn feminine capacity for empathy and their innate maternal feelings. Such thinking was distinctly different from that of abolitionist-feminist women such as Angelina Grimké, Sarah Grimké, and Lucretia Mott, who argued that women deserved greater rights in American society primarily because of the commonalities they shared with men as Christians and as citizens.[3] In the literature they published during the 1830s, female antislavery authors articulated an ideology of female empowerment that was firmly rooted in women's differences from men, rather than in their similarities to them.

As such, this chapter adds to historiographical discussions about the connections between female activism and women's assertion of their rights as citizens during the antebellum era. In her study of female abolitionists' petitions in the decades before the Civil War, Susan Zaeske traces their growing willingness, over the course of the 1830s, to define themselves as citizens and political actors, rather than solely as pious advocates of moral suasion.[4] Alisse Portnoy locates a similar trend in her scholarship on women's petitions against Indian removal and slavery during the 1820s and 1830s. The authors of these petitions gradually came to argue that, as female citizens, it was appropriate for them to voice disapproval of their government through petitioning. Over the course of these decades, white women shed their discomfort with using the explicitly political medium of petitions to make their public protests and claimed that their right to speak was rooted in the common citizenship they shared with men.[5]

This chapter suggests a less direct path from women's involvement in antislavery activity to claims of citizenship identified in Portnoy's and Zaeske's work. While over the course of the 1830s the authors whom this chapter examines also became more willing to claim their right to directly comment on political questions, they did not use the bold language of equal citizenship to do so. They did not argue that their right to discuss political questions came from the rights they held in common with men as fellow American citizens; instead, they maintained that these rights came from their differences from men, specifically their moral superiority to them.

This chapter also enters into larger scholarly discussions about how antislavery women built and sustained community. In her monograph, Beth Salerno traces the development of female antislavery societies across the Northeast and Midwest during the antebellum era. She maintains that female antislavery societies offered women vital spaces in which to forge close emotional bonds, which sustained them throughout their often challenging lives as public advocates of an extremely unpopular cause.[6] This chapter demonstrates that literary spaces such as ladies' and juvenile departments served a similar function for antislavery women, offering them opportunities to discuss antislavery ideas, debate how women could best be involved in abolitionism, and build a sense of community with one another.

For women who lived outside of the urban centers of Boston and Philadelphia, in communities often distinctly hostile to abolitionism, antislavery literature was an important site to connect with each other, and to develop an activist consciousness. Not only could women's literary spaces be places in which to forge solidarity among antislavery women, but they could also serve as significant public forums through which women could discuss antislavery tactics and ideologies.

Women's fiction from the 1830s also provides a unique opportunity to see African American and white women's antislavery literary works appearing in the same literary spaces, placed in implicit dialogue with one another. In a country as deeply segregated as antebellum America, this relatively egalitarian literary intermingling was as notable as it was unusual. Yet, though black and white women's writings appeared together in the *Liberator*'s pages, this did not mean that white and African American authors consistently addressed the same issues, tackled the same questions, or made similar arguments about abolition and racial equality. Both made their female characters crucial to the fight to end slavery and placed particular value on mothers raising their sons to be good abolitionists, but African American women's literature also differed in notable ways from that of white women writers. African American authors made their enslaved female characters more vivid, fully realized characters, reflecting on their interior lives and emotional experiences in more depth than white female writers did. Black writers also noted the fundamental interconnectedness of the struggle for civil rights in the North and emancipation in the South in ways white female authors did not.

African American authors also dedicated significant space to debating the fraught relationship between black people and the American nation. Could African American women and men ever find true equality in a nation that had been built on the institution of slavery and was so fundamentally structured by racial inequality? While black female writers asked and grappled with these questions, white authors largely ignored the issue of free African Americans' relationship to the state, concentrating instead on the plight of the enslaved. Women's literature in the 1830s thus provides valuable insights into the commonalities and differences in how African American and white women writers thought about the future of the antislavery movement and the fight for racial equality in the antebellum era.

Abolitionist Print Culture during the 1830s

Antislavery female authors who published during the 1830s did so within a rapidly growing national print culture. New transportation networks and advancing printing technologies made the dissemination of periodicals and books throughout the United States much more viable in the 1830s than had it been in previous decades.[7] Abolitionists were extremely eager to take advantage of these new opportunities to spread their message throughout the country. Despite white southerners' fierce resistance to the antislavery movement, abolitionists nonetheless hoped that an expanding print culture might enable them to distribute their literature throughout the South, as well as the North and Midwest. "Is it slander to say that God had made Southern consciences as susceptible, Southern hearts as warm as our own?" Boston Female Anti-Slavery Society member Anne Warren Weston asked in 1838, confidently answering her own question: "The omnipotent power of truth calmly & candidly laid before them must produce an effect."[8]

Antislavery advocates produced print materials in significant numbers during the 1830s, publishing 100 million antislavery tracts in 1834 and 1835 alone.[9] Abolitionists' efforts to get their literary works into the hands of readers presented significant challenges, however. Particularly in the wake of Nat Turner's 1831 rebellion, which white southerners partly blamed on the dissemination of David Walker's *Appeal to the Coloured Citizens of the*

World in the South, it became increasingly difficult for antislavery authors to distribute their works throughout the region.[10] Many southern postal facilities burned the antislavery literature that did make its way into the region, and white southern journalists frequently called for a wholesale boycott of antislavery tracts. Yet, despite these significant barriers, antislavery authors continued to write as though their works did reach a southern audience, hoping they would have the chance to sway the hearts and minds of their white southern, as well as their northern and midwestern, readers.

Disseminating antislavery literature in the North and Midwest was also quite challenging during the 1830s, given the ongoing hostility of most white northerners and midwesterners toward abolitionism. Abolitionist printers and editors were routinely condemned and attacked, sometimes violently, by antagonistic members of the white public in the North and Midwest. Garrison was dragged through the streets of Boston and nearly killed by a mob in 1835, and fellow newspaper editor Elijah Lovejoy was murdered in 1837, while trying to defend his press from angry proslavery members of his Alton, Illinois, community.[11] Because of their unshakeable belief that antislavery literature would play an essential role in bringing the peculiar institution to an end, antislavery authors and editors nonetheless continued to print and publish despite the significant danger of doing so.[12]

As noted, female authors seeking to publish their antislavery writing had an increased number of potential venues for doing so during the 1830s. In 1834, Lydia Maria Child published her antislavery gift book *The Oasis,* which featured her own fiction as well as works by fellow New England abolitionist writers Eliza Lee Follen and Hannah F. Gould. The Cincinnati-based *Philanthropist* newspaper, which launched in 1836, also published literature by female writers. Additionally, the 1830s witnessed the beginnings of a distinctive child-centered abolitionist literature, with the newly formed American Anti-Slavery Society issuing its children's periodical *The Slave's Friend* and Child infusing her children's magazine the *Juvenile Miscellany* with her abolitionist fiction during the early 1830s.

Important as all of these venues were, the central site for the publication of women's antislavery fiction in the 1830s was undoubtedly Garrison's *Liberator.* The *Liberator* commenced publication on January 1, 1831, in Boston, with perilously little in the way of financial backing, and not one single subscriber. The paper would have surely failed during its early years if not for the staunch support of African American abolitionists in Boston,

New York, and Philadelphia. Not only did African American activists such as James Forten provide vital financial resources, African Americans also constituted the majority of subscribers and a significant number of *Liberator* contributors during this decade.[13]

Although the *Liberator* struggled for survival in its early years, it nonetheless also quickly became a significant presence in American print culture. The controversial Garrison and his provocative newspaper were often flashpoints for discussion, his words often angrily reprinted and indignantly criticized both north and south of the Mason-Dixon line. Garrison may have had a difficult time attracting either large numbers of subscribers or considerable funds during the first years of the *Liberator*'s existence, but he had no difficulty whatsoever in getting attention.

Eager to provoke public discussions about slavery, Garrison was also very much interested in making women a central part of his paper. He began publishing ladies' and juvenile departments very early in the *Liberator*'s run (in 1831 and 1832, respectively) and actively courted women's participation in both of these spaces. Believing "the Ladies' Department in the *Genius of Universal Emancipation* adds vastly to the value of that able periodical," Garrison hoped his own paper's Ladies' Department would be similarly successful and influential. Like *Genius* editor Benjamin Lundy, Garrison believed ladies' departments were vital parts of antislavery periodicals, because of their potential to bring free women into the antislavery movement. "The fact that one million of the female sex are reduced by the slave system, to the most deplorable condition . . . ought to excite the sympathy and indignation of American women," Garrison wrote in his introduction to the *Liberator*'s first Ladies' Department. "We have therefore concluded, that a Ladies' Department in the *Liberator* would add greatly to its interests, and give a new impetus to the cause of emancipation." It was especially important that Garrison reach a female audience effectively because, as he asserted, "in their hands is the destiny of the slaves."[14]

By creating the *Liberator*'s Ladies' Department, Garrison also hoped to make a female-centered space in which antislavery women could safely discuss slavery and abolition with one another, without masculine interference or having to step outside the confines of bourgeois feminine propriety. This presentation of the department as a sealed-off, exclusively female-centered and controlled literary space was not an entirely accurate one. Although Garrison had hired Elizabeth Margaret Chandler to serve as editor of his

Ladies' Department (much as she served as the editor of the *Genius*'s department during these same years), he still held ultimate editorial power.

The separateness of the Ladies' Department from the rest of the paper also had some potentially problematic implications for antislavery women and the public presentation of their ideas. As Elizabeth McHenry has argued, Garrison's creation of a distinct Ladies' Department revealed the troubling "assumptions under which he operated regarding the circumscribed place of women's voices and their intellectual work in the abolitionist movement."[15] The lines between separation and marginalization could be perilously blurry ones for antislavery women writers. From its very inception, the Ladies' Department ran the risk of being a mere sideline, in which female antislavery activists wrote trivial, domestically focused fiction, while male abolitionists debated real issues of substance in the male-focused and dominated sections of the *Liberator*.

Yet despite this potential for female marginalization, ladies' and juvenile departments also had positive implications and empowering potential for antislavery women. The dedication of entire sections of the *Liberator* specifically to female readers and writers served as a noteworthy indicator of women's importance within the antislavery movement. Dedicating so much precious space in his costly-to-produce periodical to women's voices underlined Garrison's commitment to making women central in antislavery activism. Literary spaces such as ladies' and juvenile departments were also particularly valuable for antislavery women who wanted to publicly express their ideas about slavery but were uncomfortable at the prospect of doing so through such overtly-gender-transgressive means as speaking at, or even attending, public antislavery meetings.

As Deborah C. DeRosa has explored in her scholarship on juvenile abolitionist literature, some antislavery women specifically welcomed the chance to write for young readers, as the juvenile literary marketplace represented "a public but more acceptable forum" for female abolitionists.[16] Although being an abolitionist was, by its very nature, a daring act, DeRosa persuasively maintains that juvenile antislavery literature provided women with a relatively safe, socially acceptable venue through which to express their abolitionist ideas. While they could not necessarily justify public speaking as a straightforward extension of their roles as domestic, maternal educators, writing stories intended to convey moral messages to children much more readily lent itself to such justifications. Writing antislavery fiction explicitly intended for female and child audiences thus opened an important public space for antislavery women to relatively uncontroversially make their voices heard on the slave question.

Female Antislavery Authors during the 1830s

Before considering the content of the literary work they published during the 1830s, it is worth contemplating who, exactly, these antislavery women writers were. Several of this decade's authors, Lydia Maria Child, Eliza Lee Follen, and Hannah F. Gould, had wide-ranging literary careers during the antebellum era, writing novels, short stories, and poems on a range of reform and Christian subjects, in addition to abolitionist texts. It is more difficult to know a great deal about the literary careers of some of the other authors working during this decade, as several chose to publish either anonymously or pseudonymously. In early antebellum literary culture, publishing under a pseudonym was still relatively common, especially for those contributing to American newspapers. Women writers who chose to publish as "A Lady" rather than under their own names entered into the long-standing practice of female authors modestly refusing to publicly take credit for their published work.

The pseudonyms female writers published under revealed varying amounts of information about their true identities and chosen authorial personas. A few writers chose to use initials, such as "Y.N." or "N.S.," which, without directly revealing authors' names, might have signaled their identities to members of the still quite small radical abolitionist community. (During the 1820s and 1830s, Elizabeth Margaret Chandler, for example, published several of her pieces in the *Genius* as "E.M.C.," initials many of the paper's readers would have easily deciphered.) Other writers chose pseudonyms that emphasized their regional origins, like "Philadelphia," while others selected pseudonyms that carefully framed them as quasi-maternal figures—such as "Aunt Margery," who published a series of stories for young readers in the *Liberator*'s Juvenile Department.

African American women who published in the *Liberator* sometimes picked pen names that directly invoked white women's literature of the era. Abolitionist Sarah Forten, for example, used the pseudonym "Magawisca" (the Native American heroine of Catharine Maria Sedgwick's novel *Hope Leslie*) for her essays and poems. Thus, Forten quite literally wrote herself into white women's literature, reclaiming a white-created heroine's name to express her ideas. Other African American writers publishing in the *Liberator* similarly drew on names of notable women from literature and history, such as "Sophonisba," an ancient noblewoman who killed herself rather than submit to her Roman enemies and "Zelmire," the courageous heroine of a popular 1822 opera.[17] Through their pseudonyms, African American authors emphasized their immersion in and knowledge of the literary and musical cultures of the antebellum era. Writing during an era in which stereotypes about African American intellectual inferiority abounded in white America, these pseudonyms were thus a powerful means for black women to both assert their cultural sophistication and emphasize their similarity to other brave and virtuous women from history.

African American female writers also sometimes selected pseudonyms that highlighted their racial pride. One published her pieces under the name "Colored Female of Philadelphia," making her status as an author of color central to the presentation of her literary work. One of Philadelphia abolitionist Sarah Mapps Douglass's pseudonyms, "Zillah," also emphasized racial identity. A name drawn from the Old Testament, "Zillah" is variously translated as "darkness," "shade," or "shadow." By invoking not just biblical authority but also positively asserting blackness, Douglass signaled her status as not just a female Christian writer generally, but as a black, female Christian writer specifically.

Much abolitionist women's literature being published during the 1830s came from authors who were members of African American female literary societies in Philadelphia and Boston. Garrison actively sought contributions from these writers, reaching out to society leaders like Douglass and soliciting submissions from society members. In their scholarship on women's literary societies, Michelle Garfield, Elizabeth McHenry, and Julie Winch demonstrate that these organizations gave women a significant space in which to develop writing and oratory skills and to share thoughts on controversial topics.

Having such spaces was also especially important for African American female authors since, as Frances Smith Foster and Carla Peterson have demonstrated, African American women writing during the antebellum era faced significant tensions and pressures that male and white female authors did not. In addition to broader structural inequalities that made their ability to access print culture considerably more challenging, African

American female authors also had to contend with internalized racial prejudice, which had the potential to make them doubt or denigrate their own rhetorical abilities and right to speak out on social issues.[18] Female literary societies were thus an important space in which to discuss and combat such anxieties and to find support and encouragement from a community of other African American women. While they were often crucial sites in which women could express ideas without having to grapple with the racism of whites or the sexism of their male peers, Winch notes that literary societies were also problematic spaces since, much like the *Liberator*'s Ladies' Department, they remained separate from the male-dominated mainstream of free African American communities' intellectual life.[19]

Despite their separation into these racially and gender-segregated organizations, literary society members nonetheless hoped their work would have a broad impact on both the fight to end slavery and larger struggles for African American civil rights.[20] By producing original literary work, discussing these works with one another, and seeking the publication of their writings, authors hoped they could improve white Americans' opinions of African Americans' intellectual capabilities and moral probity, which would in turn benefit both the antislavery cause and the social standing of free African Americans. As one member of the Female Literary Association of Philadelphia wrote, society members needed to always remember that the interests of free and enslaved African Americans "are one, that we rise or fall together, and that we can never be elevated to our proper standing while they are in bondage." Through their involvement in literary societies, women could demonstrate to the white American public that, as one literary society member asserted, "you love literature, that you love your people, and that nothing shall be wanting on your part to elevate them." The work women did in literary societies was, as such, of value to broader struggles for racial equality, as free women's "most gratifying and astonishing progress . . . in intellectual improvement and in the virtues of the heart" undermined racist justifications for the perpetuation of slavery and ongoing racial inequalities for free blacks.[21] Unlike their white counterparts, black female authors frequently emphasized the importance of writing and publishing to move the cause of African American equality forward and to uplift the entire African American community.

Garrison had similar hopes for female literary societies, writing to Sarah Mapps Douglass, "If the traducers of the colored race could be acquainted with the moral worth, just refinement, and large intelligence of this association [her literary society], their mouths would hereafter be dumb."²² He hoped that by publishing literature written by members of existing female literary societies and praising and publicizing their work, he might help "induce the colored ladies of other places to go and do likewise" and form yet more literary societies.²³ A staunch, if far from perfect, advocate of racial equality, Garrison also sought to publish works by African American women as a means of providing these authors with a rare public platform to voice their ideas, proving to a skeptical white public that African American female writers possessed literary skill, intellectual sophistication, and moral perspicacity on par with that of white women. Hoping to increase the representation of African American female authors in his periodical, Garrison urged Douglass to "remember that we have now a Ladies' Department for the *Liberator*. Pray occupy it as often as possible with your productions, and get others of your Society to do the same."²⁴

Although Garrison strongly supported literary societies of African American women, his presentation of works by African American female abolitionists was nonetheless problematic. As scholars such as Harriet Hyman Alonso, David W. Blight, and Henry Mayer have demonstrated, though significantly more progressive in his ideas about race than many white abolitionists of his era, Garrison was by no means free from a belief in white superiority.²⁵ Even as he published a considerable amount of African American women's fiction in the *Liberator,* he marked these contributions. While he presented white female authors' writings without comment, he made notations to African American authors' works, often adding "by a young lady of color" to their bylines.²⁶

Not only did Garrison explicitly draw attention to the race of African American contributors, he also frequently added complimentary remarks to their writings, something he did not do with works by white female authors. Publishing one of Douglass's pieces in the *Liberator* in 1832, Garrison noted, "This accomplished young colored lady we are indebted to for several original and truly beautiful articles that have appeared in the Ladies' Department of the *Liberator*."²⁷ He similarly noted of "A.F.M.," the author of the 1832 "An Address to the Daughters of New England": "In intelligence and philanthropy, she is in advance of a large number of her sex."²⁸ Such comments were likely intended to emphasize to white readers that black authors' pieces were just as accomplished and insightful as white women's literary works and to further encourage African American readers' pride in literary productions from talented black female writers.

Yet while these remarks seem designed to further develop a sense of community pride among African American readers and to combat negative stereotypes about black writers in white audiences, Garrison's insistent marking of black authors' texts may not have been entirely effective. By forcefully insisting on African American women's abilities, he potentially created the impression that African American women's possession of literary skill and intellectual ability was startling and unusual. While white women might be expected to write polished literary works by default, Garrison consistently underlined African American women's ability to do so as extraordinary, thus working against African American women's pieces being considered equal to white women's.

It is certainly also worth noting that some of Garrison's compliments focused not on the literary flair or intellectual distinction of women's pieces but rather on other facets of their work. In his introduction to Zelmire's "Unnatural Distinction," for example, he declared, "Our word for it, there are few young white ladies who can prepare an essay for the press with more accuracy in regard to orthography and punctuation, or written in a more beautiful hand, than the following, by a young colored lady."[29] By highlighting not this writer's skill with words or the complexity and importance of her ideas, but rather the daintiness and femininity of her handwriting, he trivialized her work, placing her writing in the category of genteel feminine accomplishment rather than of important intellectual contribution to antislavery thought. Though admitting African American women into the white-defined realm of ladylike feminine accomplishment was in and of itself something of a radical act, such commentary nonetheless further served to indicate that African American women's literature was a surprising demonstration of unexpected ability, more than it was a contribution to serious discussions about the future of abolitionism.

Fiction in Antislavery Periodicals

While editors of antislavery periodicals also printed poems and essays written by women during the 1830s, fiction continued to be heavily represented in antislavery publications during this decade. Editors remained eager to publish fiction in their ladies' departments in large part because of their awareness that fiction was an extremely popular genre and because they believed it could activate female readers' potent imaginations in ways other kinds of texts could not. As contributor "Lady in Worcester County" asserted in 1837, "'fiction may throw as far a light as truth,' and its beams are often permitted to penetrate those recesses from which Truth is carefully excluded."[30] While female readers might shrink away from a dry pamphlet about slavery's evils, an engaging work of fiction might reach them.

Fiction would be especially valuable in touching a female audience, authors and editors indicated, as it had a unique potential to engage women's powerful feelings and imaginations. As she told her female readers in 1832, one *Liberator*'s Ladies' Department contributor had elected to convey her antislavery ideas in the form of a story, since fiction was "particularly likely to imprin[t] on your imagination . . . thus really affecting your heart."[31] Similarly, in an 1834 piece published in the Ladies' Department titled "What Have the Ladies to Do with Anti-Slavery?" the author urges women reading stories about slavery: "Suffer your imagination to paint, with vivid hues, this sad picture (it will not be too highly colored), gaze upon it, dreadful as it is, until you have formed the solemn, deliberate resolution, that you will do every thing in your power to destroy its still more dreadful original."[32] Often depicted negatively in American culture, women's capacity for feeling and imagination was reclaimed as a positive good in women's antislavery literature: women's unique ability to feel deeply and vividly imagine the evils of slavery could be vitally important in making female readers into dedicated antislavery advocates.

Fiction was also important for female readers, as it was a significant means through which mothers could convert their children to abolitionism. Writing in the *Liberator*'s Juvenile Department in 1832, "Paulina" encouraged her female audience to read the department's stories "seated with thy loved ones by thy fireside, and thy children are gathered about."[33] The heroine of Zelmire's 1831 "An Evening at Home" similarly advocated blending abolitionist storytelling with women's domestic work as mothers. Readying herself to tell her young daughter a story about slavery, the mother in this tale coaxes her, "Come hither, dear little girl" and is then careful to "make room for Emma to sit on her lap."[34] Reading their children morally engaging stories about slavery could, authors stressed, easily take place in the private sphere of the home and be incorporated into mothers' preexisting rituals of physical intimacy with and nurture of their children.

Mothers could thus use fiction to disseminate antislavery ideas in their homes in nonconfrontational ways. As Sarah Robbins argues in *Managing Literacy, Mothering America: Women's Narratives on Reading and Writing in the Nineteenth Century,* shaping their children's literary taste came to be defined as a central part of middle-class women's maternal work during the antebellum era. It was no longer sufficient for mothers to teach the rudiments of literacy, but they were also expected to ensure that their children developed a taste for worthwhile, moral literature. One of mothers' chief responsibilities was to keep their children away from potentially corrupting texts and to guide them toward works that would help them to become staunch Christians and upright American citizens.[35] Antislavery women writers entered into such discourses by insisting that mothers were also obliged to encourage their children to develop a taste for antislavery literature. This form of antislavery activism was particularly desirable, as it did not ask female readers to step outside of their proper domestic roles.

Abolitionist Mothers in Women's Fiction

This emphasis on the ways abolitionist advocacy could blend seamlessly into middle-class women's preexisting domestic responsibilities was a powerful theme of both white and African American women's literature during the 1830s. While both African American and white writers insisted that mothers played crucial roles in abolitionism through their moral influence over their children, African American authors also paid attention to how mothers could address the oppression of both free and enslaved African Americans—something white writers did not do.

In discussing motherhood, female writers argued that women demonstrated whether they were virtuous mothers through their participation in (or their abstention from) antislavery activity. Publishing their works in a culture in which being a "good mother" was defined as an essential, if not *the* essential, part of being a good woman, accusing nonabolitionist mothers of being failures constituted a very damning attack.[36] Antislavery women writers argued that caring about the plight of the enslaved ought to be an inevitable extension of free women's maternal concern for all children. No free woman could claim to have a true mother's heart, antislavery women writers declared, if she was willing to let enslaved mothers suffer. In the 1832 tale "A Dialogue on Slavery," two friends discuss their reasons for being involved in abolitionism or not, both seeking to justify their decisions in terms of motherhood. "Attention to my family is my first duty," the antiabolitionist insists to her friend, "and that fully occupies my time."[37] Because of her wholehearted devotion to her children, she simply does not have time to dedicate to anything external to her family circle; her failure to become an abolitionist, she argues, is thus not a sign of her failure to be a good mother but rather strong evidence that she is exactly that.

In this story, the abolitionist mother firmly rejects this argument: "I wish the slaves were allowed to devote a reasonable portion of theirs to such attention. No doubt it is your first duty, but it cannot I think so completely occupy the time of any lady, or of any woman above the poorest class, as to form a conscientious excuse for not devoting a few minutes now and then, to help any of her fellow creatures."[38] The antiabolitionist's failure to become an antislavery activist is thus, in part, a failure to be a good mother who exhibits concern for the well-being of those outside of her own household. Yet her sin is even graver than this, as her inaction also constitutes a direct betrayal of the sisterhood of shared maternity. After all, while the antiabolitionist character is contentedly looking after her children, enslaved mothers are consistently facing very likely permanent separation from theirs. Women's responsibilities, "A Dialogue" indicates, certainly include being conscientious mothers and caring for their families. But, as the abolitionist character in the tale contends, this role does not preclude but rather rightfully *in*cludes reserving time, energy, and thought for enslaved mothers. No truly loving mother could selfishly enjoy time with her own children, while other American mothers had no rights to protect and nurture theirs.

In addition to arguing that embracing abolitionism was the mark of virtuous motherhood, "A Dialogue on Slavery" also pointed to the class implications of failing to become involved in antislavery activity. Only genuinely poor mothers had a legitimate excuse for not participating in the antislavery movement, since all of their time was necessarily taken up by the basic struggle to survive. Middle-class mothers had leisure time to devote to worthwhile causes such as abolition. In an era when the middle class was taking shape, and falling out of this emerging class was perilously common due to pervasive economic instability, middle-class people were particularly eager to differentiate themselves culturally and behaviorally from members of the working class. Appealing to class status was thus a particularly potent means of speaking to readers seeking to achieve or maintain middle-class status. As Stuart Blumin has argued, one of the primary ways middle-class people publicly demonstrated their status during the antebellum era was through benevolent activism that benefited the less fortunate.[39] Thus, middle-class women had several powerful incentives in addition to the underlying moral imperative for becoming abolitionists.

In her contributions to the *Liberator,* Douglass also appealed to mothers and used rhetoric about motherhood to make the case against slavery. She stressed the power of enslaved women's maternal feelings throughout her 1832 tale "A Mother's Love," asking "Dost thou, poor slave, feel this holy passion? Does thy heart swell with anguish, when thy helpless infant is torn from thy arms, and carried thou knowest not whither?" Lest there be any doubt about the answer, Douglass promptly responded to her question with a resounding "yes I know thou dost feel all this."[40] She thus sought to vividly, intimately imagine the terrible sufferings of enslaved mothers, who needed to live with the persistent possibility and the all-too-common reality of permanent separation from their beloved children. Unlike her white contemporaries such as Chandler, who wrote about the gender-specific horrors of slavery in more general terms, Douglass sought to bring her readers much more closely and personally into the sufferings of enslaved mothers. By emphasizing the "anguish" and "passion" of enslaved women facing separation from their children and intimately addressing enslaved mothers as "thou," Douglass's piece brings her readers into enslaved women's experiences more extensively than the more abstract fiction written by white writers like Chandler did.

In this piece, Douglass directly addressed her free female readers, emphasizing that enslaved mothers felt "as tenderly for her offspring as you do for yours." Once they acknowledged the profound love enslaved women felt for their children, free readers who were themselves mothers were obligated to "raise your voices, and plead for her emancipation—her immediate emancipation."[41] Douglass thus challenged her free African American readers to reach across the line that separated them from enslaved women and recognize the common bonds of maternity—or, at least, of maternal feeling—that united all African American women. And, writing in a culture in which stereotypes about African American women's alleged inability to be loving, conscientious mothers predominated, Douglass stressed to her white female readers that enslaved mothers loved their children as deeply and fully as white mothers did theirs—and as such deserved the same rights to protect their children as white mothers did.

In her reflections on enslaved women and motherhood, Douglass also raised the specter of enslaved mothers potentially engaging in violent resistance to slavery, only to carefully disavow and diffuse this possibility. The enslaved heroine of "A Mother's Love," for example, endures terrible beatings from her cruel mistress and frequent separations from her beloved child. After her mistress hits her while she is nursing her baby, the heroine finds that "rage against her mistress almost emboldened her to return the blow."[42] By declaring that her heroine had the *capacity* to contemplate striking her mistress, Douglass initially seems to be echoing stereotypes of African American women as innately disposed toward impulsive violence. Her assertion at first raises anxieties similar to those that surface in white female authors' literature, about enslaved women's tendency toward troublingly unladylike resistance to slavery.

Yet Douglass quickly dispelled any concerns that her heroine's impulse toward violent resistance might have raised, emphasizing that her heroine successfully restrains her anger: "When she reflected that her child would probably be the sufferer, maternal tenderness triumphed over every other feeling."[43] Douglass thus stressed her heroine's womanly capacity for maternal self-sacrifice. Originally inspired to anger because of the damage her mistress's blow might have done to her child, the heroine is able to resist the temptation because of that same protective maternal love. Douglass thus demonstrated that maternal feeling was a central force in enslaved women's lives and that this emotion was the primary determiner of their behavior. By so doing, she pointed to significant commonalities between enslaved African American and free African American and white women, all of whom were ostensibly governed by their emotions, specifically their deep devotion to their children.

Mothers Raising Sons in Abolitionist Literature

Free readers who were mothers could, authors indicated, not just contribute to the antislavery cause by feeling empathy for suffering enslaved mothers but also by raising their children to become abolitionist activists. This maternal work took on particular significance when it came to raising sons, as boys had the potential to become the public leaders of the antislavery movement. In Y.N.'s "Family Colloquy," upset after learning about the evils of slavery from his mother, a "little boy was comforted after a while, by being told that he was a man, perhaps he could do something to help and comfort the little black children."[44] In an 1833 installment of her short story series "Aunt Margery's Evenings with the Young Folks," "Aunt Margery" similarly tells a young boy, "If you will but think and care much about slavery, dear George, when you are a man, you can help very much in getting them [the enslaved] restored to their liberty."[45] The mother in Elizabeth Margaret Chandler's 1831 "Edward and Mary" also diligently educates her son about slavery, informing him that once he becomes a man it will be his duty "to assist in removing this disgrace from your country."[46]

In Hannah F. Gould's 1831 tale "The Prisoners Set Free," Mrs. Elsworth similarly pins her hopes for the future of abolition on boys. In the story, she lauds the power that "good and philanthropic men" have "to better the condition of these unfortunate people." Mrs. Elsworth further expresses her desire that her son will grow up to join the ranks of "philanthropic men." She tells him, "If you live to be a man, you will have it in your power to tread in the steps of Clarkson." Because of her encouragement, her son becomes eager to undertake just such a role: "If ever I am a man, and slavery is not abolished then, you shall see that I have not forgotten what you have told me to-day."[47]

It is noteworthy that the mother here extracts no such promises and paints no such pictures of future leadership for her daughter, who, unlike her brother, had manifested an ardent abolitionism from the beginning of the story. Though her daughter already possessed a strong antislavery conscience and her son has to be coaxed into caring about slavery, Mrs. Elsworth nonetheless clearly sees her son as the one who will grow up to enact her antislavery principles out in the world. Her daughter, presumably, will have to wait until she has sons of her own to groom for abolitionist leadership, as her gender bars her from becoming a "Clarkson" in her own right.

In their pieces in the *Liberator*, African American female authors similarly argued that it was boys, rather than girls, whom mothers needed to mold to become the future leaders of the antislavery movement. Unlike white authors, however, African American writers also insisted that their sons needed to advocate for full racial equality for African Americans in the

North as well as grow up to condemn slavery in the South. In Douglass's 1832 story "A Dialogue between a Mother and Her Children," the titular mother lectures both her son and her daughter about the evils of slavery. However, she specifically exhorts her son, "Save your money, and when you have collected a handsome sum, uncle will put it into the funds now preparing to build a College for our youth."[48] Frequently deprived of the right to a college education that well-to-do white men enjoyed, African American boys needed to do their part to ensure that men in their communities received good educations, which would demonstrate African American men's capacity for intellectual achievement and train them to undertake public roles. The paths to be taken by the daughter and the son in this tale are therefore quite different. The boy will have economic means—as he will have money he can save and spend as he wishes, which the daughter will not—and hopefully also a formal education to enable him to become a public voice for abolition. The girl's future, by contrast, is not even considered worthy of discussion. The reader is left to assume that she will one day be in the same position as her mother, with sons of her own to instruct in abolitionist ideals.

In some respects, this vision of free African American women's and men's involvement in the antislavery cause is quite a radical one. By depicting the mother as the shaper of her children's principles, Douglass claimed the mantle of "republican mother" for African American women. Although republican motherhood was an ideal focused on elite white women, Douglass insisted that black women possessed the same virtue and maternal wisdom as their white counterparts and, as such, had the same obligation to educate their sons for virtuous citizenship and public leadership that white women did. Refusing to accept definitions of citizenship that excluded African Americans, she contended that African American mothers had the right and, indeed, the duty to raise their sons to be equal participants in American society. Once middle-class African American men routinely enjoyed the kinds of educations that their white counterparts did and took their proper places as public leaders, racist claims about the natural inferiority of African Americans would, Douglass's text suggests, inevitably erode.[49] By ensuring that their sons received good educations and became virtuous public leaders, free African American mothers could consequently do a great deal to simultaneously dismantle both slavery and broader systems of racial inequality.

Empowering as this vision was, it nonetheless also placed significant pressure on free African American women to concentrate their antislavery activity purely in the private sphere, specifically in their roles as mothers. Assumed by many members of the white public to be incapable of living up to ideals of proper, domestic womanhood and motherhood, middle-class African American women also faced considerable pressure from members of their own communities to faultlessly embody respectable femininity. Any woman who deviated from the ideal of decorous, bourgeois womanhood put herself at considerable risk for disapproval and censure. Abolitionist orator Maria W. Stewart faced this reality when she embarked on her brief career as a public speaker during the 1830s. Some of the public derision she experienced came from male African American community leaders and ministers, who disapproved of her perceived transgression of domestic femininity. Stewart abandoned her oratory work a mere two years after she began it, citing the hostility she had faced from African American men as a primary factor.[50] By arguing African American women could become republican mothers and pillars of bourgeois femininity, authors such as Douglass defied racist stereotypes that insisted that African American women were incapable of embodying these ideals. Yet her arguments also potentially reinforced suspicions of women engaged in antislavery activism that was not thoroughly rooted in their domestic work as wives and mothers.

Mothers Raising Daughters in Abolitionist Literature

Convinced that boys would ultimately become the rightful leaders of the antislavery movement, writers nonetheless also spent considerable time considering what roles girls ought to play.[51] Stressing the importance of mothers raising abolitionist sons and arguing that men ought to be the primary public abolitionist actors, authors also maintained that there was a special, gender-specific connection between girls and abolitionism. Female authors emphasized that girls were naturally more receptive to the antislavery message, stronger in their abolitionist principles, and more willing to defy the status quo on behalf of abolitionism, than boys were. Writers thus gave the clearest moral vision and the most ardent commitment to abolitionism, not to those whom they envisioned as the future leaders of their movement but rather to young girls, who were relatively powerless.

Abolitionist authors and editors signaled the powerful connection between girls and antislavery ideals in part by indicating that they expected their most devoted readers to be female children. Writing in the *Philanthropist,* one author noted that she had "presented to one of the little daughters a late number of the 'Slave's Friend,'" not mentioning whether she had made similar presentations to any friends' sons.[52] In her 1831 tale "Family Colloquy," published in the *Liberator,* author Y.N. wrote that she knew "a little girl [who] always inquires for the '*Liberator*' . . . and is quite disappointed if [the *Liberator*] does not contain a 'Juvenile Department.'"[53] Whether she knew of any little boys who felt the same way about the periodical significantly goes unmentioned. Author Aunt Margery made a similar allusion to the popularity of the Juvenile Department with girls, specifically, in one of her stories: "A little friend of mine, who is about six years old, came to me a few weeks ago, after hearing the story of 'An Evening at Home' read from the '*Liberator*,' to ask me to tell her more about the poor slave people. I did so."[54]

It does not seem coincidental that all of the children whom authors claimed loved their stories and actively sought them out were female. Assuming women and girls innately found literature more appealing than men and boys did, authors also indicated that girls were more likely to be emotionally stirred by antislavery stories than boys were. This was likely due in part to the ideologies of childhood and femininity developing during the antebellum era, which gave female children a double advantage over their adult male counterparts when it came to the capacity for both feeling and moral purity. After all, if women were more morally perspicacious than men and children were more innately virtuous than adults, then female children were necessarily the most principled, morally sensitive people of all. As such, girls were also the most likely to be interested in and responsive to tales focused on the moral outrages of slavery and enslaved people's sufferings.[55]

Given these larger cultural understandings about the nature of female children, it is perhaps unsurprising that authors made their girl characters central in educating their families about the evils of slavery. In "Family Colloquy," Y.N. noted approvingly that one of her young readers had taken to "reading to her mother from the *Liberator*," a striking reversal of usual depictions of moral education within the family unit.[56] Although the Juvenile Department was permeated with stories of mothers educating their children about slavery, Y.N.'s tale suggested that in some cases this educational process could be reversed: virtuous daughters could be the ones to instruct their mothers about the peculiar institution.

An author writing in the *Philanthropist* in 1836 described a similar scenario in her "Interesting Anecdote," telling a story about a little girl who took the initiative and asked a traveling antislavery agent for a juvenile antislavery periodical. "On calling again a day or two afterward," the agent "was informed by the mother, that she [the daughter] had been found weeping and apparently in great distress; and that, on being asked to tell the cause of her tears, she said she could not help crying, when she thought of the poor little negro boy about whom s[h]e had been reading in her little book."[57] Like grown women, girls instinctively responded to learning about the sufferings of the enslaved by shedding sorrowful tears of sympathy over their plight and encouraging those around them to do so likewise.

The boys in women's antislavery narratives notably do not respond to stories about slavery in the same powerfully emotional ways that their female counterparts do. While they respond favorably to their mother's calls to become abolitionists, it is only girls who actually cried after learning about slavery's injustices.[58] This response was significant, since the very act of shedding tears could, according to female writers, be a potent form of antislavery activism.[59] In "Interesting Anecdote," seeing the little girl cry over the antislavery text she is reading inspires her family members to read this work for themselves. The agent in this story remarks, "This same little book was, after this, read by all the family. The cause of the oppressed is not likely to fail, whilst their God provides for it so sure a refuge in the sympathies of the young and virtuous."[60] The *Philanthropist* author credited this young girl with securing the conversion of her entire family to abolitionism, purely because of her tears over antislavery literature. Herself converted by the strong emotions inspired by an antislavery story, the girl successfully induces her family to read the same text, and themselves likewise be moved to embrace abolitionist ideas.

Armed with a heady combination of youthful innocence and virtuous femininity, girls march through the pages of women's antislavery fiction not just weeping over the plight of the enslaved but also questioning the corrupt, proslavery political systems in which men (including their own fathers) are enmeshed. While boys in tales like "A Dialogue between a Mother and Her Children" and "Edward and Mary" are confident in their abilities to contribute to abolitionism as future public leaders and citizens, girls actively question and criticize the morality of America's existing social and political structures. Unlike their brothers, they could not imagine themselves as future public leaders, voters, or politicians. Indeed, authors indicated that it was girls' very exclusion from public political power that enabled them to clearly see and effectively critique their government's deep moral corruption.

Informed that laws written and passed by white American men perpetuated slavery in the United States, Emma, the child heroine of the "Evening at Home" series, is indignant and incredulous. "'Oh, mamma,'" Emma exclaims, "the blood crimsoning in her cheeks, and her eyes filling with tears, 'is it possible?'"[61] After being brought to her abolitionist awakening by her virtuous mother, Emma quickly becomes a firm believer in the antislavery cause, as staunch and vocal an antislavery advocate as her mother is. Both excluded from full participation in the political sphere, mother and daughter are sharply aware of and deeply upset by the immorality of their government's support for slavery.

Throughout women's antislavery fiction, girls prove themselves willing to directly challenge the wisdom of a government that upholds slavery in ways that boys are not. U.I.E.'s "Family Circle" stories, for example, focus on a mother's discussions of slavery with her three children, Lucy, Henry, and George. Throughout the series, Lucy and Helen challenge the status quo, demanding to know how an evil such as slavery is allowed to continue in an ostensibly moral country like the United States. "But why do free states allow this?" Lucy asks her mother, "as they think it wicked to keep people in slavery I should think there would be some law to punish any of their own people that had anything to do with it."[62] In answer, her mother sparks a discussion about the morality of the American government among the three children:

> "Because, my dear," said her mother, "the laws of the slave states allow people to keep slaves, and do not punish such kinds of cruelty."
>
> "That is very strange," said Helen, "who makes the laws?"
>
> "Why, the people, to be sure," said George, "in a republican country like ours, the people choose the laws makes, and will be sure to choose men that will make such laws as they like. But Helen, dear, you cannot understand about this."

"Nor I either, very well," said Lucy, "only it seems as if they must all be very wicked, to make such laws."[63]

Within this dialogue, Lucy, Helen, and their mother are far more critical of the government than George is. Through George, U.I.E. suggested that boys possessed an unjustified faith in their government that more skeptical, morally clear-sighted girls did not. George, and George alone, defends America as a "republican nation" and praises the country for being a democracy, in which the American people freely choose their leaders.

By using the word "people" to describe those who participate in the electoral process, George erases voters' genders and glosses over the reality of women's political disempowerment. He deliberately makes it appear as though *all* American people are equally responsible for making the laws of the land and choosing the leaders by whom they are governed, overlooking that women are excluded from this kind of direct political decision-making. George's remarks thus erase white men's culpability for being the primary creators and upholders of proslavery legislation and institutions. His sisters do not allow him to shrug off proslavery laws as the will of all American people, however; instead, they insist that such legislation is unjust and that the men who support it are fundamentally immoral. George is profoundly misguided in his condescending assumption that his sisters will not be able to even comprehend the basic workings of their government. Lucy and Helen understand these workings perfectly well—better, indeed, than George does. These politically disempowered girls are the most perceptive about the ugly, proslavery reality at the heart of American political structures.

Conscious of their status as outsiders in politics, girls such as Lucy and Helen are fearless in challenging the justice of laws that uphold slavery and are quick to condemn male voters and government officials for creating and supporting such legislation. Unlike their brother, who is willing to accept the existence of proslavery laws as the democratic will of the people, Lucy and Helen refuse to accept the wisdom of an unjust government that protects the slave power. Baffled by her brother's willingness to defend an immoral political system, Lucy tells him, "When I think about all the abominable wickedness of the slaveholder, I have no patience, and I do not want to find any excuse for them; and I do not see why you want to."[64] Unlike the measured, patient George, Lucy wishes her country's leaders would act immediately to end slavery. This divide between a hasty, emotional girl and a cool, rational boy at first appears to confirm negative stereotypes about feminine unfitness for political power. Given that one of the primary arguments against female enfranchisement in the nineteenth century (and into the twentieth) was that women were too emotional to make thoughtful political decisions, representing Lucy as a girl whose potent emotions determine her statements and actions initially seems problematic.[65]

But U.I.E. did not represent Lucy's strong feelings, fierce commitment to abolitionism, or desire for immediate emancipation negatively. Instead, she indicated that the girl's naturally strong emotions helped her see the injustice of a proslavery government—an injustice her more reasonable brother, notably, does not. U.I.E. thus suggested that girls' and women's more powerful feelings had the potential not only to make them better abolitionists but also more discerning evaluators of their country's policies on slavery than boys and men were. By arguing that women's emotional natures made them more rather than less politically discerning than men, U.I.E. questioned one of the most powerful objections to female political empowerment in nineteenth-century America. Yet she did not do so to make an argument in favor of giving women access to political power; to the contrary, she suggested that one of the things that made girls and women so perceptive about the immorality of their government was their very distance from it. Gifted by nature with stronger feelings and more reliable moral compasses than men, girls and women were also privileged by their distance from (and their lack of complicity in) America's corrupt governmental structures.

Female children in these stories are therefore demanding not the right to vote or even to have more access to formal political power but rather to freely voice their opposition to their government's policies. Thus, the sole power they call for is not really power at all but rather influence. Like their mothers, girl characters in antislavery literature are seeking the right to influence men to think correctly about the slave question. In the 1836 narrative "The Coffle Yoke," for example, young Ellen is shocked when her father informs her that slave-trading is legal in the District of Columbia. "In the city of Washington, father! where Congress sits!" Ellen exclaims, "Is it possible?" After her father admits it is, Ellen gazes at a flag and declares, "The stripes in the national flag make me think of the stripes the poor slaves suffer. Won[']t the rest of the world ridicule us, dear father, for having such a flag?"[66] Unlike her father, the girl does not have any part in voting for a government that willfully trades in human beings or in supporting a government that protects the slave trade. And also unlike her father, she is willing to condemn American hypocrisy in upholding slavery and to raise questions about how America's ongoing support for the institution would affect its moral standing in the eyes of the world. By voicing these ideas, Ellen seeks to make her father understand the slave trade as a moral failing of the entire American nation, which needs to be addressed if the country wishes to live up to its own high ideals.

The young heroine of N.S.'s 1837 story "Talk by the Fireside," Martha, takes this willingness to enter discussions of political matters a step further, informing her father, "I don't know any members of Congress; if I did, I would beg of them not to let little children be bought and sold any more."[67] While such direct political involvement might initially seem startling for a young girl, Martha is careful to present this activism as a straightforward extension of proper feminine moral influence over men. Deliberately using submissive language such as "beg" and emphasizing her desire to act purely to prevent the suffering of her fellow children, Martha stresses that her appeal to congressmen would be a suitably deferential, gender-appropriate one. She simply wants to extend her moral appeals beyond the men of her household to the men of her government, bringing her concerns about the exploitation of children to the attention of male legislators who are currently, and wrongly, unconcerned by these issues. By calling for Martha to have the right to appeal directly to government officials, N.S. seemed to risk making Martha complicit in the government she is criticizing. Yet even as they appeal to officials, girls like Martha nonetheless remain independent from and outside of their country's political system. They simply assert their right to remind male legislators of moral principles they had all too often lost, working in the morally suspect realm of government.

Throughout their fiction, female antislavery authors represented girls as more strongly, naturally abolitionist in their sentiments, and more willing to challenge the American government regarding its morally untenable support for slavery, than boys. Depicting their female and male characters as profoundly different from one another, writers argued that both nonetheless had crucial roles to play in the struggle against slavery. They thus created a tidily organized universe, in which girls and boys recognized their proper places in the existing gendered order: boys would be groomed by their mothers to assume positions of abolitionist leadership, and girls would share their moral insights with their brothers, their fathers, and, subsequently, their own sons. Girls would consequently remain suitably domestic and distant from politics, maintaining their moral perspicacity through this very distance. Recognizing the moral purity of their wives and daughters, men would heed women's moral guidance in their work as public, political actors against slavery.

This vision of gendered participation in the abolitionist movement was problematic in several respects. Maintaining that girls' status as political outsiders was an advantage which enabled them to see clearly on moral issues troublingly echoed assertions made by anti-feminists and anti-suffragists during the antebellum era. Opponents to women's rights often drew on similar ideas, highlighting the need for women to remain independent from politics in order to successfully retain their feminine moral purity.[68] Female antislavery authors expressed comparable distaste at the idea of girls and women becoming involved in the morally suspect realm of politics. They hoped girls' and women's primary political involvement would instead lie in shaping the moral ideals of their politically empowered male family members. Expressing confidence that men would take the moral principles they learned in the home out into the public sphere, faint uneasiness nonetheless lurked beneath the placid surface of women's antislavery fiction. Although it did not fully grapple with the issue, women's fiction in the 1830s nonetheless implicitly raised the question of what would happen if morally inferior men failed to implement morally superior women's ideals.

African American Authors on Civil Rights and Racial Prejudice

While African American and white female authors both addressed how women could best use their roles as mothers to serve the antislavery movement and considered how female and male children could most effectively participate in abolitionism, other issues were raised exclusively by African American writers. Black female authors emphasized the need to combat racial prejudice as well as slavery, called for civil rights for free African Americans, and debated whether African Americans should remain in a country that systematically discriminated against them. In the fiction they published in the *Liberator,* African American female writers advocated for an abolitionism that was not just female-centered but also dedicated to racial equality for all African Americans, free and enslaved. This more radical, egalitarian vision, troublingly, was not present in white female antislavery authors' literary work.

African American female writers raised the issue of racial equality in part through their portrayals of girl characters. In "For the Children Who Read the *Liberator*," Douglass told the tale of Elizabeth, unparalleled for her modesty, piety, selflessness, and kindness. By choosing to center this tale on such a faultlessly virtuous girl, Douglass claimed the mantle of angelic femininity—explicitly coded as white in nineteenth-century America—for African American, as well as white, girls and women. In an era in which African American women were widely assumed to be innately predisposed to vice, the act of writing an African American paragon of feminine goodness was quite a radical one.[69]

It was, significantly, only at the very end of her story that Douglass disclosed that the virtuous Elizabeth was, in fact, African American. "I would now ask my little readers," the narrator inquires of her white audience, "if the character of Elizabeth appears the less lovely to them, because her complexion differed from theirs. I am sure every good child will answer, 'no!'" Yet in the story, Elizabeth's white peers *had* treated her differently, discriminating against her when it came to choosing who they wanted to socialize with. "Methinks I see the blush of conscious shame mantling the cheek of some of my little readers," Douglass's narrator asserts, "who have been guilty of the like sin."[70] Although she asserted in her 1832 "A True Tale for Children," "I hope none of my little readers are so wicked as to despise children whose complexions God has caused to differ from theirs," Douglass was well aware that such prejudices were very much present among her white child readers—as they were among their parents.[71] She consequently asked her white readers to be conscious of not just the injustice of slavery but also the evils of racism and to work equally diligently to end both.

In the literature she published in the Ladies' and the Juvenile Departments of the *Liberator*, Douglass insisted on the need to eradicate racial inequality. In her 1832 piece "To a Friend," her narrator envisions a utopian future in which slavery has been abolished and "no wailing is heard; no clanking chains, but the voice of peace and love and joy is wafted to my ear on every breeze." Not only will the chains of slavery have been broken, but "black and white [will] mingle together in social intercourse, without a shadow of disgust appearing on the countenance of either."[72] In Douglass's work, abolishing slavery would not be enough to create a truly free society; instead, racial equality also needed to be achieved, and white racial prejudice wholly done away with. By using evocative language of "mingling" and "social intercourse," Douglass even went so far as to invoke one of the chief anxieties expressed by antiabolitionists: that ending slavery would inevitably lead to widespread acceptance of interracial love, sex, and marriage. Raising this possibility through her word choices, Douglass boldly framed all "social intercourse" between African Americans and whites as a positive outcome of the abolition of slavery and the dawn of true equality. While white authors tended to carefully sidestep the question of what the end of slavery would mean for free African Americans, Douglass directly linked the causes of racial equality and immediate abolition, daring to imagine a future in which the two were achieved simultaneously.

Yet whether such a reality could, indeed, ever be achieved in the United States was a topic of some debate among African American female authors. As Gary Nash and Julie Winch have argued, free African Americans often experienced significant conflict during the antebellum era, in seeking to reconcile the seemingly contradictory realities of their blackness and their Americanness.[73] In a world in which the archetypal American citizen was a white man, and "American" was often constructed as an exclusively white category, how could African Americans claim an American identity without denying their racial heritage? David Walker considered such questions at length in his 1829 *Appeal to the Coloured Citizens of the World,* acknowledging the many barriers to the realization of full African American citizenship but maintaining that that such citizenship was nonetheless African Americans' by right and that they needed to fight for it.[74]

African American female authors who published in the *Liberator* held differing views about whether they would, indeed, be able to successfully achieve full equality in American society. During an era in which the colonizationist movement remained active and possessed a small but vocal group of African American supporters, such questions were far from theoretical. Black women writers engaged in these debates throughout the Ladies' Department. Some contributors, such as "A Colored Female of Philadelphia," insisted that African Americans needed to find a government "under whose protection we may safely reside, where it is no disgrace to wear a sable complexion, and where our rights will not continually be trampled upon, on that account." "We too," "A Colored Female" argued, "ought to manifest that spirit of independence that shines so conspicuously in that character of Europeans, by leaving the land of oppression, and emigrating where we may be received and treated as brothers."⁷⁵ Remaining in a country that so shamefully mistreated African Americans, she insisted, demonstrated an unacceptable lack of spirit and will.

Publishing her piece in a ladies' department, "A Colored Female" was, of course, addressing herself to a primarily female audience. Yet her assertion that African Americans needed to find a land where they would be accepted as "brothers" nonetheless gendered the struggle for full citizenship as masculine. In her piece, "A Colored Female" might have invoked the rights of "brothers and sisters," but she instead indicated that the "new world" she envisioned for African Americans away from the United States was still one in which women and men would have very different, and seemingly unequal, relationships to the state.⁷⁶ Much like the white women who published their literature during this decade, this author was careful to indicate that men were the proper leaders of society—whether that society was in the United States or in Africa.

With her piece, "A Colored Female" opened up the question of African American civil rights and colonization for discussion among female readers of the Ladies' Department. In a series of sketches published in the department throughout 1832, Douglass (writing as "Zillah") and "Woodby" (an unidentified member of the Female Literary Association of Philadelphia) exchanged their views on colonization. These narratives almost certainly had their roots in the female literary society of which these authors were both members. It was common practice in such societies for female members to write essays, stories, and sketches on a common theme, place these pieces anonymously in a box, pull each work out individually, and then critique and discuss them as a group.⁷⁷ It is thus likely that Woodby and Douglass's writings stemmed from just such an exchange within their literary society. The Ladies' Department offered a significant opportunity to make this internal discussion public, inviting all female readers of the department to join in the debate.

Woodby's and Douglass's pieces discussed many of the same issues that "A Colored Female" had raised in her piece about the relationship between African Americans and the state and whether America could ever be a true home for African Americans. In her work, Douglass asserted that the United States was African Americans' rightful home: "Believe me, my friend there is no spot in the known world where people are happier than America. . . . [B]ethink thee, dearest, it is home! Think of this one moment, and memory will call up so many fond and soothing recollections as will make thee loth to leave it."⁷⁸ Although racist whites might deny it, "this is my own, my native land," Douglass declared, and "though she unkindly strives to throw me from her bosom, I will but embrace her the closer, determining never to part with her."⁷⁹ Acknowledging that the United States was not a society that truly valued its African American members or protected their rights, Douglass indicated she was nonetheless profoundly attached to the country and had no intention of leaving it.⁸⁰ Woodby was skeptical about such patriotic devotion, however, affirming that it would be valuable for the African American community to identify "a place of refuge we might adopt, if driven by oppression from our native country."⁸¹

Woodby's and "A Colored Female"'s assertions that their desire for independence and respect demanded they live in a new land that fully recognized their humanity notably differed from Douglass's seemingly hopeless devotion to a country that did not value her. Yet Douglass's assertion of her right to be a patriotic American, love her country, and be respected and protected by its government in return was a powerful declaration of African Americans' right to be full participants in American society. Deeply conscious of the terrible racial injustices that plagued the American nation, Douglass nonetheless indicated that she would remain in the United States, to fight to improve the country where she had been born and raised.

These kinds of debates notably did not arise in white women's antislavery literature, which concentrated on women's emancipation from slavery, and paid little attention to what women's lives might be like once this liberation had been achieved. African American writers like Douglass, by contrast, devoted as much time to discussions of free African American women and the viability of their future in the United States as they did to discussions of the need to liberate enslaved women. As the voices of free black female writers were severely marginalized in women's antislavery literature after the 1830s, likewise did the sustained discussions of racial discrimination they had brought with them also all too often disappear.

In her 1832 series of "Dialogues," African American *Liberator* contributor Bera had her four female characters engage in debates about how and whether free women ought to become involved in abolitionism. When a couple of these characters express concerns about the gendered propriety of women becoming involved in the political question of slavery, the abolitionist Ella asserts, "I suppose the objection must mean that the object aimed at is an alteration in the laws, and that as women are not legislators, they should not interfere in a question that is to come before a legislative body. I cannot see the slightest force in the argument, that because women can have no part in the final decision, they ought not to take any in helping on the subject toward that decision."[82] While the law of the land surrounding slavery would hopefully radically change through the public actions of men, this did not, Ella insists, mean that free women ought to remain uninvolved in the slave question. To the contrary, they need to play in active role in helping men make the correct public decisions about emancipation.

It was how, exactly, women could help men take the necessary steps against slavery that remained an open question in the literature women wrote and published during the 1830s. Women clearly needed to speak out against slavery in the domestic sphere and raise abolitionist sons to become future leaders of the antislavery movement. But by crafting imaginary worlds in which female characters were more consistently abolitionist than male ones, who were more politically and socially powerful, female authors raised implicit questions about the ultimate viability of this approach. This unease, and larger questions about how women could both effectively and decorously make their voices heard about slavery, continued in the literature women published during the 1840s.

CHAPTER THREE

"They Did Not Relinquish Freedom without a Struggle"

Violence, Empowerment, and Moral Suasion, 1839-1851

> The abolitionists are, for the most part, rather doers and thinkers than writers; yet here are many pages excellent as writings . . . pages which are actions rather than words, for they express the adhesion of the writers to a despised, but most noble and righteous cause. Such adhesions are the stuff that the literature of after ages is made of, although they cannot claim affinity with the literature of today, for the very reason that they must be classed not with letters, but with acts.
> —"The Tenth Massachusetts Antislavery Fair,"
> *National Anti-Slavery Standard,* February 1, 1844

Eliza Lee Follen concluded her 1843 story "The Courage and Truth of Jesus" by directing a few encouraging words to her young female readers struggling to be moral people in an often immoral world. She assured her audience, "The girl that ever speaks the truth fearlessly, though she may be laughed at, or blamed for it, gives the promise of a woman, that shall be the glory and support of the circle in which she moves. Who can tell her worth?"[1] Follen offered her readers no promises that the abolitionist path they had chosen (or, at least, that she hoped they would choose) was an easy one. Instead, she emphasized that girls and women who advocated for unpopular causes such as abolition would inevitably be mocked and reproached by those around them; yet they could not allow such condemnations to prevent them from being advocates for justice, given the tremendous potential they possessed to morally transform the fallen world in which they lived.

This chapter examines the antislavery fiction that female antislavery writers published during the 1840s, and the complex ways they envisioned free and enslaved women's resistance to slavery during this decade. The 1840s witnessed a notable widening of the reach of abolitionist literature, with more newspapers and gift books capable of attracting broader audiences beginning publication during these years. The rise of more popular, mainstream antislavery literary spaces during this decade caused as much unease in antislavery circles as it did celebration. Some abolitionists worried that efforts to reach a larger audience would necessarily involve a dangerous dilution of the antislavery message, which might damage their cause as much as it benefited it. Others hoped these more mainstream periodicals might successfully reach a large audience (including previously elusive white southerners) in ways smaller-circulation abolitionist periodicals had not. Female antislavery authors of the 1840s consequently addressed more of their fiction directly to elite white southern women, offering them advice about how to best contribute to the fight against slavery, from their unique positions within slave society.

Women who published their fiction during the 1840s did so in a decade of tremendous upheaval, in both antislavery organizations and in antislavery thought. The 1840s witnessed the rise of the first antislavery political parties in American history, with the formation of the Liberty Party in 1840 and the Free Soil Party in 1848. While neither party was by any means abolitionist, both, at least, called for the containment of slavery and offered antislavery advocates some hope that they might have allies, however imperfect, inside the American government. Worried about the rise of the slave power in the House and Senate—especially in the wake of the outbreak of the Mexican-American War, which they saw as benefiting proslavery interests—some antislavery activists began to think it was increasingly important to have their cause represented in the halls of government.

This shift toward political abolitionism was by no means universal, as many abolitionists continued to believe politics was not a useful or desirable means of creating social change and to resist the idea of allying with any party or organization that did not endorse the immediate abolition of slavery. During these years, the debate about the appeal of using politics as a means of creating abolitionist change was an active one in women's literature, as it was in the antislavery movement overall. As the movement began to shift toward the political, female writers remained insistent that for their cause to be successful, feminine moral suasion, rather than masculine political activity, needed to remain the core of abolitionism.

During the 1840s, abolitionism was also seized by increasingly active discussions about whether violent resistance, on the part of enslaved people and their free allies, was a viable means of undermining slavery. Having begun as a largely pacifist movement, some abolitionists were increasingly despairing that nonviolent activism would ever be effective in ending slavery; they consequently began to embrace the possibility of violence by enslaved men as an important means of undermining the institution. White women publishing antislavery works during the 1840s were uneasy about violent activism as a central form of resistance. They continued to see the male-dominated realms of violence and politics as fundamentally morally corrupt and to believe peaceful, feminine moral influence ought to remain the primary means of creating abolitionist change.

By analyzing debates about these questions in women's fiction, this chapter enters vibrant historiographies concerning the evolution of abolitionism during the 1840s and larger shifts within the antislavery movement toward violent activism. Although the increasing acceptance of violent abolitionism has long been acknowledged in the historiography of the abolitionist movement, only in recent decades has violent antislavery activism received sustained, significant attention from scholars. Stanley Harrold and John McKivigan's anthology *Antislavery Violence: Sectional, Racial, and Cultural Conflict in Antebellum America* was an important development in this scholarship, providing valuable essays about the ways enslaved people and free abolitionists drew on violent methods to resist slavery. The majority of the articles in this collection center on men, with one highlighting white female settlers' participation in the guerilla wars between proslavery and antislavery factions in Kansas during the 1850s.[2] Harrold's monograph and anthology *The Rise of Violent Abolitionism* continued this work, reprinting and analyzing tracts written by three African American and white male abolitionists about the use of violence in the antislavery struggle.[3] Much like Harrold's work, the articles about violence in Timothy Patrick McCarthy and John Stauffer's essay collection *Prophets of Protest: Reconsidering the History of American Abolitionism* similarly focus on discussions of violence among white and African American men, specifically on the connections between violence and public demonstrations of masculinity.[4] Authors in these collections have drawn readers' attention to the significant ways white and black male abolitionists used ideas about violence in the construction of their racial and gender identities. Seeking to break from a culture that defined free abolitionist men as deficient in masculinity and that denied enslaved men the right to be considered men at all, male abolitionists asserted that participation in violent antislavery activity could be an important means for black and white men to assert their manhood.

This chapter examines these issues from a different angle, refocusing discussions about violence in a changing antislavery movement to focus on white women and their anxieties about violent antislavery activity. While antislavery women have often been absent from historians' discussions of violent abolitionism, these women brought important, gender-specific perspectives to public debates about this issue. Unlike many abolitionist men, white antislavery women expressed concerns about an abolitionism centered on violence, in large part because of the ways such an approach would marginalize female abolitionists and the ostensibly feminine practices of pacifism and moral suasion.

This chapter also enters scholarly discussions of how enslaved women were represented in white women's fiction. In their groundbreaking scholarship, Karen Sánchez-Eppler and Jean Fagan Yellin examine power dynamics between white authors and their African American subjects, arguing that white female authors frequently used tales about enslaved women as an oblique means of examining their anxieties about white women's experiences of sexuality and marriage. Telling stories about enslaved women's powerlessness to control their lives and bodies also served as a means for white women to explore their anger at their disempowerment within the institution of marriage while problematically conflating the radically different types of sexual oppression experienced by white and enslaved women.[5] Scholars including Eve Allegra Raimon have expanded on Sánchez-Eppler and Yellin's work on the "tragic mulatta," the lovely, nearly white figure who was the heroine of many white female authors' antislavery narratives. Raimon argues that by demonstrating the racial hybridity at the heart of the American nation, the very presence of tragic mulattas in these texts challenged definitions of America as a white country.[6] This chapter maintains that white female authors also created enslaved female characters in part to underline their arguments that white women were the people best suited to be the moral center of the antislavery movement. Believing that African American women possessed the same gender-specific virtues white women did, white female authors nonetheless expressed anxiety that slavery had rendered enslaved women incapable of being fully effective antislavery actors.

Antislavery Literary Culture during the 1840s

Before turning to discussions about how women's fiction reflected on these questions of race, gender, and activism, it is worth thinking about who the authors of these stories were. Four of the seven writers considered in this chapter (Maria Weston Chapman, Lydia Maria Child, Caroline W. Healey Dall, and Frances H. Green) came from New England, two (Eliza Leslie and E. D. E. N. Southworth) from the mid-Atlantic, and one (Jane Elizabeth Jones) from the Midwest. Jones, Leslie, and Southworth were sympathetic to antislavery ideals but did not have any official ties with the formal antislavery movement. Although the literary works examined in this chapter come from perspectives ranging from gradual emancipationist to radical abolitionist, several of the most prolific authors under consideration were firmly entrenched in Garrisonian abolitionist circles. Chapman, Child, Dall, Follen, and Green were all Garrisonians who endorsed his principles of immediate abolition, moral suasion, and nonviolence. The majority of authors considered in this chapter thus shared Garrison's distrust of electoral politics and his strong endorsement of moral influence as the most useful form of abolitionist advocacy, expressing their suspicion and displeasure about the larger antislavery movement's shift away from moral influence toward political activism over the course of the 1840s.

This chapter centers not only on the works of these specific authors but also on the six literary venues in which their fiction appeared: the *Child's Friend,* the *National Anti-Slavery Standard,* the *National Era,* the *Liberty Cap, Liberty Chimes,* and the *Liberty Bell.* Even the four of these issued by Garrisonian authors or organizations—the *Standard,* the *Liberty Cap, Liberty Chimes,* and the *Liberty Bell*—made a concerted effort to address a popular audience and to publish works written by non-Garrisonian abolitionists. Three of the six—*The Child's Friend,* the *Liberty Bell,* and the *National Era*— achieved a degree of success with a popular audience, and the remaining three, while not widely circulated outside of it, were influential within the antislavery movement.⁷

The *National Anti-Slavery Standard* (1840–70) and the *National Era* (1847–60) proved quite controversial in antislavery circles, in large part because of their sustained, explicit efforts to become popular newspapers that would appeal to nonabolitionist readers. Child, who served as editor of the *Standard* between 1841 and 1843, articulated her hopes for the paper early in her editorial tenure, declaring that it was "not intended to meet the wants of ultra abolitionists, but to gain the ear of the people at large."⁸ As part of her efforts to make the *Standard* a more mainstream paper, Child persuaded much-loved authors such as Eliza Leslie to publish their fiction in its pages and began printing a literary items section that provided readers with news about contemporary popular literature.⁹

Child also sought to diffuse any controversy that might surround her work as a female editor of a politically minded, activist newspaper.¹⁰ On assuming the reins of the *Standard,* Child was careful to stress that she felt humbled at the idea of taking on this traditionally masculine role. Insisting that she would have been delighted to have her husband step into the editor's chair in her stead, she modestly informed readers, "Such as I am, I am here—ready to work, according to my conscience and ability; promising nothing, but diligence and fidelity . . . with very quiet resolution I go to my new work: asking only such confidence as I may deserve, and ready to pass away whenever a fitter instrument of God's will offers to take my place."¹¹ Assuming the editorship of the *Standard* nearly fifteen years after Chandler had taken up her post as Ladies' Department editor at the *Genius,* Child used very similar language to describe her work.

Like Chandler, Child emphasized her sense of awe and unworthiness at having been chosen for such an exalted position and hastened to reassure readers of her willingness to step aside should an editor more qualified than she—that is, a man—be found. Thus, as she embarked on the controversial work of seeking to transform the *Standard* into a popular newspaper, Child sought to present her own headship of the paper in a nonthreatening way.

Child's desire to make the *Standard* into a widely read periodical drew mixed reactions from other members of the abolitionist community. Garrison regarded her editorial work positively, writing to Elizabeth Pease in 1841, "Mrs. Child is now at the head of the Standard, and every thing looks well."¹² Others were more skeptical about the value of such a periodical focused on pleasing its audience and welcoming readers not wholeheartedly committed to abolitionism. As Oliver Johnson wrote anxiously to Maria Weston Chapman in 1841, "the Standard is a very *agreeable* paper under Mrs. Child's administration.... [I]ts agreeableness is attracting the support of some half-and-half, milk-and-water sort of abolitionists.... I don't want our papers to become too popular."¹³

This fear also swirled around the *National Era,* which also sought to be agreeably literary and attractive to a wide readership.¹⁴ Much like Child, Gamaliel Bailey, founder and editor of the *Era,* hoped his paper would play a crucial role in bringing antislavery ideas before audiences who had not previously been exposed to them. This even extended to white southerners. As Bailey told readers of his paper's inaugural 1847 issue, "it must never be forgotten that it is a leading part of our design to reach the mind of the South—disarm prejudice, correct misconception, win respectful attention." Bailey hoped his northern readers would see the wisdom of this approach and second his desire to create a newspaper that would entice rather than alienate white southern readers. "A majority of anti-slavery people of the free states, without abating their zeal, or comprising their principles," he asserted, "clearly see that mere denunciation may inflame, but not convince—may terrify the cowardly, but must arouse the indignation and resistance of men of courage and intelligence."¹⁵

Carefully giving no names, Bailey nonetheless sought to distance himself from radical abolitionist publications such as the *Liberator,* which regularly featured uncompromising, blunt denunciations of white southern society. While wishing to be unwavering in his condemnations of the South's peculiar institution, he nonetheless hoped to avoid alienating white southerners.¹⁶ An important means of making the *Era* a pleasant, popular periodical for all of its readers regardless of region, Bailey indicated, would be a heavy inclusion of fiction; as he noted in his first issue, "literature will receive a large share of attention."¹⁷ He was as good as his word, featuring numerous short stories and serializing several novels by popular female authors over the course of the *Era*'s existence.¹⁸

The *Standard* and the *Era* were not the only periodicals launched during this decade that offered female antislavery authors a new, more popular platform for their work. The 1840s also witnessed the rise of the antislavery gift book and female antislavery editors' and authors' efforts to bring abolitionism into middle-class readers' parlors through this medium. Gift books were beautifully bound, lavishly illustrated collections of poetry and prose intended for display in their middle-class owners' homes. Ideally, a gift book would be a powerful symbol of its owner's material prosperity, discernment as a consumer, and refinement as an individual. As were other examples of the genre, abolitionist gift books were very much female-centered texts. Published by female antislavery societies, edited by female abolitionists, prominently featuring women's literary work, and primarily intended for a female audience, gift books strongly reinforced the association of literary production and consumption with femininity. Expensive to produce and difficult to assemble, most—such as Massachusetts Female Emancipation Society's *Star of Emancipation* and the Providence Ladies' Anti-Slavery Society's *Liberty Chimes*—only lasted for a year or two. But one gift book, the Boston Female Anti-Slavery Society's (BFASS) *Liberty Bell* (1839–58), flourished for nearly two decades. Its survival and success had a great deal to do with the considerable wealth and social influence of its editor, Maria Weston Chapman.[19]

Born into the prominent Weston family and married to wealthy Boston abolitionist Henry Grafton Chapman, throughout her life Chapman used her affluence and social standing in the service of the antislavery cause. A dynamic, seemingly tireless activist, Chapman was a founding member of the BFASS, worked for the Massachusetts Anti-Slavery Society, and served on the American Anti-Slavery Society's executive board. She was also extensively involved in antislavery print culture, having a close working relationship with Garrison and stepping in to guest-edit the *Liberator* when he was ill or absent. Chapman also published a tract about women's rights in the antislavery movement, *Right and Wrong in Massachusetts*, in 1839; facilitated the launch of the *National Anti-Slavery Standard* in 1840; published her novella *Pinda: A True Tale* that same year; and served as editor of the *Liberty Bell* for virtually all of its existence.

Under Chapman's editorship, the *Liberty Bell* grew into a periodical notable for not only its beautiful design but also for the fame of its British, American, and European contributors. Chapman used her significant social connections to persuade popular authors to endorse, support, and publish their work in the *Liberty Bell*. Because of her efforts, writers including Elizabeth Barrett Browning, Alexis de Tocqueville, Ralph Waldo Emerson, Victor Hugo, Henry Wadsworth Longfellow, and Harriet Martineau all contributed to the gift book. Securing such prominent contributors, Chapman hoped, would attract readers otherwise uninterested in abolitionism and subsequently convert them to the cause.

And Chapman had very definite ideas about what the American reading public would require to become interested in antislavery issues. She was convinced the *Liberty Bell*'s prospective readers were "like children, to whom a medicine is made as pleasant as its nature permits. A childish mind receives a small measure of truth in gilt edges where it would reject it in 'whity-brown.'"[20] There is no small trace of condescension in Chapman's declaration; yet though she expressed some ambivalence about readers who required frothy fiction to engage with the slave question, as editor of the *Liberty Bell,* Chapman nonetheless did everything in her power to attract and retain them.[21] On assuming control of the BFASS's Anti-Slavery Bazaar in the mid-1830s, she became convinced that a popular volume of antislavery literature would be the ideal item to market to the bazaar's many visitors. Already seeking to induce middle-class female consumers to become interested in abolition through the sale of goods including slavery-themed potholders, pen wipes, and fire screens, she hoped attractively packaged antislavery literature would be another desirable commodity that could be sold to female purchasers for the benefit of abolitionism. As Chapman asserted, she was very much aware that "the opportunity afforded by the Fair for the introduction of Anti Slavery publications to the attention of great numbers makes it a most valuable instrumentality in the cause."[22]

Antislavery reviewers praised the *Liberty Bell* as the ideal volume for the discerning, virtuous female reader. Lauding the *Liberty Bell* for its consistently high quality, a *Standard* reviewer wrote, "The contents of this beautifully printed little volume are extremely interesting. How could they be otherwise . . . when such women as Maria W. Chapman, Lydia M. Child, Anne W. Weston, Caroline Weston, Eliza Lee Follen, Henrietta Sergeant, Harriet Martineau, Mary Clark, and Mary E. Robinson,—are among its contributors?"[23] During an era in which female readers were avid consumers of literature written by what Nathaniel Hawthorne contemptuously dismissed as "that damned mob of scribbling women," highlighting the presence of popular female writers within the *Liberty Bell*'s pages seems to have been a deliberate bid to attract a female audience.[24]

The reviewer also stressed the physical beauty of the *Liberty Bell:* "We know no American Annual, got up as they are, for the especial adornment of parlour tables, that excells the Liberty Bell in the beauty of its type, the excellence of its paper, and the general elegance of its appearance."[25] Given the pressures placed on middle-class women to make their parlors sites of both moral discernment and material beauty, this gift book was thus positioned as the perfect item for the principled, refined woman's home. Elegant in its appearance, the *Liberty Bell* also contained works written by some of the day's most popular, well-respected female authors. By purchasing it, a female consumer could at once make her parlor more beautiful, display the refinement of her literary taste, and demonstrate her moral commitment to the worthy cause of abolition.

Another popular female-centered literary medium that female antislavery authors increasingly drew on during the 1840s was children's literature. Fiction intended for children had been an important part of antislavery print culture since the 1830s.[26] As Deborah C. DeRosa notes, the 1840s witnessed a further flowering of literature intended for young readers not only in abolitionist circles but also in the American literary marketplace more broadly.[27] Antislavery women such as Eliza Lee Follen followed in Child's footsteps by infusing their children's periodicals with antislavery messages. A powerful voice in antislavery children's literature during the 1840s, Follen both published gift books intended for young readers and incorporated abolitionism into the stories she wrote for her mainstream children's periodical *The Child's Friend* (1843–58).[28]

As white women's antislavery literary work expanded outward into children's literature, gift books, and more mainstream antislavery periodicals, African American female authors' voices largely disappeared from antislavery fiction. One significant factor in this was that the primary venues in which African American women had published their literature during the 1830s, the *Liberator*'s Juvenile and Ladies' Departments, no longer existed. Although Garrison continued to sporadically publish women's fiction in the *Liberator* during the 1840s and 1850s, he ceased including separate Ladies' and Juvenile Departments as of 1839. While still receptive to printing female authors' works, he thus severed the close ties between his newspaper and African American female literary societies. Literary society members (already reticent about publishing their work in a public forum) seem to have been yet more uncomfortable with publishing in the *Liberator* generally, rather than in its women's pages specifically. After all, its Ladies' and Juvenile Departments had been explicitly gendered spaces, for which African American women's literature had been directly solicited and in which it had been explicitly welcomed.

The types of antislavery periodicals rising to prominence in the 1840s may also have made the publication of African American women's literature significantly less likely than it had been in previous decades. Dedicated to not alienating white southerners and to publishing fiction from authors who had the largest possible name recognition, the editors of periodicals like the *Standard* and the *Era* may well have been reluctant to accept submissions from African American female authors, even if the writers had wanted to publish their work in these publications' pages. African American female authors also would likely not have been as eager to submit their work to more moderate, less racially progressive publications such as the *Era,* which lacked the dedication to the dual causes of abolition and racial equality expressed by more radical periodicals such as the *Liberator.* Similar impediments existed for African American women seeking to publish in antislavery gift books. Issued by white-led female antislavery societies, and with a similar desire to include works by the most famous, popular literary figures of the day, gift books such as the *Liberty Bell* were also far from welcoming spaces for African American female authors. As writers such as Harriet Wilson discovered in subsequent decades, while the antislavery literary marketplace was hungry for formerly enslaved people's narratives about their lives in the peculiar institution, it was nowhere near as receptive to the writings of free African American women focused on racial injustice in the North.[29]

Another possible cause of this re-whitening of mainstream antislavery literary culture was the slow but steady rise of African American–edited periodicals, which may have offered more attractive options for publication for black female writers than white-edited and -dominated publications and presses did. The 1840s witnessed the beginnings of a more extensive, sustainable African American newspaper culture than had existed in previous decades. The first such newspaper, *Freedom's Journal,* had begun publication in 1827 and closed its doors in 1828. The *Colored American,* which published its first issue in 1837, was also relatively short-lived, ending publication in 1842. 1847 saw the beginnings of Frederick Douglass's career as newspaper editor, as he began issuing the *North Star.* This newspaper reconstituted itself as *Frederick Douglass' Paper* in 1851 and ran until 1863.

While black newspapers were still far from numerous and still often struggled for both funding and survival, the late antebellum era nonetheless offered more chances for black writers to seek publication in periodicals edited by African Americans than had existed in previous years. As will be discussed more extensively in chapter 4, such opportunities were clearly significant for black authors such as Frances E. Watkins Harper, who chose to publish her pioneering short story "The Two Offers" in the African American-edited *Anglo-African Magazine* in 1859. In the 1840s, likewise, African American female authors may have chosen to withdraw their literary contributions from moderate, white-edited antislavery periodicals, in favor of writing for more progressive, black-run newspapers. The combination of these factors led to a mainstream antislavery literary culture made up almost exclusively of white writers' voices, which had numerous implications. Questions about civil rights and racial equality largely disappeared in the literature published in white-edited periodicals, and enslaved female characters became increasingly passive victims of the slave system in white women's writings, rather than active resistors of it.

The 1840s were a very tumultuous decade in the history of abolitionism; in addition to upheavals in antislavery print culture, the movement was seized with a new wave of debates about the place of women in the antislavery movement. In 1839 and 1840, these discussions reached a crisis point, when Abby Kelley was appointed to the business committee of the American Anti-Slavery Society (AASS). Some members, unwilling to accept a woman in such a leadership position, left to form a rival organization, the American and Foreign Anti-Slavery Society (AFASS).

Kelley's appointment and the related questions about women's roles in the antislavery movement it raised were not the only factors driving this division in organized abolitionism. Members of the AASS and AFASS also disagreed over Garrison's controversial leadership, the use of political action in the service of abolitionism, the principle of nonresistance, and the connections between activists' religious affiliations and their abolitionism. The woman question was, however, a particularly explosive one in antislavery circles, sparking strong feelings and fierce debates.[30]

Of the antislavery women writers whose works are discussed in this chapter, some remained loyal to Garrison and AASS, whereas others felt more comfortable with the AFASS's more moderate views.[31] None of these writers explicitly addressed the contentious issue of the schism in the abolitionist movement in their fiction, however. Wary of making their work partisan, female antislavery authors nonetheless continued to discuss questions about women's roles in abolitionism. Yet they did so without naming names, pointing fingers, or directly alluding to the organizational and ideological divisions then wracking the larger movement.

Enslaved Women in White Authors' Texts

In the fiction they published during the 1840s, white female antislavery authors dedicated considerable time and attention to considering the plight of enslaved women. They placed significant emphasis on enslaved women's victimization, lingering over descriptions of the harassment, beatings, and sexual violence women endured in slavery. As previous scholars have noted, this focus on physical and sexual abuse at once reflected the reality of enslaved women's lives as perpetually vulnerable to sexual assault while also having troublingly exploitative, pornographic overtones, and providing white female authors with a means of exploring their own fears and anxieties about sexuality. I argue that these representations of enslaved women's gender-specific sufferings were also a means of stressing enslaved women's maternal virtue and their desire to preserve and maintain their chastity.

By emphasizing that their enslaved female characters wanted only the right to be faithful wives and loving mothers, white female writers highlighted enslaved women's commonalities with white women, their high standards of feminine moral virtue, and their subsequent fitness to successfully manage the challenges of freedom and citizenship. While these representations favorably depicted enslaved women, they nonetheless also rendered them passive figures in these narratives. During a decade in which debates about enslaved people's violent resistance to slavery were prevalent in abolitionist circles, white female writers denied enslaved women virtually any agency through which to effectively work for their own liberation. Their fiction thus created a vision of enslaved women who were morally virtuous but fundamentally in need of white guidance—both within slavery and, implicitly, after slavery had ended.

Throughout their work, white female writers stressed that one of slavery's chief evils was that it deprived enslaved women of their right to care for and protect their children. This was an especially cruel facet of the peculiar institution, white female authors insisted, since enslaved women possessed the same deep maternal feelings that white mothers did. For example, the heroine of Child's 1842 "The Quadroons," Rosalie, is discussed primarily in terms of her status as a loving mother. Resigned to the injustices she herself suffers in slavery, Rosalie begins to worry about her own enslavement only when she reflects on the impact it will have on her young and beautiful daughter. "For herself she cared but little," Child wrote of her selfless heroine, "but when she looked at her beloved Xarifa, and reflected upon the unavoidable and dangerous position which the tyranny of society had awarded her, her soul was filled with anguish."[32] Profoundly conscious of the gender-specific perils that confronted women in slavery, Rosalie suffers greatly in contemplating the dark future of sexual violence and exploitation that almost certainly awaited her beloved daughter. After Rosalie's owner, who is also Xarifa's father, abandons his plans to emancipate both women, Rosalie dies of heartbreak and despair. The protagonist of Caroline W. Healey Dall's 1848 "Annie Gray" similarly focuses on the plight of a devoted enslaved mother, the titular Annie, who is inspired to resist slavery only after she becomes pregnant. Uncertain about whether to make a bid for freedom by running away, Annie confides in the reader, "I debated, until I remembered that this child would be a Slave,—perhaps a daughter,—and horror-struck at the thought, I hurried my preparations for my departure."[33]

Whether enslaved mothers responded to the threats slavery posed to their beloved children with flight or with death, white female writers stressed that maternal love was the center of these women's lives and invited their white female readers to empathize with mothers' desires to protect their children, particularly their sexually vulnerable daughters, from harm. Authors highlighted that white female readers needed to resist slavery because of their common bonds with enslaved women, as mothers or prospective mothers. Right-thinking white women had to join the abolitionist fight unless they were prepared to live in a country in which their fellow loving, virtuous mothers' rights were persistently, viciously denied.

White female readers also needed to take up the antislavery cause to aid enslaved women whose sexual purity had been cruelly violated by brutal white men. Several narratives written during this era centered on heroines who had been the victims of sexual exploitation and abuse. In Child's "The Quadroons," Rosalie's death is caused because her fickle white master-lover has abandoned her and her daughter Xarifa, and Xarifa dies after her vicious owner rapes her.[34] The heroine of Child's 1843 tale "Slavery's Pleasant Homes," Rosa, similarly dies after having been forcibly parted from the enslaved man she loves and repeatedly raped by her master. Dall's title character in her story "Amy" is also coerced into an unwanted sexual relationship with her master, and the titular Annie Gray's master "marries" her to a series of enslaved men against her will.[35]

Green's "The Slave Wife" similarly centers on a sexually abused and exploited enslaved heroine, Clygy, whose story is told to the tale's narrator by Clygy's widower, Laco. Laco has escaped from slavery to Canada, and when the narrator asks after his family, he embarks on the tragic tale of his beloved Clygy's short life and brutal death. The pair were happily married, when their master took notice of and began regularly raping Clygy. She became pregnant—by her husband, she insisted—and was whipped to death while in labor with their child for refusing to renounce her relationship with him. After describing Clygy's tragic death, the narrator urges her female readers, "Think of that, wives! Think of it, all ye modest and virtuous women, who have husbands, and brothers, and friends, and the laws, to wall round, and protect your purity."[36] As Sánchez-Eppler and Yellin have argued, white female writers often focused on the sexual violence endured by enslaved women as a means of exploring their anxieties about married white women's lack of control over their sexual and reproductive lives, often problematically conflating these two forms of oppression.[37] Yet Green's story notably highlighted her awareness of the considerable differences between white and enslaved women's experiences of sexual violence.

In "The Slave Wife," Green emphasized that her white female readers had significantly more ability to control their sexual lives than enslaved women did, since they were part of a culture that at least recognized the existence of white, middle-class women's sexual "purity." White men sometimes stripped white women of sexual agency, but they could and did also sometimes offer protection for white, middle-class women facing sexual violation. Defined as unrapeable under American law and in American culture, enslaved women were offered no such protections. White women, Green insisted, thus needed both to be aware that they possessed a considerable degree of sexual privilege and to fight to ensure that *all* women were granted the same control over their sexual and reproductive lives.

White writers stressed that rape was not the only threat to sexual purity that enslaved women faced in slavery. They also highlighted the ways modest enslaved women consistently endured obscene, sexualized assessment by crude slave traders. When the gently reared Xarifa is put on the auction block in Child's "The Quadroons" she is "compelled to listen to the grossest language, and shrink . . . from the rude hands that examined the graceful proportions of her beautiful frame."[38] The enslaved heroine of E. D. E. N. Southworth's *The Mother-in-Law,* Anna, finds herself in a similar plight, as a slave trader's "sensual eyes roved all over her girlish figure, gloating on her beauty, he muttered an exclamation—'She is a handsome girl. . . . She'd bring twelve or fifteen hundred dollars!'"[39] By vividly rendering the horrors of enslaved women being sold into the "fancy trade" of sexual slavery, writers emphasized shame and horror endured by refined young women who possessed the same innate sexual modesty as white, middle-class women. Enslaved women had exactly the same feelings when forced to reveal their bodies to crass, violent men and to face the prospect of selling their bodies in forced prostitution, authors stressed, that white female readers would have if they were forced into an identical situation.[40]

White female writers emphasized that enslaved female characters in these narratives held themselves to the same high standards of chastity expected of white, middle-class readers. Highlighting the significant value that enslaved women placed on their sexual virtue, white writers worked to counter pervasive cultural stereotypes that defined African American women as innately, inescapably hypersexual. Recalling how his wife recounted the story of her sexual assault, "The Slave Wife"'s Laco exclaims, "O I wish some of those fine ladies, who think the slave woman has no virtue—no delicacy—could have seen with what a sweet and shrinking modesty she told me the revolting tale."[41] Possessing the delicate sensibilities expected of middle-class white women, Clygy shrinks from telling even her loving husband about the sexual violence that she has endured. In Child's "The Quadroons," Xarifa also feels powerful shame about her sexual violation, and after being raped by her master, she becomes "a raving maniac. The pure temple was desecrated."[42] Rather than live with the deep shame she felt about her rape, Xarifa quickly descends into madness and death.[43]

By creating these scenarios, white female authors defined enslaved women as true ladies who cared more about preserving their sexual honor (defined according to white, middle-class codes of sexuality, which prioritized female virginity and chastity) than they did about their own lives. White authors thus emphasized that enslaved women were not only naturally inclined to live up to strict codes of female sexual respectability but were also willing to die for these ideals if they violated them, however unwillingly. Such representations were quite subversive in a country in which enslaved women had no legal right to bodily integrity and were culturally defined as hypersexual and unrapeable. Yet, holding enslaved women to the same strict sexual code white, middle-class women were expected to follow, which defined death as preferable to the perceived shame of living as a rape victim, also had many disempowering aspects. This ideology did not, after all, leave any room for the many enslaved women who had endured sexual assault, or whose lives had not followed the pattern of premarital chastity and lifelong sexual fidelity to one man, to lead productive lives in a postemancipation world—or, indeed, to live to see emancipation, at all.

Narratives of enslaved women's repeated sexual violation also had the potential to be read in pornographic as well as abolitionist ways. These texts might have offered not only white female readers the chance to empathize with enslaved women's sufferings but also white male readers the opportunity to read tales that contained descriptions of young, beautiful enslaved women's bodies, and their sexual vulnerability to white men.[44] Designed to combat the hypersexualization of African American women in American culture, white women's stories had the potential to do the exact opposite, subjecting enslaved women's bodily experiences to a scrutiny to which white female characters in these texts were never exposed.

While these stories may have had a male readership, which was potentially less sympathetic, female authors remained most concerned with their white female readers and how they would respond to tales of enslaved women's exploitation and suffering. Authors insisted to white women that if they could peruse these heartrending tales about women's sexual victimization unmoved, doubt would be cast on their own purity of mind. Having told Clygy's story, the narrator of Green's "The Slave Wife" urged female readers, "Think of this, all ye virtuous—all ye pious women of the land; and if your virtue, your piety, are not a mere sham—are not a damning lie." Green insisted that no free woman could call herself truly sexually virtuous if she lived peacefully in a land that whipped expectant mothers to death for the "sin" of wishing to be sexually faithful to the men they loved. Green's Laco takes this argument a step further: "If any woman can bear it [hearing about Clygy's repeated sexual assault and eventual death] without a wish—a determination to labor with all her might to abolish

THE SLAVERY OF WOMAN, I impeach her virtue—She is *not* TRUE—she is not PURE."[45] In an era in which the ideal of white, middle-class female "passionlessness" held sway, and a crucial part of bourgeois femininity was chastity, impugning female readers' sexual virtue was a compelling (if also a controversial) argument.[46] Free women needed to sympathize with enslaved women who had been sexually abused not only because it was the right thing for a woman of true feeling to do but also because *not* to do so indicated her willingness to turn a blind eye to sexual immorality. And to thus condone sexual immorality was, Green contended, to render one's self sexually impure.

As this focus on enslaved women's sexual exploitation and the violation of their maternal feelings indicates, when enslaved women appeared in the pages of women's antislavery fiction, they did so primarily as the passive victims of slavery's gender-specific cruelties. As Child declared in "The Quadroons," the plight of her unfortunate heroine Xarifa embodied the horrors suffered by "that docile and injured race."[47] Numerous narratives conformed to this model, following enslaved women as they passively endured physical abuse, suffered rape, and then died, asking for white female readers' sympathy and aid before doing so. In some ways, authors represented this passivity in the face of terrible suffering as its own kind of strength: like Christ, enslaved women demonstrated that they were morally powerful enough to endure horrible cruelties, and even death, at their tormentors' hands rather than compromise their moral ideals.

Authors sometimes made enslaved female characters' likeness to an all-forgiving, long-suffering, self-sacrificing Christ explicit. Speaking about the enslaved Anna in Southworth's *The Mother-in-Law,* the abolitionist Susan remarks admiringly, "She never speaks of her position, her sorrow; I never heard her utter a word of complaint, impatience, or repining, in my life. I have seen her suffer excruciating bodily pain, and when I have been distressed to death at her agony, she has smiled a mournful smile."[48] When Anna faces a future of sexual slavery in New Orleans, she prays directly to the Christ whom she so strongly resembles: "Thou Crucified! who remembered amid the agony of the cross that Thy executioners knew not what they did, and prayed for them, give me a portion of Thine own divine calmness, patience, and justice." Like Christ, she not only freely forgives those who torment her but also patiently accepts a martyr-like death, if that is God's will.[49]

Anna was far from being the only enslaved female character to die tragically in the pages of white women's antislavery fiction. After suffering betrayal at the hands of her owner and lover in "The Quadroons," Rosalie "was found dead in her bed."[50] Child's "Slavery's Pleasant Homes" and Green's "The Slave Wife" both bring their enslaved heroines to the stake to be whipped to death while they are pregnant, because they refused to abandon their marriage vows to enslaved men.[51] Describing her heroine's death, Green used overtly Christlike language, noting that "she endured with the spirit of a lamb."[52]

Explicitly linking their heroines to Christ for their willing submission to suffering and death, female antislavery authors gave enslaved protagonists positions at once tremendously morally potent and essentially passive.[53] If Christ was the model to which Christian Americans ought to aspire, then it seemed enslaved women had the opportunity to come the closest to reaching this ideal. By accepting a lowly position on earth, stoically facing terrible physical sufferings and the likelihood of an early, brutal death, and benevolently forgiving those who wronged them, enslaved female characters undoubtedly conformed to Christ's example. Yet this model of enslaved women's acceptance of suffering and death obviously provided a very narrow vision of the ways enslaved women could live within and fight against slavery. These tales worrisomely indicated that enslaved women could play the most significant role in the antislavery struggle by dying—becoming martyrs whose deaths would serve as rallying cries for white women's antislavery action, rather than by being abolitionist actors themselves.

Enslaved female characters' deaths in white women's abolitionist fiction were thus not as much about enslaved women as about the impacts their deaths would have on white female readers. White female audiences were expected to read these harrowing narratives and be spurred to take abolitionist action. Because enslaved women could not successfully fight for their own freedom, it was white women's obligation to fight for them; in a post-emancipation world, virtuous enslaved women would be able to join white women's efforts to morally purify American society. However, these narratives indicated that they would not do so as equal partners but rather as deferential followers, accepting more active, effective white women's leadership and guidance.

It is notable that even in the handful of stories in which they did succeed in escaping from slavery and building new lives for themselves as free women, enslaved women still ultimately owed their freedom to white initiative and assistance. When the title character in Chapman's *Pinda* finds herself separated from her master on a visit to the North, she is approached by a white male abolitionist who asks her, "Do you wish to be free?" Receiving an affirmative answer, he tells her, "'Come with me, then;'—and he conducted her to the nearest antislavery dwelling."[54]

The enslaved protagonist of Dall's "Annie Gray" also experiences her abolitionist awakening at the hands of a white male activist, Arthur, who comes to her household preaching the antislavery gospel. "He set it before us in such a true light," Annie recalls. "He pleaded against it; and in our hours of leisure he read to us from the books he most valued. Under his influence my mind and heart greatly expanded; a great change worked itself within me." Having been educated about slavery's evils by the benevolent Arthur, Annie becomes an active voice for abolition on her plantation. "I interested myself in the other Slaves," she recollects. "I tried to teach them; I talked to them of freedom, when now, for the first time, I understood it." After Annie becomes pregnant and is terrified that her child might be a daughter, Arthur instructs her, "'Fly, with the rising sun. You know your route.' He pointed to the north, dropped a purse at my feet, and was gone."[55] At the end of their respective stories, Annie has successfully made a happy life for herself and her child in Canada, and Pinda and her husband have found contentment living free in the North.

In these narratives, the authors made it clear that enslaved women had an innate desire for liberty, even before their fateful encounters with white male abolitionists. Pinda unhesitatingly agrees to seek her freedom when an abolitionist approaches her, suggesting she had already contemplated freeing herself. After meeting Arthur, Annie takes to the role of antislavery activist with alacrity, educating her fellow slaves about freedom and seizing the chance to flee North as soon as the opportunity arises. Yet without white men, these stories also make clear, the liberation of these two women would not have happened. It is the economic prosperity and social power of white male characters in these tales that makes enslaved women's freedom viable.

While on one level, such narratives simply reflected the reality that white men had significantly more access to material resources and freedom of motion than enslaved women did, on another, it rendered enslaved women problematically passive, even in narratives about their own self-emancipation.[56] Though Annie had lived in slavery her entire life, it took a white man to awaken her to the institution's injustice, and while Pinda managed to find herself unsupervised by her master when in the North, it took a white man's prompting to induce her to escape. The women in these stories clearly desire freedom, but their decisions to fight for it are prompted by benevolent white abolitionist men. Given that white female writers emphasized that white men were much less morally trustworthy than white women, the idea that enslaved women needed to rely on white men to secure their freedom was a troubling one. While Chapman's and Dall's stories feature white male abolitionists who *are* reliable and principled, these depictions are the exception, rather than the rule, in women's antislavery fiction. As such, the idea that enslaved women might need to rely on economically and politically powerful white men to secure their freedom was a distinctly disquieting one.

Uncomfortable with the concept of enslaved women relying on morally suspect white men for their freedom, white writers nonetheless also indicated that when enslaved girls and women took action against slavery independently of white abolitionists' careful guidance, they revealed a disturbing nonconformity to the proper ideals of decorous feminine activism. The forms their resistance took often proved radically different from the restrained antislavery activity that white female abolitionists praised in their white female characters. In Eliza Leslie's story "The Traveling Tinman," two white Quaker girls, Amy and Orphy, find an African American child concealed in the title character's van. The girl, Dinah, tells them that the tinman has kidnapped her from her freeborn parents and plans to sell her into slavery. "I hate him," she tells Amy and Orphy. "And yesterday, when I know he didn't see me, I spit in the crown of his hat." Only five years old and powerless to resist the tinman in more significant ways, Dinah finds her own small means of revenging herself on her captor. Rather than validating her feelings and actions, however, Amy exclaims, "Hush! Thee must never say thee hates anybody."[57] Thus, not even having been kidnapped into slavery justified a young girl expressing feelings of hatred toward anyone.

By claiming that she hated her captor and spitting into his hat, Dinah had violated the code of ladylike behavior that even the youngest girls in the antebellum era were expected to live up to. While sympathetic to her plight, Leslie nonetheless condemned Diana for the indecorous nature of both her actions and her sentiments. "The Traveling Tinman" notably ends with the feisty, raucous Dinah being brought into Amy and Orphy's household as a servant, to be schooled there into sedate, virtuous womanhood. "The Traveling Tinman" indicated that African American girls could not be relied on to resist slavery in the gender-appropriate ways. Leslie thus signified that African American girls and women needed to be trained in proper femininity by white women, who were more naturally decorous; despite that Dinah was born and raised in freedom, she nonetheless does not share the same standards of ladylike comportment and speech as white girls like Amy and Orphy. Troublingly, this suggests that African American girls' failure to live up to the ideals of bourgeois white womanhood might come not from their status as free or enslaved but rather from innate racial difference; even when free, African American women needed white women to carefully educate them in the standards of genteel femininity.[58]

The vision of enslaved women that emerged from white women's literature was thus a problematic one. Taking pains to emphasize that enslaved women possessed the same deep maternal feelings and high standards of sexual virtue that white, middle-class women did, white female writers made a powerful case for white female readers becoming involved in the antislavery movement specifically to liberate innocent enslaved women. While they in some ways represented enslaved and white women as equals in their dedication to selfless maternity and spotless chastity, these literary works also created a definite hierarchy. Enslaved women still needed white abolitionists to help guide them to freedom and to instruct them about how to resist slavery effectively and appropriately. This depiction of enslaved women had concerning implications for the place white female abolitionists envisioned for free women of color in a postemancipation world.

Violent Resistance to Slavery in Women's Fiction

When white antislavery authors did depict enslaved people taking violent action against slavery, they represented this violence as a decidedly problematic form of resistance. Writers expressed sympathy for the injustices that motivated their enslaved male characters to violently resist their enslavement. However, they also represented the willingness to embrace violence as a moral failing and as ultimately unhelpful in moving the antislavery cause forward. Men's violent activism pushed the abolitionist movement troublingly far away from what these authors insisted should be its true center—the moral values of pacifist women.

The specter of violent abolitionism loomed particularly large for antislavery female authors writing during the 1840s, as many activists became more receptive to violence as a form of antislavery activity during this decade. This was by no means a universal shift, as many abolitionists remained committed to pacifism (a commitment some would retain until the outbreak of the Civil War). Yet some abolitionists who had previously been staunchly opposed to the use of force began to argue that violence would sometimes be necessary to resist slavery effectively.[59] White abolitionists who came to advocate violence during the 1840s often focused on defensive forms of violence, in which enslaved men used violence to protect themselves and their families. For men who had been enslaved, such self-assertion was often framed as an important reclamation of the masculinity that slavery had deprived them of. In accounts such as Frederick Douglass's 1845 *Narrative of the Life of Frederick Douglass, An American Slave*, formerly enslaved men emphasized that defending themselves and their loved ones against their masters and overseers was a crucial part of reclaiming identity and self-respect as not just human beings generally but as men specifically. These links between the assertion of masculinity and morally justifiable violence were ones white female authors staunchly refused to affirm.

In their depictions of violence in enslaved communities, female authors praised enslaved men who embraced pacifism. An elderly enslaved man in Child's "The Black Saxons," for example, is the lone pacifist voice in a large gathering of insurrectionary enslaved men. "The blessed Jesus always talked of mercy," this man tells the crowd, "I know we have been fed like hogs, and shot at like wild beasts. Myself found the body of my likeliest boy under the tree where buckra rifles reached him. But thanks to the blessed Jesus, I feel it in my poor old heart to forgive them. . . . Now I say, let us love our enemies; let us pray for them."[60] This man is clearly an admirable character, emulating Christ in his willingness to forgive those who have grievously wronged him.[61] However, this male pacifist is in the minority among enslaved male characters in the story and is quickly silenced by the tale's pro-violent-uprising male majority.

Throughout their representations of enslaved men's antislavery violence, female writers demonstrated an uneasy blend of sympathy for enslaved men's anger and condemnation of the violent feelings and actions that anger led to. Aware that the flagrant injustices of slavery had sparked retaliatory violence, white authors nonetheless remained uncomfortable with this violence. Writing in a culture saturated with stereotypes about animalistic, violent African American men—and with slave uprisings like Nat Turner's, in which white women and children had been killed, in the very recent past—racially charged anxieties about potentially uncontrollable violence was present even in the most committed and progressive white abolitionists.

Child's "Slavery's Pleasant Homes," for example, contains this uncomfortable blend of sympathy for enslaved men's violent resistance and doubts about that violence's moral justifiability. Toward the end of the story, the noble enslaved character George murders his master, Frederic—to avenge the loss of his wife, Rosa, whom Frederic had repeatedly raped and beaten to the point where she had miscarried her and George's unborn child and subsequently died. "I murdered him," George confesses, "for he killed my wife, and hell was in my bosom."[62] The story concludes by quoting northern newspaper reports of George's execution, which make no mention of the repeated rapes or violent death of Rosa and insist that cases like George's prove the natural violence of African American men and the consequent need for the restraining institution of slavery. As Carolyn Karcher notes, "Slavery's Pleasant Homes" thus highlighted the ways the American media erased the pervasiveness of violence against enslaved people and depicted any violent acts committed by the enslaved as proof of innate racial inferiority and volatility.[63]

Presenting George as a sympathetic character throughout the story, Child expected her readers to empathize with his sufferings and to comprehend his actions. Yet she nonetheless also introduced an element of moral ambiguity by having him affirm that he committed the murder when "hell" had overtaken him. Linking George's actions to a hellish, un-Christian desire for vengeance, Child indicated that this murder was against the basic codes of religion and morality, however comprehensible the motivations behind it were.

A similar ambivalence suffuses Child's "The Black Saxons." This narrative (as its title indicates) argues that enslaved people's desire for freedom was parallel to the struggles of Saxons, who had resisted Norman occupation in medieval England. Having eavesdropped on a secret gathering of enslaved men planning a rebellion, slave owner Mr. Dixon reflects, "Was not their spirit that gleamed forth there as brave as theirs [the Saxons]? And who shall calculate what even such hopeless endeavors may do for the future freedom of their race?"[64] By drawing a parallel between the Saxons and enslaved people, Mr. Dixon affirms that, contrary to prevalent stereotypes, the desire for liberty and self-determination transcends the category of race. Violence thus had the potential to be noble when directed against a worthy foe such as the Normans—or white slave owners.⁶⁵ Efforts to resist slavery through violence might be comprehensible and even laudable, yet at the same time, as Mr. Dixon asserts, they are also "hopeless" and doomed to failure.

Raising doubts about whether such violence could ever even be successful, in "The Black Saxons," Child also expressed discomfort with black men's resistance that uneasily echoed proslavery denunciations of black men as naturally, dangerously violent. One of the story's protagonists is the rebel leader Bob, described by the narrator as "a tall, sinewy mulatto . . . with fierce gestures." Possessing a "high, bold forehead, and flashing eye, indicating an intellect too active and daring for servitude," Bob seeks to persuade his fellow slaves to violently rise up against their masters, showing them only as much mercy as they have been shown. He declares that enslaved men ought to "ravish their wives and daughters before their eyes, as they have done to *us*. Hunt them with hounds, as they have hunted *us*. Shoot them down with rifles, as they have shot *us*. Throw their carcasses to the crows, as they have fattened on *our* bones; and then let the Devil take them where they never rake up the fire of nights."⁶⁶

Admirable for his intelligence, daring, and desire for independence, Bob is nonetheless a disquieting figure.⁶⁷ In terms that emphasize his physical strength and fiery nature, Child's descriptions are uncomfortably close to those of enslaved man as barely tamed savages, prevalent in proslavery literature. Presenting Bob's anger as comprehensible in the face of the pervasive rape, murder, and abuse that enslaved people endure in slavery, Child also directly linked violence by enslaved people with the suffering of innocent white women and children. Calling for enslaved men to rape white women in retribution for the sexual violence enslaved women suffered, "The Black Saxons" uneasily echoed proslavery tracts that represented the sexual violation of white women as an inevitable outcome of enslaved men's emancipation.⁶⁸

As Karcher observes, "The Black Saxons" ends on a decidedly uneasy note, with the specific uprising that the narrative discusses quashed but future plots and uprisings clearly inevitable. As long as the injustices of slavery continued, enslaved people would unavoidably be pushed into considering violent resistance.⁶⁹ This inevitability was troubling, since, however rooted in justifiable anger at the brutality of slavery they may have been, in Child's fiction male-led slave uprisings were ultimately neither a moral nor a desirable form of antislavery activity.

In their fiction, female authors condemned not just the violent resistance of enslaved men but also white men's decision to support American participation in the Mexican-American War. Female writers were quick to decry white male decision-makers for choosing to wage war with Mexico, condemning them for starting a violent conflict, as Eliza Lee Follen asserted in her 1846 story "Dialogue," "for the purpose of making this infamous system [of slavery] more secure and extending it farther."[70] Critical of the white-male-controlled state's use of violence on behalf of proslavery interests, female authors also condemned violence directed *against* those interests. After listening to his mother's denunciations of the Mexican-American War, Phil Selden, the young boy at the center of Jane Elizabeth Jones's 1848 "The Young Abolitionists," asserts that he will try to undo the evils of slavery by becoming a soldier and going to war against the immoral proslavery men his mother has so powerfully condemned.

Instead of praising her son for his bravery or his desire for martial valor, Mrs. Selden questions his assumption that the best way to stop violence is to engage in yet more violence: "Some think that those who go to war and slay their brethren and trample out their life's blood on the red field of battle as you talk of doing, are good men."[71] But her statement indicates that no truly good man would find any moral value in killing another human being and emphasizes her desire to raise her son to be a man who will seek nonviolent solutions to slavery. In a culture that often conflated the capacity for violence with the possession of vigorous manhood, Mrs. Selden constructs an alternate model of masculinity, in which men demonstrate their strength and virtue not through violence but rather through their ability to work for change through peaceful means.[72] Whether her efforts to persuade her son to embrace her pacifist values will ultimately be successful is left unclear, however. If even a son raised by a pacifist mother has a natural predilection for violence, then the prospects of the slave question being resolved nonviolently seem questionable.

In white women's antislavery literature, authors expressed discomfort with both enslaved and free men's seeming inclination toward, and appetite for, violence. Whether it was white male characters voting to support, or itching to fight in, unjust wars or enslaved male characters taking the law into their hands to resist slavery, female writers drew uneasy connections between men and an innate, dangerous propensity for potentially uncontainable violence. Questioning the efficacy and the justness of violent activism, female writers insisted that, for reasons of morality and practicality, peaceful feminine influence should remain the primary form of action against the peculiar institution.

White Women and Moral Suasion in Antislavery Texts

Uncomfortable with the idea of violent men being at the forefront of the antislavery cause, authors continued to hope that women (specifically, white women) would remain the heart and moral center of abolitionism. Throughout their literature, writers continued to insist that white women were naturally better abolitionists than men, because of their deeper feelings and sharper moral consciences.[73] To put these keen moral values into practice, white women needed to influence white men to feel, think, and act rightly on the slave question. However, in the literature they published during the 1840s, successfully exercising a benevolent moral influence over men proved to be no easy task for white female characters.

In the fiction women published during the 1820s and 1830s, husbands and fathers were typically distant, but benevolent, presences. While white women took the initiative in embracing abolitionism and converting their loved ones to antislavery ideals, white men were at least supportive of these efforts. In the fiction women wrote during the 1840s, by contrast, white men appeared not so much shadowy supporters of abolitionism as vividly present impediments to antislavery progress. In Jones's "The Young Abolitionists," Mr. Selden urges his wife not to tell their children anything about slavery. Though by no means a supporter of the institution, he does not want his innocent children to know anything about slavery's cruel realities. "He loved them so well, and was so desirous to make them happy," the narrator informs the reader, "that he shrunk from the thought of having a single shadow fall on the sunlight of their young existence."[74] However well-meant this attitude, Jones indicated, it was nonetheless also a profoundly misguided and even dangerous one. Mrs. Selden insists to her husband that their son needs to be fully informed about slavery, if he is to grow up to be a morally responsible citizen and voter.[75] Thus, over her husband's objections, she educates her son about the brutalities of slavery and the need for abolition.

In this story, Jones thus indicated that women needed to be willing to place moral duty to their children and nation over obligations to their husbands.[76] Antislavery women needed to be aware that defying their husbands' wishes might become necessary. Such defiance had not been required of white female characters in antislavery literature of previous decades, as white male characters had either already been heartily committed to abolitionism or had quickly been convinced of their wives' right to bring antislavery principles into their households. Jones's narrative raised the disquieting possibility that such scenarios could no longer be relied on and that an abolitionist mother might need to convey her principles to her children over her husband's objections. This could certainly present some female readers with the unpleasant prospect of going against their husbands' wishes—including going against the will of husbands who might not be as obliging as Jones's Mr. Selden was.

White men in these stories not only sought to prevent their children from being educated about slavery, they also played more definitive roles in upholding the peculiar institution. As the mother-heroine of Eliza Lee Follen's 1846 "Dialogue" tells her son after outlining slavery's evils, "your father pays taxes to support the government that sanctions and defends these crimes against innocent beings."[77] In "The Young Abolitionists," Mrs. Selden makes a comparable assertion when she informs her son, "The men all around us, Charlie . . . our very neighbors and friends, join with the slaveholders in sustaining this wicked Constitution and all the laws that are made under it, even those that justify the master in all the terrible cruelties that I have mentioned. They sustain a government under which the poor mother is robbed of all her little ones, and left with nothing to love, nothing to hope for." These mothers make it painfully clear that when it comes to important political and moral decisions about slavery the men these young boys know and love best are not to be trusted. When young Charlie Selden seeks reassurance that his own father had no part in supporting a proslavery government that cruelly persecuted enslaved mothers, the best his mother can offer him is a weak "I hope not. . . . I trust he will never enter into a government with the oppressors of his race; and that he will give no voluntary support to laws that deny equal liberty to all."[78] But she can give no definite assurances.

In these narratives, white female characters stressed their husbands' power to make political decisions that profoundly affected the lives of enslaved people. The heroines were often anxious, because white male characters' political choices were typically dangerously misguided. While wives could clearly see their husbands were sustaining an immoral, proslavery government, the men did not have this same moral awareness. The issue of men's political actions took on a new urgency in the 1840s, in part because of the development of the first political antislavery parties during this decade. The emergence of the Liberty Party and the Free Soil Party raised some hopes for a counterbalance to the powerful proslavery forces then predominating in the American government.[79]

In their fiction, however, Follen and Jones expressed profound distrust about the possibility for any kind of antislavery change to happen in the realm of politics. Very much aware that the decisions made by male politicians and voters were shaping the future of slavery, Follen and Jones were clearly troubled, as in their stories, even good white men prove incapable of making good political decisions. Married to staunchly abolitionist wives, these men make poor choices in polling places, consistently using their political power to elect leaders who support slavery.

Female antislavery writers stressed that white men's misguided political decisions had dire consequences and often meant the difference between not just between slavery and freedom but also peace and war. Discussing her husband's vote in favor of the proslavery Mexican-American War with their sons, the heroine of Follen's 1846 "Reformatory" declares:

> I think your father was very wrong in praising such a wicked thing as the War with Mexico. I think it is vile and vindictive beyond all words to tell, and I was grieved to my soul from the first that your father's political views stood in the way of his seeing what was just and noble.... He has known that I disagreed with him, that I thought him wrong, but I should not have said this to you if I did not think it a solemn duty which I owe you, to say what I think about the crimes of our Government.[80]

She thus places the blame for the war squarely on the shoulders of male politicians and voters, not exempting her own husband but instead highlighting that it was ill-advised political decision-making such as his which had made such a criminal war possible in the first place.

Troublingly, in these stories abolitionist female characters' efforts to persuade their husbands of injustices are neither immediately nor completely successful. In "Reformatory," after listening to his wife's antiwar speech, the husband informs their children, "Had their mother always spoken to them and to me as she has to-day, her higher and purer moral sense would perhaps have taken hold.... [H]enceforward I will bid my boys learn justice and humanity from their mother."[81] To some extent, then, Follen restored order at the end of her story, with the morally insightful wife and mother successfully making her morally misguided husband realize the error of his political actions. Yet even this seemingly happy ending did not fully resolve the fundamental problem the story had raised, as in the husband comes to his epiphany too late. His voting decisions have, after all, been part of a larger movement that already put a powerful proslavery government in place and set a destructive proslavery war in motion. Follen suggested that the heroine's moral influence over her husband was not a complete failure, as there is some hope that he might hereafter be inspired to take political action against both slavery and the war. The story also indicates that its heroine will be able to shape the ideals of the next generation of male voters, through her influence over her sons. Yet her attempts to shape the ideals of the men of her family were less successful than those of women in the antislavery literature of previous decades.

Follen and Jones painted a relatively dark picture for their female readers, one in which even well-intentioned men had voted a proslavery government into power and continued to misguidedly support its immoral actions. These authors created a stark dichotomy between the values of politically disempowered women and those of male voters and the male-led American government. While the women in these tales are steadfastly abolitionist, their government most certainly is not; to the contrary, it consistently upholds the interests of slaveholders, even to the point of waging a costly, unjust war simply to gain more land for slave states. Most troubling of all is that this unprincipled government was voted into office, and has been systematically sustained, by these characters' own husbands.

While heroines in narratives from the 1820s and 1830s effortlessly use moral suasion to convert men to abolitionism, women in stories from 1840s consistently struggle to do so. As scholars such as Lori Ginzberg and James Brewer Stewart have argued, the 1840s was a decade in which moral suasion died out as a central approach in many American reform movements.[82] Antislavery women writers did, however, continue to endorse moral suasion in their fiction during this decade. Yet their faith in feminine moral influence, while not entirely destroyed, sustained considerable damage during the 1840s.

Voicing awareness and unease about the rising importance of political activism within the antislavery cause, antislavery women writers entered into broader discussions about women, politics, and power taking place during the 1840s. This was a decade in which public debates about women's roles and rights intensified, with the first women's rights convention being held in Seneca Falls, New York in 1848.[83] Antislavery women writers were certainly not calling for the same kinds of radical social changes that the women's rights activists of Seneca Falls were; they made no claims, for example, for the direct political empowerment of women. Female antislavery authors wrote about women and politics in very different ways than the activists of Seneca Falls did, not emphasizing the rights women deserved because of their status as citizens. Instead, female antislavery writers stressed not women's similarities with men but rather their differences from them, hoping women's moral influence might yet effectively permeate the masculine realm of government. However, their literature indicates a growing anxiety about a society in which morally unsound men possessed considerably more political power than morally pure women did.

White Southern Women and Moral Suasion in Antislavery Texts

During the 1840s, female antislavery authors' explorations of feminine moral influence and political antislavery activism focused not only on white northern women but also on white southern women. While white southern female characters had not been entirely absent from the fiction of the 1820s and 1830s, most narratives from these decades focused on the experiences and activism of white northern women. Authors writing during the 1840s more fully included white southern women, in part because of increased hopes that antislavery literature might actually reach this constituency. With periodicals such as the *Standard* and the *Era* launching with the explicit purpose of reaching out to white southern readers—the *Era* also being based solidly below the Mason-Dixon line in Washington, D.C.—female antislavery authors were more hopeful than ever that their arguments might actually reach white elite and middle-class southern female readers.

In the literature of the 1840s, white slave-owning female characters faced difficult choices about whether to follow their consciences and defy the authority of proslavery male relatives or continue to uphold a system they knew to be unjust. Female antislavery authors hoped to influence white southern women to place loyalty to their sensitive female consciences above loyalty to the men of their families. If slave-owning women would only allow their actions to be dictated by their innate feminine moral principles, authors argued, slavery would be severely undermined. White southern women just needed the strength of will to follow their consciences and to challenge the proslavery values of their husbands, fathers, and fiancés, who were, of course, less morally astute.

Of course, these fictional visions of white, elite southern women as natural, staunch abolitionists did not reflect the reality of how the majority of planter-class women thought about slavery and abolition. As the diaries of wealthy southern women such as Mary Chestnut and Ella Gertrude Clanton Thomas and the scholarship of historians including Drew Gilpin Faust and Anya Jabour have powerfully demonstrated, the majority of slave-owning women were deeply invested in the slave system and had no interest in seeing it undermined or destroyed. Keenly aware that their wealth and social standing depended on the labor of enslaved people, most planter women at most expressed distaste for the peculiar institution. Often lamenting how much work "caring for" and managing enslaved people was and sometimes expressing disapproval of white men's sexual involvement with enslaved women, planter women were nonetheless very far from being abolitionists. Instead of sympathizing with enslaved women, they far more often blamed them for any sexual contact with white men, seldom acknowledging the fundamentally nonconsensual and frequently violent nature of such contact, and further criticized enslaved women for being unladylike, unintelligent, and difficult to work with. In the real world outside the pages of antislavery fiction, planter women usually identified with men of their race and class, typically expressing little sympathy for or solidarity with enslaved women.[84]

But despite this reality, female antislavery authors still created worlds in which slave-owning women were prevented from participating in abolitionist activity, not because of their own beliefs but because they were under the control of proslavery white men. Ignoring the majority of white elite women's actual support for slavery, writers insisted that women of this race and class, like all right-thinking white northern women, were natural and inevitable abolitionists. This argument stemmed from writers' larger belief that gender, rather than race or class, was the most significant dividing line in American society and that all women possessed common attributes and values denied to men. Though it flew in the face of most white southern women's expressed beliefs about slavery, authors insisted that all women, regardless of class or region, shared sensitive moral consciences and tender feelings that invariably lead them to endorse abolitionism.

Creating this stark gender divide, authors contended that if (abolitionist, moral) white southern female characters wanted to put their antislavery values into action, they would need to defy the authority of (proslavery, immoral) male family members. Writers acknowledged that such defiance would be even more difficult for white southern women than it was for white northern women. While it was largely considered respectable for middle-class women in the North to take an interest in reform movements and to have relatively egalitarian, companionate marriages, this was certainly not the case for elite southern women. As scholars such as Cynthia Kierner and Elizabeth Varon have documented, white middle- and upper-class southern women did not actually live their lives on a pedestal far removed from the world but rather were very active in politics, and in benevolent and reform work.[85] Yet despite this, the ideal of passive, submissive white womanhood nonetheless remained important in elite southern culture. To differentiate women of the planter class from their poor white and enslaved counterparts and to underline slave-owning men's absolute authority over their plantations, the ideal of elite white femininity remained a rigid one throughout the antebellum era.[86] This ideal insisted that white women ought to live lives of carefully sheltered domesticity and be absolutely dependent on and submissive to the male heads of their households. Although this vision did not fully reflect the reality of elite women's lives, it placed considerable pressure on women of the planter class to at least aspire to an image of strictly deferential, domestic femininity.[87]

Convinced that white southern women shared the same innate feminine morality as white northern women, authors created white southern female characters sympathetic to antislavery ideals. Despite this sympathy, however, southern female characters were often unable to put their antislavery values into practice, as both the individual men in their lives and broader patriarchal power structures prevented them from doing so. For example, the female protagonists of Child's "Slavery's Pleasant Homes," Marion and her slave Rosa, grow up side by side and affectionately regard each other as sisters. Marion consequently seeks to persuade her husband, Frederic, to secure Rosa's happiness by allowing her to marry George, the enslaved man she loves. When her husband refuses, Marion "tried to remonstrate with him ... but he answered sharply, and left her in tears."[88] Marion soon learns the reason for her husband's refusal to allow Rosa's marriage: he is repeatedly raping Rosa and is jealous at the idea of her having a freely chosen sexual relationship. On learning of her husband's attacks, Marion initially blames Rosa, and instead of expressing sympathy or concern for her, hits her in a fit of displaced anger. As historians such as Catherine Clinton and Elizabeth Fox-Genovese and narratives by formerly enslaved women like Harriet Jacobs have amply detailed, white women blaming and violently punishing enslaved women for their own sexual assaults was an all too common reality in the antebellum South.[89]

In Child's fictional world, however, Marion quickly repents of her violence against Rosa, and the two women collapse into each other's arms, weeping tears of sympathy for one another. After this exchange, the narrator informs readers, "neither sought any further to learn the other's secrets," and the two never again speak of the rapes Rosa continues to endure. Marion disappears from the story thereafter, and "Slavery's Pleasant Homes" ends with Rosa's death after a severe whipping by Frederic causes her to miscarry her unborn child. As Carolyn Karcher and Carolyn Sorisio have argued, "Slavery's Pleasant Homes" thus served as a multifaceted critique of southern patriarchy and the ways it perverted familial relationships, destroyed marriages, and subjected both enslaved and white women to the control of sexually corrupt, morally bankrupt white men. The story underlines that however much white southern female characters may have pitied enslaved women, they were powerless to protect them against white, slave-owning men who had been granted—and did not hesitate to use—virtually unlimited physical power over both their wives and enslaved women.[90]

Unlike their married counterparts, who were subject to the control of violent, immoral husbands, single white southern female characters possessed a much greater ability to make change. Susan, the unmarried heroine of Southworth's novel *The Mother-in-Law,* firmly rejects her future as a slave-owning plantation mistress. Whenever she is congratulated on being the heiress to a plantation with a large enslaved population, Susan affirms, "I do not for a moment acknowledge any right in myself to hold them."[91] The single protagonist of Southworth's 1849 *Retribution,* Julie, similarly rejects her expected future as a wealthy slave owner. Having long said she would liberate her family's enslaved population as soon as she came into her inheritance, Julie is as good as her word and carries out "her purpose of emancipation" as soon as she legally can.[92] The single women in these stories successfully undermine slavery by liberating the enslaved people they own the moment they can, and on the rare occasions they are given the legal power to take antislavery action in these narratives, they do so decisively and efficiently.

Through characters such as Susan and Julie, Southworth argued that white southern women shared white northern women's innate abolitionism, despite having been born into a society that insisted they had every right to own their human property. White southern female characters thus proved stronger in the face of the moral temptations of slavery than their male counterparts were. While slave-owning men in these stories fully exploit the power slavery gave them over enslaved women, single, slave-owning women fully reject such unjust control and set free the enslaved people whom they, unwillingly, own. Thus, through their stark juxtaposition of deeply virtuous female and hopelessly corrupt male slave-owning characters, female antislavery authors further highlighted women's innate moral superiority to men.

White antislavery women's writings hence also contain an implicit criticism of marriage and the tremendous power it gave husbands. If abolitionist women like Susan or Julie had been married to proslavery men, they would have been unable to emancipate the enslaved people they owned. Although married women's property rights acts had begun to be passed in individual states beginning in the 1830s, such legislation did not make any significant inroads in the South during the antebellum era.[93] By depicting unmarried female characters as capable of taking abolitionist action, but married ones as unable to do so, writers raised questions about married women's rights in both the North and the South. They indicated that giving married women more rights over their property would be an advantage not only for free women but also for the antislavery cause; white southern women would liberate enslaved people if they were only given the opportunity to do so. Strong as this vision of female-driven emancipation and legal empowerment was, it nonetheless also further underlined depictions of enslaved women as passive property whose futures were to be determined by the actions of either white women or white men.

Authors recognized that most white southern women would not be able to make their own independent, legal decisions about slavery. Most would eventually marry and, as such, turn over to their husbands all rights to any enslaved people they owned. And since white southern women had been taught since birth to defer to the authority of male family members, white female characters also sometimes made the mistake of privileging their husbands' and fathers' wishes over their own antislavery principles. Not only were white southern women stripped of all practical ability to take abolitionist action, but their gender socialization further subordinated them and, more dangerously still, enslaved women to the men of their households. In Dall's 1849 "Amy, A True Tale," wealthy plantation mistress Elsie, for example, responds to queries about whether she will emancipate her virtuous slave Amy by replying, "That will be as Meredith says."[94] Since Meredith, Elsie's dissolute fiancé, has sexual designs on Amy, all hopes for Amy's liberation are thus unfortunately dashed. According to the codes of southern society, Elsie correctly yields household decisions to her future husband. Yet Dall argued that her choice to give authority over her slaves to Meredith was profoundly unwise, and tragically destructive for enslaved women like Amy.[95]

The enslaved Rosalie in Child's "The Quadroons" makes a comparable error of judgment in entrusting her future to her lover and master, the weak-willed, indolent Edward. She trusts in his promises to liberate her and their child, but after Edward dies, it transpires that he has "carelessly omitted to have papers of manumission recorded."[96] In *The Mother-in-Law,* Susan similarly hopes she can prevail on the men of her family to help secure the release of the enslaved Anna, after she has been sold into the fancy trade of sexual slavery. "Ah," affirms the more hardheaded, realistic Anna, "they will have but one answer to your prayers, Miss Susan—the law."[97]

Throughout these narratives, white men were more likely to abuse the legal rights given to them over enslaved people than white women were. Growing up in a culture that emphasized their absolute right to the bodies of enslaved women, and already subject to the greater sexual temptations that ostensibly plagued all men, white male characters frequently use their power to sexually exploit and rape enslaved women.[98] Writers raised significant concerns about giving sexually corrupt men absolute power over enslaved women and, implicitly, over their wives as well. White women, allegedly free from sexual temptation, would clearly make much better decisions about the lives of enslaved women than white men would.

Authors acknowledged, however, that there were significant practical and cultural barriers to white southern women taking effective action against slavery. Often prevented by law from liberating or protecting enslaved women, white women were also prohibited from taking abolitionist action by their strict training to defer to the men of their families. Writers thus advocated a profound challenge to multiple hierarchies in southern households. They wished not only to undo white power over the enslaved but also to undermine white men's authority over white women. Overlooking the reality of most white planter women's support for their society's racial and gender hierarchies, authors argued that gender was a more powerful factor than class or region and that, given the opportunity, virtuous white women (both North and South) would come together to ensure slavery's demise.

Yet hopeful as authors were about white southern women's desire to contribute to the antislavery cause, female characters' efforts to make their male family members recognize slavery's evils nonetheless often end in failure. In Southworth's *The Mother-In-Law,* Susan has high hopes she will be able to persuade her doting grandfather of slavery's injustice. When she comes to him with a plan to liberate her family's slaves, however, "he smilingly caressed me, and told me that my patrimony in land and negroes was too small to bear abatement, and that young girls knew nothing about such things." Alerted to his granddaughter's abolitionist tendencies, the grandfather becomes increasingly resistant to her appeals on behalf of the enslaved. She then laments that ever since she first expressed her abolitionist ideas, her grandfather had become "exceedingly jealous of my influence, exceedingly suspicious of any plan I may propose to him, and the more anxious I feel for the accomplishment of my wishes, the firmer he shows himself in the rejection of the proposition, whatever it may be."[99]

Susan's trust that her grandfather's love for her would lead him to adopt her antislavery ideals was thus profoundly misguided. White men may be fond of their female family members, but this affection did not make them likely to accept women's moral judgments or to act on their antislavery counsel. Praising white southern female characters for their devotion to abolitionism, authors also worried about their ability to engage in meaningful antislavery activity. Blocked by the law, expectations of feminine deference, and white men's staunch dedication to slavery, white southern female characters' antislavery commitments in these stories often remained more theoretical than actual. In their depictions of both white northern and white southern female characters, female antislavery authors at once insisted that women were morally superior to white men and raised doubts about the ability of more virtuous, but less powerful, women to successfully put their antislavery ideals into practice.

As their movement debated the merits of embracing political and violent abolitionism during the 1840s, female antislavery authors remained staunchly in favor of peaceful feminine moral influence as the primary mode of antislavery activism. Distrustful of the morally corrupt political realm and uneasy about violent resistance, writers hoped feminine moral suasion would stay the central force in undermining slavery. However, their fiction during this decade contained a newly strong undercurrent of doubt about whether women's abolitionist values could, indeed, be successfully implemented in American society. Expressing growing unease about the American government's power to control the destinies of enslaved people and the unwillingness of white men to heed the moral counsel of virtuous female family members, authors publishing during the 1840s worried about the future of their movement and the place of women within it.

As national debates about slavery became increasingly heated and contentious in the 1850s, writers would continue their discussions about the best way forward for abolitionists. A decade filled with numerous setbacks for the antislavery cause, the development of a powerful new antislavery political party, and ever-growing fears about the seemingly invincible slave power, the 1850s offered new challenges for female antislavery authors to consider in their fiction. Worried about abolitionism's apparent inability to prevent the entrenchment and expansion of the peculiar institution, writers began to offer startling new visions of white women's proper place in their movement.

CHAPTER FOUR

"We Women Will Set All Things Right"

Moral Suasion and Political Empowerment, 1851-1861

> I dwell thus long political matters, women of America, because I feel that all reform in politics, in philanthropy, and in social life, depends upon you for purity and vigor. Do not be afraid to assume your responsibility.
> —CAROLINE W. HEALEY DALL, "Pictures of Southern Life, for Drawing Rooms of American Women" (1851)

> We women will set all things right.
> —ELIZABETH D. LIVERMORE, Zoë; or The Quadroon's Triumph (1855)

In 1855, a contributor to the *Liberator* reflected on the significance of antislavery fiction in a post-*Uncle Tom's Cabin* world. The writer asserted that in the wake of the novel's dazzling popular success, abolitionists could consider every work of antislavery fiction in circulation "an eloquent lecturer perpetually on the stump."[1] This author was not alone in expressing considerable hope that fiction would be an especially potent means of spreading the abolitionist gospel to the free American public during the 1850s. Always optimistic that fiction could be a powerful tool to convert skeptical American readers to abolitionism, these hopes reached new heights after Harriet Beecher Stowe's *Uncle Tom's Cabin* became a massive bestseller and an unprecedented literary phenomenon in American culture.

Female antislavery authors who wrote and published in the wake of *Uncle Tom's Cabin* continued to define women as naturally abolitionist in ways that men were not. Yet at the same time, they also expressed deepening anxieties about women's abilities to successfully translate their abolitionist values into concrete change. They worried about women's ability to effectively act on their antislavery ideals in a movement increasingly dominated by male-centered political activism. Arguing by the end of the 1850s that moral suasion was no longer a viable activist strategy, antislavery writers struggled to define what a new, gender-appropriate, and efficacious role for women in the abolitionist movement might be.

By analyzing the complex ways writers discussed moral suasion and politics in their fiction, this chapter helps reshape our understandings of abolitionists' shift away from moral suasion to political activism during the late antebellum era. In his influential work, James Brewer Stewart argues that over the course of the 1840s the majority of male abolitionists rejected moral suasion, instead putting their faith in antislavery political parties and violent resistance. Focusing her attention on women in the antislavery movement, Lori D. Ginzberg maintains that by 1850, female abolitionists had similarly rejected moral suasion, in favor of institutional and electoral forms of activism.[2] I assert that this shift was not quite so clear-cut or straightforward, with antislavery authors abandoning moral suasion only gradually and with great reluctance by the end of the 1850s. In some respects, these authors did shift away from advocating moral suasion toward (at least considering) the value of electoral politics. In the stories they published before the mid-1850s, writers continued to counsel female readers to persuade men to adopt abolitionist ideals. But in their publications during and after the mid-1850s, by contrast, they spoke for the first time to male readers, instructing them not about broader moral principles but rather about which specific political parties and candidates to support.

Yet despite this new political awareness, authors nonetheless did not wholeheartedly embrace political activism or easily relinquish their beliefs in moral suasion. I argue that writers tenaciously held onto their faith in moral influence into the mid-1850s and relinquished that faith only after a painful struggle.[3] Conceding that moral suasion was a failure, authors nonetheless deeply mourned the loss of feminine moral influence and painted a troubling, uneasy picture of male-led political abolitionism.

This chapter thus enriches existing understandings of white women and their involvement in electoral politics during the late antebellum era. As scholars such as Mary Ryan and Elizabeth Varon have noted, during the

1840s and 1850s white, middle-class women became increasingly involved in partisan politics. Contrary to visions of white, middle-class women as supposedly confined to the private sphere, Ryan and Varon argue that white women were very much involved in politics, making banners, attending rallies, and serving as enthusiastic audiences for political speakers.[4] In his examination of antislavery women's involvement in electoral politics during this era, Michael Pierson traces a similar trend—noting the important ways women served as symbols of political virtue in both Free Soil and Republican Party literature and at public events for these parties.[5] As these historians skillfully demonstrate, women regarded attendance at political rallies, the display of party paraphernalia in their homes, and the use of political symbols in their fashion choices as significant means of voicing their political consciousness and ideals. Historians of women have done invaluable work by thus tracing the myriad ways women were dynamically involved in electoral politics during the antebellum era. Their scholarship has moved us away from defining white, middle-class women purely as passive onlookers to a political system in which they played no meaningful roles.

This chapter builds on and complicates these insights, focusing on the ways antislavery women writers defined the political. In their discussions of women's involvement in electoral politics, authors insisted that if women did not have the right to vote, any other forms of female political expression were futile. As such, writers defined "politics" and "political power" in much different, far narrower ways than historians of the antebellum era have done, as their white female characters' exclusion from the franchise left them entirely without a political voice. Authors thus expressed a distinctive vision of what it meant for white women to possess political agency in the mid-nineteenth-century United States. In writers' works, political power *was* the vote, and if white women did not possess this core political right, then any other forms of political participation were ultimately meaningless.

Women's Antislavery Literature in the Era of Uncle Tom

The antislavery literary landscape changed dramatically after the publication of *Uncle Tom's Cabin*. Stowe's novel, serialized in the *National Era* in 1851 and 1852 and subsequently published in book form in 1852, was astonishingly successful, selling at a remarkable rate throughout the North and Midwest. Although troubled by the novel's refusal to call for immediate abolition and its endorsement of colonization, the majority of antislavery activists nonetheless warmly embraced the book. "'Uncle Tom's Cabin,'" Wendell Phillips declared to a crowd of abolitionists in 1853, "is an event more than a book."[6] Phillips's sense of *Uncle Tom's Cabin* as a transformative moment in the history of the antislavery movement was one shared by many of his fellow abolitionists.[7] Antislavery activists were particularly pleased by the novel's ability to reach audiences that would otherwise not have been exposed to antislavery ideas. "Many who were too prejudiced or too timid to read an Anti-slavery paper or pamphlet have been induced by the quaintness of the title of the work and its unprecedented popularity to peruse it," the *National Anti-Slavery Standard* noted approvingly in 1852, "and are now strongly Anti-slavery."[8]

The novel's phenomenal success made opportunistic publishers throughout the North hopeful that they, too, could turn the American reading public's new interest in the slave question to their economic advantage. In the wake of *Uncle Tom's Cabin*'s publication, antislavery fiction writers therefore experienced unprecedented opportunities to have their novels issued by more mainstream publishers and to potentially reach larger numbers of readers than ever before.[9] Antislavery advocates even hoped, vainly, that *Uncle Tom's Cabin* and other antislavery novels might finally effectively reach the homes and hearts of significant numbers of white southerners.[10] While *Uncle Tom* did, to some extent, create new opportunities for antislavery writers, no work could parallel the spectacular success of Stowe's volume or realize abolitionists' dreams of antislavery fiction uniting the entire American nation against the peculiar institution.

Yet though *Uncle Tom's Cabin* did not ultimately create the sea change in American attitudes toward slavery that abolitionists had hoped it might, it did generate a new wave of antislavery literature. The *National Era* was one of many antislavery periodicals to notice this trend, asserting in 1856, "Mrs. Stowe has founded a new 'school' in literature, of which no one can foresee the end."[11] By the mid-1850s, the *Era* was able to declare, "If we may judge by the number and range of volumes on these subjects issued from the press, *Anti-Slavery* literature is very popular."[12] Given the strong associations abolitionists had long drawn between women and fiction, antislavery activists were thus particularly hopeful that novels would be useful in reaching, converting, and energizing female readers.[13]

The authors considered in this chapter certainly hoped *Uncle Tom's Cabin*'s success would enable them to reach a wider audience than had previously been possible. Of the fifteen named authors considered here, only two (Caroline W. Healey Dall and Lydia Maria Child) had published explicitly antislavery literature prior to the 1850s.[14] The other thirteen published their first antislavery novel or story after *Uncle Tom's Cabin* emerged on the literary marketplace. One potential motivation for this new influx of women into antislavery literature might be female authors' hopes of becoming popular successes (and perhaps also wealthy and famous, as Stowe had done) by writing a book in the *Uncle Tom* vein. While it is certainly possible that some female authors may have hoped to capitalize on *Uncle Tom's Cabin*'s popularity, given the riskiness of publishing on the controversial topic of slavery (especially as a means of building a mainstream literary career), it seems much more likely that genuine commitment to antislavery ideals inspired much of women's abolitionist literature.

The underrepresentation of free African American female writers in antislavery literary spaces continued throughout the 1850s, with publication opportunities in white-edited periodicals and presses largely unavailable to free African American women. This does not mean that African American women's voices were entirely absent from the antislavery print marketplace during the 1850s, however. In 1859, Harriet Wilson published her novel, *Our Nig: Sketches from the Life of a Free Black,* which detailed the systematic economic and social oppression faced by free African Americans in the North. Focusing on racial injustice in the North rather than slavery in the South, the novel went largely unremarked on in white abolitionist circles.[15] Eager to reach the mainstream white public, white abolitionist editors and publishers in the 1850s avoided publishing fiction like Wilson's, which extensively grappled with the ugly realities of racial discrimination and inequality in the North.

African American poet Frances E. Watkins Harper enjoyed considerably more literary success than Wilson during the 1850s.[16] A popular antislavery orator, the Baltimore-born writer published *Poems on Miscellaneous Subjects* in 1854. The book would subsequently go through twenty printings. One of its poems, "Eliza Harris," proved especially popular, being reprinted in the *Liberator, Frederick Douglass' Paper,* and Cleveland's African American newspaper *Aliened American* during the 1850s. The poem blends reflections about the courage of Harris, an enslaved female character who flees slavery with her child in *Uncle Tom's Cabin,* with condemnations of the American nation for allowing the immoral institution to continue. Other poems in the collection tout the value of free labor; attack Christians who use the Bible to defend slavery; praise the mother of slain antislavery newspaper editor Elijah Lovejoy; and tell vivid, harrowing tales about the separation of enslaved mothers and children, enslaved people being sold at auction, and an enslaved man being executed for his heroic participation in a slave uprising. Subsequent editions of the collection also included a poem celebrating the life and mourning the death of Margaret Garner, who killed one of her children when fleeing slavery, rather than see her child reenslaved.

In the 1850s, Harper also published the pioneering "The Two Offers," thought to be the first short story published by an African American author, in the African American–edited *Anglo-African Magazine.* The tale does not directly tackle issues of slavery or racial equality, instead focusing on the lives of two young women, Laura and Janette, as they make crucial decisions about their future paths in life. Though in the text these heroines are not explicitly noted to be African American, since Harper was an African American author, writing for an African American audience in an African American periodical, it is likely that she intended Laura and Janette to be read as African American. Throughout her career as a poet and novelist, Harper was dedicated to reflecting on African American women's lives, much like African American periodicals such as the *Anglo-African Magazine* were particularly eager to publish work focused on the black experience. In the tale, Laura decides to marry a charming but dissolute man, and Janette eventually dedicates her life to "single blessedness," good works, and social activism. "The Two Offers" makes it clear that Janette has chosen the better path, as she lives a pleasant life of virtuous activity, whereas the unfortunate Laura endures an unhappy marriage and a premature, tragic death.

By not including the voices of African American writers like Wilson and Harper, white-edited, mainstream antislavery literary publications lost important perspectives on slavery, activism, and civil rights. White female authors did not systematically examine the challenges facing free African American women or seek to imaginatively enter the experiences of enslaved people in the same ways African American women writers did. Much as had been the case in the 1820s and 1840s, the racial uniformity of writers publishing in antislavery periodicals and with antislavery presses in the 1850s, unfortunately, limited the discussions of race and slavery present in the fiction from this decade.

Of the white authors examined in this chapter, a significant number—eight of fifteen—were published authors and/or had professional careers as writers either before or after the publication of their antislavery fiction in the 1850s. Harriet Newell Greene Butts, Lydia Maria Child, Caroline W. Healey Dall, Phebe Ann Coffin Hanaford, Mary Irving, Sophia Little, and Harriet Beecher Stowe published before this decade, with Butts, Child, Irving, and Stowe enjoying wider popular success, and Dall, Hanaford, and Little remaining largely confined to reform-oriented and Christian literary spaces. W. H. Corning published a handful of short stories after her antislavery novel, and Mary Hayden Green Pike published one additional novel after her first work of antislavery fiction. That so many of the authors analyzed in this chapter were known names prior to the publication of their antislavery fiction may have had made them more able to attract readers than obscurer writers would have been.

The writers analyzed here also came from a range of regions. Of the fifteen discussed, seven were from New England (Butts, Child, Dall, Hanaford, Little, Pike, and Stowe), four from the Midwest (Harriet Hamline Bigelow, W. H. Corning, Elizabeth D. Livermore, and Hattia M'Keehan), two from Kentucky (Mattie Griffith and Elizabeth A. Roe), and the regional origins of two (Mary Harlan and Mary Irving) are unclear. The dominance of women from New England is perhaps unsurprising, since New England was a hub of antislavery activity throughout the antebellum era.

Four of this chapter's authors (Child, Dall, Griffith, and Hanaford) were actively involved in the postbellum women's rights and suffrage movements. That several of these authors subsequently became involved in women's rights activism likely helps account for the frustrations expressed in these narratives about women's disempowerment, marginalization, and exploitation in American society.[17] Given that almost a third of the writers analyzed in this chapter became advocates of female suffrage after the Civil War, it is notable that none directly endorsed female enfranchisement in their fiction. The reasons for this silence about female suffrage may have several explanations, including that the authors simply did not yet advocate women's suffrage. During the antebellum era, endorsing the vote for women was an extremely radical step even in abolitionist circles, and these authors, much like the overwhelming majority of even progressive, reform-oriented Americans, may not have yet believed in the value or viability of female enfranchisement. After the Civil War, the end of slavery, and subsequent redefinitions of freedpeople's citizenship, female suffrage may have seemed much more feasible and desirable.

Authors may also have refrained from endorsing female enfranchisement because they feared taking attention away from the primary issues of abolition and slavery. Writing in a climate in which some antislavery activists insisted that discussing women's rights was a distraction from the central topic of abolition, authors may have hesitated to raise the seeming side issue of free women's political empowerment. And in a culture that frequently defined women's rights activists as dangerous agitators, it may also have seemed wiser to avoid explicit, sustained discussions of female political empowerment. Yet while writers did not directly advocate for women's access to political power, they nonetheless persistently raised questions about the wisdom of having morally corrupt white men be the only ones making political decisions about slavery.

Enslaved Women's Resistance in White Women's Texts

In their fiction published during the 1850s, white female writers focused the bulk of their attention on white women and the actions they could or could not take against the peculiar institution. Enslaved women were not entirely absent from their texts, however; as had been the case in previous decades, white writers created enslaved female characters who demonstrated to their (presumably white) audiences the full horrors of slavery, because of the abuse, rape, and separation from their children that women frequently suffered. In the 1850s, however, enslaved female characters exercise more agency and overt resistance to slavery than they had in previous decades; they take proactive steps to speak out against slavery, and they seek to liberate themselves from it.

This new wave of enslaved females' resistance to slavery in women's fictionmay be rooted in the overall darkening landscape for enslaved people and abolitionists' growing frustration with their inability to effectively undermine the peculiar institution. Several legal challenges to slavery failed dramatically during the 1850s, to abolitionists' great disappointment and indignation. In 1850, Congress passed the Fugitive Slave Law, which mandated, among other rigorous provisions, that all enslaved people who escaped to the North be returned to their owners. The enforcement of this controversial law faced a significant challenge in the 1854 Anthony Burns case, in which the self-emancipated Burns sought to retain his freedom but was eventually ordered to return to slavery. Throughout his trial, Burns received sympathetic coverage from the northern press, and his court-mandated re-enslavement caused extensive public outcry.[18] In 1857, Dred Scott's efforts to claim freedom for himself and his wife, Harriet—on the grounds that they had become free after having been taken by their owners to live in free states—ended with a Supreme Court decision that decreed African American people were not citizens and possessed no rights under American law.

These well-publicized challenges to, and defeats of, enslaved people's efforts at self-liberation seem to have affected women's antislavery writing in the 1850s, giving a new urgency to their discussions of enslaved people's struggles for freedom. These writers considered the concrete steps enslaved women could take to secure their own emancipation. While authors sometimes optimistically represented women's efforts to escape slavery as effective, they remained ambivalent about whether enslaved women would, indeed, successfully become autonomous, free American citizens after emancipation.

The 1850s was a decade in which discussions about enslaved women and violent resistance to slavery were particularly heated and pervasive. These years witnessed two high-profile cases in which enslaved women were put on trial for murder, resulting in widespread public discussion about what these cases demonstrated about enslaved women's moral character, capacity for violence, and fitness for freedom and citizenship. These discussions about the meanings of enslaved women's resistance to slavery were, of course, far from new in American society. As historians including Stephanie M. H. Camp, Patricia Hunt, Cynthia Lynn Lyerly, and Deborah Gray White have documented, enslaved women consistently both covertly and overtly struggled against slavery. Enslaved women's resistance frequently took daily, subtle forms involving choices in dress, modes of religious expression, and efforts to take control of their labor through either feigned illness or temporary absences from work.

Often the primary caregivers of children, enslaved women did not permanently escape from slavery at the same rates enslaved men did, nor did they as commonly engage in violent resistance, which might have resulted in severe reprisals for themselves and their families.[19] This does not mean enslaved women did not undertake violent resistance, engaging in self-injury, killing their children, or attacking or killing their masters and overseers. The murder cases that became infamous during the 1850s, of Celia Newsom and Margaret Garner, were by no means the only instances of enslaved women using violence in their struggle against slavery, though these cases received the most media attention. In 1855, Newsom killed her master, Robert Newsom, who had repeatedly raped her since he had purchased her as a teenage girl and had fathered two of her children. A year later, Margaret Garner killed her two-year-old daughter during a failed escape attempt, rather than see her child reenslaved. Debates about these women and their violent actions became national discussions about the nature, character, and capacities of enslaved women. Proslavery advocates argued these cases illustrated the inherently savage, violent nature of enslaved women. Abolitionists countered by arguing that these acts proved the innate depravity and callousness not of enslaved women but rather of the entire slave system, which forced gentle women and loving mothers to engage in such horrific acts of protective, retaliatory violence.

Depictions of enslaved women as violent are rare in women's fiction, and when they do appear, authors carefully explain them as the result of enslaved women's maternal feelings and desires for sexual purity having been brutally, repeatedly violated. In Stowe's *Uncle Tom's Cabin,* Cassy poisons one of her daughters rather than see her grow up to be sexually exploited and abused the way Cassy has been. In Mary Hayden Green Pike's 1854 *Ida May,* Chloe abuses the enslaved children in her charge because of the psychological damage caused by her own severe sufferings in slavery.[20] When Chloe was a young woman, the narrator informs the reader, "the whole energy of affection in her fierce nature was centered on her children, whom she loved with a fondness that, coupled as it was with the fear of losing them, made life and love itself a torture. When the last one was taken from her, she fell down in a fit, and, from that moment, no one ever saw her manifest any trace of the kindlier feelings of our nature."[21] Having already suffered sexual violation and exploitation at the hands of several different men, the selling of all her beloved children away from her finally breaks Chloe's spirit and destroys her capacity for empathy and compassion, even for her fellow enslaved people.

These representations thus depict this violence as at once deeply disquieting and decidedly comprehensible. Cassy kills her child to prevent her from experiencing a future of sexual abuse and attendant physical and mental suffering. It is also noteworthy that Cassy's story ends with her moral redemption and her explicit renunciation of any form of violence. After she meets the Christlike, pacifist Uncle Tom, he convinces her that her plan to kill her sexually abusive master is immoral. Cassy eventually successfully escapes from slavery without using violence and builds a happy, peaceful life in Liberia. While Cassy's killing of her daughter remains a painful, difficult facet of the text, her story is, in the end, primarily a hopeful one. Although Cassy has demonstrated her capacity for violence, the end of *Uncle Tom's Cabin* emphasizes that she is no longer a force for violent disorder. Not only has she been converted to pacifism because of the wise Uncle Tom, but she has also been removed from the American continent. In *Uncle Tom's Cabin,* the specter of enslaved women's violence is raised but also carefully removed as any real threat to American society.

The character of Chloe presents a rather more unsettling vision of the nature and possible implications of enslaved women's capacity for violence. The type of violence Chloe engages in is not protective violence designed to spare her own child suffering, but rather more generalized brutality, designed to wound others' children. The anger she feels about her own abuse has the potential not to just to turn itself toward enslaved children but also, perhaps most troublingly of all, for white readers, to become violence against all enslaved people and all whites. "Toward all of the white race," the narrator notes, "she displayed a hatred that might be called inhuman . . . even towards those of her own race, who were in happier circumstances than herself, she was willing to do all the injury in her power."[22] While readers do not see Chloe act on this violent hatred toward whites, her possession of it would likely have been disturbing to white readers, particularly as she disappears from the novel early on, still full of hatred for all, and without having made a redemptive pacifist turn as *Uncle Tom's* Cassy had done.

Ida May thus asked whether the cruel institution of slavery had morally and emotionally damaged women like Chloe to the point where they had lost their capacity to live as peaceful citizens. Representing enslaved women's violence as entirely comprehensible, given the persistent, vicious brutality of slavery, Stowe and Pike nonetheless raised questions about whether women could recover from the violence they had suffered, to effectively adapt to freedom in America. *Uncle Tom's Cabin* argued that women could go on to lead peaceful lives, provided that they did so outside of the United States, while *Ida May* expressed concerns that even that kind of redemptive future might not be possible. Sympathetic to what enslaved women had suffered and the violent feelings this suffering had inspired, white authors nonetheless uneasily suggested that there might not be a place for formerly violent African American women in the American republic.

Despite their unease about the role formerly enslaved women might play in the United States, writers nonetheless argued that enslaved women were an important part of the fight against slavery. In Mary Irving's 1856 story "Mirth and Melancholy," the (now emancipated) Mrs. Grey successfully converts her husband to abolitionism, through the power of her love and moral influence. After Mr. Grey falls in love with her—one of his slaves, a chaste, virtuous woman—and decides to free and marry her, the new Mrs. Gray successfully persuades him to embark on a plan of gradual emancipation. She explains, "How *could* I ever bear to own a slave, having been one myself. . . . No; Mr. Grey and I have taken a vow to each other and to Heaven; and we are preparing our slaves—*his* slaves, I mean—for the freedom he means to give them, as soon as possible!"[23] Remarkable for its positive portrayal of a happy marriage between a master and his former slave, "Mirth and Melancholy" is also noteworthy for highlighting Mrs. Grey's ability to secure emancipation not just for herself but also for all enslaved people on the Grey plantation. While it is clear that this emancipation will not be immediate, and that enslaved people will need to be "prepared" for it, Irving expresses no doubt but that, because of Mrs. Grey's moral and emotional power over her husband, Mr. Grey will "as soon as possible" free his plantation's enslaved population.

Stowe's 1856 *Dred: A Tale of the Great Dismal Swamp* similarly highlights the power of feminine moral influence to create positive change for enslaved people. The title character is prevented from undertaking the, according to Stowe, profoundly unwise slave uprising he had been planning, because of the benevolent influence of the pious, pacifist enslaved Milly. Milly's prayers and entreaties to the would-be insurrectionist Dred and his followers to forsake violent resistance and to "love yer enemies" causes Dred and his acolytes to abandon their plans to violently rebel.[24]

Having successfully prevented men's violent resistance to slavery, Milly goes on to live a peaceful life as a free woman in the North. The novel ends with her living in "a neat little tenement in one of the outer streets of New York, surrounded by about a dozen children, among whom were black, white, foreigners. These she had rescued from utter destitution in the streets to give them all the attention and affection of a mother."[25] Milly thus demonstrates the superiority of feminine pacifism over masculine violence, the power of female influence to reform morally misguided men, and the potential for freedwomen to make meaningful contributions to American society after emancipation. Having ended *Uncle Tom's Cabin* with most of her self-emancipated characters seeking new lives in Africa (and having been strongly criticized by many abolitionists for doing so), Stowe concludes *Dred* by highlighting Milly as the ideal, virtuous, *American* citizen.[26] Having lost all of her children in slavery, Milly transforms that loss not into anger or a desire for vengeance but rather into a commitment to aiding and nurturing poor children in the urban North, regardless of their race. With *Dred,* Stowe thus contended that once freed, enslaved women would turn their innate tendencies toward Christian virtue and maternal nurture to the benefit of the entire American population.

White authors thus presented their enslaved female characters in complex, contradictory ways. Convinced enslaved women possessed the same moral values as white women, writers nonetheless raised concerns about the future roles of African American women after emancipation. Could the damage the brutal institution of slavery had done to the psyches of enslaved women ever truly be undone? Was there a place for freedwomen in American society, or would citizenship for freedwomen necessarily be non-American citizenship? Expressing concerns about enslaved women's ability to adjust to freedom, white authors nonetheless emphasized that enslaved women were more morally principled and naturally abolitionist than their male counterparts, underlining their belief that gender commonalities united white and African American women, more than racial differences divided them.

White Women, Romantic Influence, Religious Activism, and Abolitionist Martyrdom in the Early 1850s

Authors' representations of white women's involvement in abolitionism were similarly ambivalent and contradictory during the 1850s. In the early years of this decade, writers continued to hope white women could use their gender-specific powers of moral suasion to benefit abolitionism. By the end of the decade, by contrast, authors insisted that change could only come about through the political actions of white men and that white women's efforts to use moral influence in the service of their cause were doomed to failure. Remaining firm believers in innate gender differences that made women morally superior to men, female antislavery authors ended the 1850s on a decidedly pessimistic note, affirming that the wisest moral voices were not the ones being heard in the (as they argued, incredibly important) halls of American government.

Writers' hopes that feminine moral influence might aid the abolitionist cause persisted into the early 1850s, however, with authors arguing that white women could reform dissolute, slave-owning men. Once these men had been persuaded to stop sexually exploiting and abusing enslaved women—in favor of consensual, monogamous marriage with abolitionist wives—it would be but a small step for these men to become full-fledged abolitionists. If women could control and redirect men's sexuality through moral influence, they could create antislavery marriages and families and, by extension, an antislavery society.

Authors writing during the early 1850s entered into fierce cultural debates about the nature of sexuality. The late antebellum era was notable for the development and expansion of several utopian and religious movements that experimented with different modes of sexual and familial organization, the rise of more accessible, sexually explicit literature, and new anxieties about the breakdown of family control over young people's (especially young men's) sexual behavior.[27] Underlying these concerns were antislavery advocates' ongoing fears about how slavery affected the sexual morality of slave-owning men, who had the power and cultural sanction to rape and sexually exploit the women they owned with impunity.

In women's literature from the early 1850s, in their abolitionist advocacy female characters draw on notions of white female sexuality prevalent during the antebellum era. Desired by sexually immoral slave-owning men, abolitionist female characters steadfastly refuse marriage proposals until these men convert to abolitionism and liberate the enslaved people whom they own.[28] The abolitionist protagonist of Phebe Ann Coffin Hanaford's 1853 *Lucretia, a Quakeress; or Principle Triumphant,* for example, refuses to marry her slave-owning suitor while he holds "a single fellow-being in bonds."[29] In Sophia Little's 1851 *Thrice through the Furnace: A Tale of the Time of the Iron Hoof,* the pious heroine Aimee Freeman converts the slave owner who loves her, Arthur St. Vallery, to abolitionism by praying for and with him. Previously a sexually unprincipled rake, by the end of the novel Arthur is a virtuous man and ardent abolitionist. His conversion came about, he declares, because "an angel has appeared before me in my downward path, warned me, awakened me."[30]

Described by their suitors as "angels" who have lived lives as notable for their chastity as men's were for licentiousness, white women in these stories drew strongly on the ideal of white, middle-class female "passionlessness."[31] As historians such as Nancy Cott have demonstrated, the ideal of passionlessness, which assumed that white, middle-class women were devoid of the sexual desires that inevitably plagued men, invested these women with significant moral power. Their moral vision unclouded by the lusts of the flesh that persistently tempted men, white, middle-class women were presumed to be better judges about issues of sexuality than men were. Paragons of sexual virtue who steadfastly refuse to associate with lascivious slave-owning men until they have forsaken their profligate ways, abolitionist female characters are able to transform proslavery men into antislavery activists by embodying sexual virtue and denying their suitors sexual access until these proslavery cads have been transformed into abolitionist husbands.

Authors writing during the early 1850s thus also drew on contemporary notions of companionate marriage and romantic love. As scholars such as Anya Jabour have argued, an ideal of marriage that focused on love and mutuality came to dominate middle-class American culture during the nineteenth century.[32] Alongside the ideal of companionate marriage came an attendant focus on the importance of romantic love in heterosexual relationships. As Karen Lystra has contended, this had empowering potential for middle-class women. Women could use this new emphasis on romantic love to undermine traditional masculine authority, and to claim more egalitarian power dynamics in their relationships with men.[33] In antislavery women's fiction, female characters employed these notions of romantic love and companionate relationships in their dealings with slave-owning men, using the rituals of courtship to candidly voice their disapproval of slavery and to urge their suitors to liberate their slaves. Authors made it clear that it was primarily men's desire and love for—and subsequent willingness to be morally influenced by—antislavery women that secured their eventual abolitionist conversions. As such, they maintained that women could make crucial contributions to abolitionism through courtship rituals that took place in the private sphere.

While most of their readers likely did not know any slave-owning men, let alone have a slave-owning man pursuing them romantically, the essential message of these stories could be translated into other situations. Single northern women could deny suitors who refused to adopt abolitionist principles and could seek to persuade their sweethearts and husbands to embrace abolitionist ideals. These narratives thus suggested that women did not need to worry about access to formal power, as the informal, romantic, and emotional influence they already possessed over men would be sufficient to make great strides for abolitionism.

Yet this argument was far from a universally positive one; that women's sexual allure was central to their activism made this form of activity primarily accessible to conventionally attractive, single women, thus marginalizing women who fell outside of these categories. Encouraging women to use their romantic and sexual influence over men in the service of abolitionism also risked reducing women to their sexuality. This type of antislavery advocacy was also, of course, heavily reliant on the men involved. Antislavery women could be as chaste, loving, and principled as they wished, but if men were not willing to listen to their wives' and sweethearts' persuasions, women's abolitionist principles would remain confined to their own hearts and minds. While abolitionist women's efforts to use moral influence over men are radiantly successful in Hanaford's and Little's texts, there is nonetheless an undercurrent of unease about what might happen should women encounter men not as receptive to this kind of feminine appeal.

Women writing during the early 1850s focused not only on the value and potential pitfalls of women using their emotional, romantic, and sexual influence over men in the service of abolitionism but also on the significance of white women's religious activism for the antislavery cause. In discussing women's religious activities, authors primarily focused on Quaker women's involvement in abolitionism, with Quaker women embodying the archetypal virtuous female activists. These decisions to concentrate on Quaker women may initially seem counterintuitive; after all, during the antebellum era, Quaker women such as Angelina Grimké, Sarah Grimké, and Lucretia Mott were at the forefront of abolitionist radicalism, boldly delivering antislavery speeches to "promiscuous," mixed-sex audiences and explicitly linking the causes of abolition and women's rights. As historians such as Margaret Hope Bacon have noted, abolitionist Quaker women were in many ways the most radical activists of the antebellum era when it came to issues of both race and gender, serving as the "mothers of feminism" in the nineteenth-century United States.³⁴

Yet by the late antebellum era, popular perceptions of Quaker women in mainstream American society were not necessarily of incendiary subversives who transgressed all existing gender hierarchies. Rather, Quaker women were often depicted in as decorous, restrained women most notable for their modest dress, disciplined behavior, and high principles.³⁵ This shift was in part a reaction to changes in Quaker communities. Though to a significantly lesser degree than those in other Christian denominations, between the Revolution and the Civil War Quaker women experienced a decline in support for, and the visibility of, their public ministry.³⁶ Although certainly still radical in their ideas about gender compared with the majority of mainline Protestants, Quaker women in the mid-nineteenth century were much more in line with many Protestants' conceptions of gender roles than they had been a century before. As such, female antislavery authors could much more readily present Quaker women not as fiery iconoclasts, but rather as pious, Christian women operating in their religious communities in ways that would have looked familiar to non-Quaker readers.

Quaker heroines may also have been a desirable choice for writers, as Quakers were no longer the divisive, religiously disruptive presence in the United States that they had been a generation before. With the rise of evangelical Christianity and the Second Great Awakening in the late eighteenth and early nineteenth centuries, Quakers, always a religious minority, became an even smaller percentage of the overall American population. In the face of the new religious elements introduced into American culture during the antebellum era, including a new influx of Catholic immigrants and the expansion of alternative religious groups such as the Oneida Community, the Mormons, and the Shakers, Quakers may also have no longer seemed quite so revolutionary. In fact, to many Protestants, they may well have seemed nonthreatening to the point of being benign.

If an antislavery novelist wanted to create an explicitly religious heroine, because of fierce debates about the rightful connections between Protestant churches and abolitionism raging during the antebellum era, a Quaker woman may have also been a less contentious choice than a mainline Protestant woman. One of the more divisive controversies in the antislavery movement centered on whether abolitionists had to be "come-outers" and leave their churches if they refused to embrace abolitionist principles.

Some antislavery activists believed this was the only proper moral course, while others maintained abolitionists ought to remain in nonabolitionist churches to encourage them to change their policies.[37] Many Protestant denominations also faced significant internal debate about the viability of remaining unified amid growing sectional strife. As a consequence of these tensions, several Protestant denominations split along regional lines during the antebellum era. Although Quaker congregations were by no means free from such internal disputes, they presented a much more united front against slavery than other religious denominations of the antebellum era.[38] Creating a Quaker heroine could thus help an author avoid becoming embroiled in debates about the connections between abolitionism and mainline Protestantism taking place during the 1850s.

Female Quaker characters serve as forces of unity and community cohesion rather than of strife and division. They are exemplary, obedient daughters to their fathers; decorous, restrained participants in Quaker meetings; and, ultimately, loving, submissive wives to their husbands. They do not work to disrupt hierarchies in either their homes or society as a whole, happy to be subordinate to the men of their households and to remain uninterested in positions of religious authority in their meetings. Slavery is the only social institution they challenge.

Quaker women figure prominently in *Uncle Tom's Cabin,* embodying loving, egalitarian care for enslaved people and successfully turning formerly violent proslavery men into gentle pacifists. Though their antislavery activism is profoundly subversive of American social systems and racial norms, it also closely conforms to middle-class feminine ideals of domesticity and maternal nurture. One Quaker character who powerfully embodies this combination of abolitionist radicalism and traditional feminine virtue is *Uncle Tom's Cabin's* Rachel Halliday. After she has fled from slavery with her son, Eliza Harris is taken in by the Halliday family. Its matriarch, Rachel is the ideal model of how a woman can influence members of her household to think and act rightly, and she does so in an appropriately feminine way. In her household, "all moved obediently to Rachel's gentle 'Thee had better,' or more gentle 'Hadn't thee better?'" Leading her family members with such quiet, feminine guidance, Rachel encouraged her family members to follow her counsel by "diffusing a sort of sunny radiance over the whole proceedings generally."[39] As such, she perfectly embodies how women can shape the behavior of those around them through feminine moral suasion, without in any way transgressing the norms of domestic womanhood.

Yet Rachel and other Quaker women pair adherence to dominant ideals of womanhood with a radical refusal to accept the racial hierarchies of mainstream American society. Rachel, for example, consistently breaks down the boundaries of racial division by calling Eliza "daughter," and her friend Ruth cares for and loves Eliza's son Harry as though he were her own, showering him with constant physical affection, "ever and anon stopping to put a cake into Harry's hand, or pat his head, or twine his long curls round her snowy fingers."[40] In *Uncle Tom's Cabin,* Quaker women model the best version of antislavery womanhood, expressing maternal love for enslaved people, refusing to abide by racial norms that emphasize distance and hierarchy between African American and white people, and influencing those around them to think rightly in only the gentlest and most feminine ways.

The novel also makes a Quaker woman central to the moral conversion of one of the text's previously most vicious proslavery characters, Tom Loker. A career slavecatcher who has been dispatched to bring Eliza and her son back to their owners, Loker is injured in the recapture attempt and sent to recover "under the motherly supervision of Aunt Dorcas." The Quaker Aunt Dorcas lives up to her maternal, nurturing name, by not just physically but also morally rehabilitating the previously depraved Loker. Because of her kindness and care, the end of the novel finds Loker living peacefully in the North, cured of his violent proslavery ways.[41]

In antislavery novels, Quaker women do not just exert a benevolent maternal influence over proslavery men but also pray that the men they love will be converted to the antislavery cause. They exert moral influence over these men until they are persuaded of the justness of antislavery ideas, doing so in part by speaking out against slavery in Quaker meetings. In Little's *Thrice through the Furnace,* for example, Aimee Freeman's prayers "reached [her slave-owning suitor's] inmost soul, and pierced through and through that long closed heart" moving him to promise to God to "free all my slaves, oh! that I could free every slave under the canopy of thy Heaven."[42] Hanaford's heroine Lucretia Barnard similarly persuades the slave-owning man who loves her of the injustice of slavery through a sermon she delivers in her Quaker meeting. Listening with "breathless attention," her would-be husband feels compelled to "release the fellow immortals who were styled his slaves."[43]

Such forms of address initially appear controversial, since they feature women not only speaking in a public religious forum but also daring to instruct men in religious spaces about moral questions, in direct contradiction of biblical injunctions that women keep silent in churches and ask their husbands for any needed religious guidance. Yet novelists hastened to reassure their readers that Quaker heroines were not threats to either religious or secular ideals of female privacy and respectability—in part by highlighting Quaker female preachers' extreme rectitude of both manner and dress. In a culture in which women who spoke in public, particularly about controversial issues such as slavery, were frequently condemned for violating contemporary norms of gender propriety and sexual morality, Quaker heroines were represented as the very antithesis of the loose, immoral "public woman." With their hair covered, dresses plain, and eyes downcast, they were the opposite of the stereotypical showy, immodest female orator, ostensibly seeking to draw attention to her body as much as to her words. Antislavery women used Quaker women's self-presentation as a means of combating claims that women who joined the public fight against slavery were necessarily sexually suspect or culturally transgressive.

Authors writing during the early 1850s also used Quaker heroines to demonstrate that even when offered it, right-thinking antislavery women would willingly renounce a form of public power in favor of moral influence and domestic activism, as soon as they had the opportunity. Quaker female characters in antislavery women's stories eagerly give up public speech once they have successfully converted the proslavery men they love to abolitionism: once they have married their newly abolitionist husbands, these women steadfastly resist speaking in public meetings or contemplating any other form of public feminine activism.[44] Although she had once been an ardent proponent of women speaking out against slavery in Quaker meetings, after her marriage, Hanaford's Lucretia regards "*home* as woman's most appropriate sphere of action and influence."[45] Heroines like her are convinced that they can have a considerable influence on abolitionism by operating exclusively in the domestic sphere. Thus, through Quaker heroines, female antislavery authors demonstrated that though women could be at once public speakers and sexually respectable, their most desirable and effective form of antislavery activism remained domestic moral suasion.

Authors writing during the early 1850s also argued that white women could have a powerful impact on abolitionism by dying in its service. By centering their narratives on girls and women who died as part of their antislavery advocacy, writers gave these characters both a tremendously powerful, and a distinctly problematic, place in abolitionism. On the one hand, dead and dying girls and women could play central roles in embedding abolitionism in the hearts and minds of their friends and loved ones. On the other, securing these antislavery conversions came at the highest possible cost, as women and girls did not live to see the beneficial effects of their redemptive deaths on the people they loved or on American society overall.

By writing about female characters who died for the sake of abolitionism, authors drew on powerful tropes within women's antebellum sentimental literature. As scholars such as Lucy Elizabeth Frank have detailed, narratives that focused on the deaths of female characters, most of whom were young, pious, and beautiful, permeated women's sentimental literary culture.[46] By including similar representations of the deaths of youthful, lovely, virtuous women and girls, female antislavery authors participated in a pervasive trend in antebellum sentimental fiction. Knowing their audience was accustomed to and had a taste for tales about the tragic deaths of attractive, saintly young women, female antislavery authors likely included such elements in their fiction as part of broader efforts to make it more appealing. In *Uncle Tom's Cabin,* Stowe allowed her readers considerable time with the angelic child character Eva prior to her death, establishing her status as a model Christian, loving daughter, and kindly benefactor to the enslaved. Investing Eva with considerable charm and stressing both her perfect piety and her extreme youth, Stowe invested the character's demise with the maximum possible pathos.[47] E. D. E. N. Southworth adopted a similar tactic in her descriptions of the peerlessly virtuous Rosalie Sutherland in her 1853 *Mark Sutherland.* Prior to Rosalie's death halfway through the text, the author consistently highlighted her compassion, thoughtfulness, and benevolence, encouraging readers to love and empathize with this gentle abolitionist.[48]

Writers made their tales about girls' and women's premature deaths as moving as possible, creating deep feeling and hopefully inspiring copious tears in their female readers. As Julie Stern has argued, shedding tears over the deaths of beloved characters became an expected part of middle-class female readers' engagement with literary culture during the antebellum era.[49] Incorporating this powerful element of popular sentimental literature, writers encouraged their female audience to transform their emotional distress into support for abolition and to take up the cause their saintly, martyred female characters had lived and ultimately died for.

By stressing the angelic virtue of female characters and the redemptive power of their deaths, authors drew implicit—and sometimes, explicit—parallels between their heroines and Christ. In a culture dominated by Protestant Christianity, such parallels were undeniably potent: by likening girls and women to the central figure of the Christian faith, writers invested them with notable moral power. Like Christ's, their deaths had the potential to morally redeem both those around them and the entire American nation. In *Uncle Tom's Cabin,* Eva directly likens herself to Christ, telling Uncle Tom she understands Christ's willingness to die for the sake of all humanity: "I would be glad to die, if my dying could stop all this misery, I *would die* for them [the enslaved.]" Although Eva's death does not secure the liberation of all enslaved people, it does spark the abolitionist conversions of her friends and family members.[50] The death of *Mark Sutherland'*s Rosalie has a similar impact on those she loved. In the mind of her previously proslavery widower, especially, the "thought of Rosalie [was] as that of some bright guardian angel, still blessing from heaven those she loved upon earth."[51] Much like Christ, Eva and Rosalie die in the hopes of redeeming others from their sins—specifically, from the sin of upholding slavery.

Powerful as these narratives were, arguing that dying was one of the primary ways women could contribute to abolitionism had some distinctly negative implications. Martyrs such as Eva and Rosalie set a moral standard virtually impossible, and certainly not terribly appealing, for any real girl or woman to follow. Flawless saints devoid of any desires of their own, they live and die purely to defend the moral right. They do not slip off of their pedestals for so much as a second, which makes them problematic figures for female readers to emulate, and, most fundamentally, these characters offer an unhelpful model for antislavery women, as their deaths are their most important means of contributing to abolitionism. This particular form of antislavery activity was thus not an especially viable or attractive option for female readers who wanted to live for their cause, rather than die for it.

By the early 1850s, female authors seemed less concerned with presenting female readers with a practical roadmap about how they could become involved in the antislavery movement and more concerned with emphasizing the direness of current conditions for the antislavery cause in the United States. Arguing that girls and women needed to go so far as to sacrifice their lives for the sake of abolitionism, female authors indicated that the antislavery movement was facing decidedly bleak odds, which necessitated dramatic action. This sense that abolitionism was in a desperate position only increased as the decade advanced.

White Women, the Death of Moral Suasion, and the Rise of Political Activism in the Mid- and Late 1850s

In the mid-1850s, female antislavery authors' arguments about white women's involvement in the abolitionist cause underwent a striking, abrupt shift. Writers moved from endorsing the power of white women's moral influence to despairing that anything but white men's political activism would benefit their cause. This shift was in many ways a troubling one for white female antislavery advocates, as it left them in a notably powerless position. If the future of slavery lay in the votes of morally suspect white men, where did that leave morally virtuous white women and the antislavery cause as a whole?

Authors shifted from asking female readers to persuade male family members and friends to feel and act rightly on the slave question to urging male readers to support specific political parties, candidates, and initiatives. Yet despite this new focus on men's political action, writers expressed strong doubts about white men's political activism as a means of successfully moving the antislavery cause forward. White female writers raised significant concerns by depicting white men as oblivious to evils of slavery at best and as the source of those evils at worst.

Ambivalent about the role of politics in the antislavery movement, authors writing in the mid- and late 1850s nonetheless consistently represented any efforts to use feminine moral suasion on behalf of abolitionism as abject, dramatic failures. By doing so, in some respects they were participating in a broader shift among female activists away from moral suasion.[52] However, authors turned away from feminine moral influence only with great regret and with no sense that political activism was a better or more ethically desirable means of creating social change. To the contrary, writers expressed profound skepticism about the white-male-dominated realm of politics and the temptation it offered men to place worldly concerns over moral considerations.

Throughout the fiction women published during the mid- and late 1850s, female characters who sought to exercise moral influence over men consistently failed miserably. In W. H. Corning's 1856 novel *Western Border Life; or, What Fanny Hunter Saw and Heard in Kanzas [sic] and Missouri*, the eponymous protagonist fails to persuade her proslavery employer of the moral necessity of abolition, despite her repeated, heartfelt entreaties that he emancipate the enslaved people he owns.[53] The abolitionist heroine of the 1856 novel *Mrs. Hadden*, Ada, faces similar difficulties, vainly encouraging the proslavery men around her to "*strive* to do right in one's own soul, and with one's hands and lips."[54] In these narratives, male characters turned away from female characters' appeals, entirely unmoved by their efforts.

Not even when moral suasion was blended with women's efforts to exert romantic and sexual influence over men did female characters enjoy any success. Much as they had done during the early 1850s, in the mid- and late 1850s, writers created a stark dichotomy between sexually dissolute, slave-owning men and sexually virtuous, antislavery women. During these years, however, chaste women who sought to influence the slave-owning men they loved to change their sexually opportunistic, violent ways did so in vain, facing only contempt, physical abuse, and a worsening of conditions for the enslaved women they were seeking to help.[55]

In these narratives, white women's attempts to prevent men's sexual violence perversely made enslaved women's plights even worse, with free women's advocacy spurring slave-owning men to yet more extreme acts of sexual abuse. Such is the case in the 1856 novel *Woman's Faith*, in which the antislavery heroine's pleading with her husband on behalf of an enslaved woman he has repeatedly raped "so far from effecting a favorable change in the conduct of her husband, seemed but to aggravate his outrageous and restless cruelty."[56] In Harriet Hamline Bigelow's 1856 novel *The Curse Entailed*, Mrs. DeWolfe similarly seeks to intervene on behalf of the enslaved Jeanette, who has been the victim of numerous rapes by her husband. Rather than ameliorating Jeanette's sufferings, however, Mrs. DeWolfe's attempts result in Mr. DeWolfe doing all in his power to "crush [Jeanette] to the earth."[57]

With these representations of white slave-owning men as hopelessly sexually corrupt and violent, female abolitionist authors entered into longstanding discussions about the impact slavery had on white slave-owning men's sexual morality. Their works indicated that living in a slave-owning society had convinced white men not only that engaging in violent acts was one of their rightful prerogatives but also that it was a key way for them to assert dominance over their wives and enslaved women.[58] Slave-owning men responded to their wives' efforts to exercise moral authority with violent reprisals against enslaved women; these men clearly expected to be absolute masters in their households and responded to any attempts to challenge their authority with brutal violence.

That white women's moral influence was no longer sufficient to persuade slave-owning men of the evils of sexual profligacy and violence inevitably raised the question of whether stronger measures were called for. If white southern men's behavior could not be curbed by the power of white women's moral suasion, did it need to be controlled through the formal channels of politics and the law? Antislavery women's fiction raised this possibility by demonstrating that white female characters' efforts were no longer sufficient to protect enslaved women from white men's sexual brutality.

In several reform movements of the late antebellum era, female activists similarly contended that it was no longer enough to hope that white men would be persuaded to be chaste before marriage and respectful of their wives' right to sexual refusal after it. Women's rights advocates placed marriage reform high on their list of priorities, arguing that married women needed to have more legal protection from their husbands' rape and sexual abuse.[59] During these same years, moral reform activists also increased efforts to legislate sexuality, petitioning legislators to pass laws making seduction a crime and cracking down on prostitution in cities.[60] In the late antebellum era, it was not uncommon for female reformers to argue that rapacious male sexuality needed to be controlled not by individual female moral influence but rather by the full power of the law.

Writers indicated the desirability of such legal constraints being placed on white slave-owning men. Demonstrating the utter inability of white women to control white men's sexual behavior, authors indicated that something more powerful than individual feminine moral influence would be necessary to end slave owners' sexual abuse of enslaved women. They did not, however, overtly advocate for laws designed to check white men's sexual power over women, perhaps because of their doubts about the possibility of such laws ever being passed. To ask a government largely comprising white, slave-owning southern men to take power away from white, slave-owning southern men may have seemed counterproductive. Uncertain about how white southern men's unjustified sexual license could effectively be ended, antislavery female authors nonetheless forcefully denounced such sexual violence.

Not only do female characters regularly find their efforts to use moral suasion ineffectual, they also sometimes find them fatal. In fiction published during the mid- and late 1850s, several female characters die in their attempts to aid the abolitionist cause. And, unlike the female protagonists who died in narratives from the early 1850s, these characters' deaths were utterly meaningless, doing nothing to benefit abolitionism. Women may have possessed the same willingness to die for their cause as those in earlier novels, but such virtue now went entirely unrewarded, as the men they sought to influence remained just as proslavery after women's deaths as they had been before them.

Pacifist female characters in antislavery fiction sometimes found themselves caught up in violent conflicts over slavery—and these were not always conflicts they survived. Lydia Maria Child's 1856 short story "The Kansas Emigrants," for example, features an uneasy, ambiguous portrayal of violent abolitionism and women's involvement in it. As part of the larger movement to bring Kansas into the Union as a free state, Alice Bruce and Kate Bradford venture into the Kansas territories with their husbands. Unfortunately for Alice and Kate, the territories are already overrun by vicious proslavery men, who systematically brutalize, rape, and murder innocent antislavery settlers. Throughout the story, Child emphasized how ardently antislavery advocates hope to stay peaceful in the face of this violent onslaught but how impossible it is to do so. Child consistently placed her antislavery characters in situations where they were obliged to defend themselves from proslavery violence. In one scene, the valiant Kate holds off proslavery marauders at gunpoint, to prevent them from attacking her family. Such threats of violence could be justifiable, Child indicated, provided they were in the service of a just moral cause and women's natural desire to protect their husbands and children. Uneasy as "The Kansas Emigrants" is about violence, persistently associating it with immoral proslavery men, Child also justified virtuous antislavery women's defense against violent attack.

Yet while the courageous Kate successfully defends her family and survives to the end of the story, the delicate Alice is not so lucky. After proslavery men shoot her beloved husband in the back, Alice quite literally dies of a broken heart, her dreams of helping her spouse to build a free Kansas entirely destroyed.[61] And Alice is not the only female character to fruitlessly die in the midst of antislavery struggle in fiction of the mid and late 1850s. In Stowe's 1856 *Dred*, abolitionist Nina Gordon dies seeking to emancipate the enslaved people whom she owns. After her death her dissolute, adamantly proslavery brother burns all of her antislavery writings, including those expressing her desire that her plantation's enslaved population be emancipated.[62] The slave-owning father of Madge Vertner (the heroine of Mattie Griffith's 1859-60 serialized novel of the same name) similarly disregards the promises about emancipation he made to his heart-broken daughter on her deathbed, "saying to himself, as many another has done, 'I'll liberate [the slaves] at my death.'"[63]

Writers allowed readers to bond with and come to care for their doomed female heroines, before sending them to deaths as premature and tragic as they were fruitless. By having female characters die for the antislavery cause without in any way benefiting that cause, authors emphasized both white women's profound commitment to abolitionism and their complete inability to contribute to it through moral influence. These novels and stories thus raise the question: if moral suasion were quite literally a dead end for white women, where did that leave the antislavery movement and its future?

Increasingly despairing about inability of white women's moral influence to move abolitionism forward, authors increasingly concentrated their hopes on the male realm of electoral politics. Yet while their fiction contended that the primary site for abolitionist change needed to be politics, antislavery writers remained wary of the American government, given that it and the men who led it were often proslavery in their sympathies and actions. During the mid- and late 1850s, the White House had two presidents, Franklin Pierce and James Buchanan, who supported white southern interests.[64] Additionally, Supreme Court decisions in cases such as *Dred Scott v. Sandford* were also tremendously discouraging for abolitionists. Antislavery activists regarded the Dred Scott decision as yet more proof that American politics had been taken over by a corrupt slave power that privileged the interests of elite, white southerners over the basic human rights of enslaved and free African Americans.[65]

These political setbacks appalled abolitionists and convinced female antislavery authors that politically mobilizing against proslavery interests was vitally necessary. Writers publishing during the mid- and late 1850s consequently stressed that every white man with antislavery principles was morally obligated to vote antislavery politicians into office and to support antislavery legislation at the polls. White men's political activism could, they argued, quite literally make or break the abolitionist cause on both the state and the national level. In her 1855 novel *Aunt Leanna; or, Early Scenes in Kentucky*, Elizabeth Roe emphasized this point, noting the potential of one man's vote to make the difference between slavery and freedom for thousands of people. Roe notes, "Twice in his life did Dr. Cadwell give the casting vote in the legislature of Illinois on the subject of slavery, and the last time the matter was settled permanently in favor of freedom."[66] Proslavery forces might currently be in the ascendant in the United States, but the political involvement of white antislavery men might be able to turn back the tide and ensure that liberty, and not slavery, predominated in state and hopefully also federal government.

White men effectively taking antislavery action at the polls might also have seemed much more viable to female authors during the mid- and late 1850s, given the rapid rise of the antislavery Republican Party. Unlike previous antislavery political parties, such as the Liberty Party and the Free Soil Party, from its very beginnings the Republican Party quickly demonstrated its potential to be a viable political threat to the proslavery Democratic Party.[67] Only two years after its founding, the party's 1856 presidential candidate, John C. Frémont, made a respectable showing at the polls, signaling the emergence of a new force to be reckoned with in American politics.

Throughout the mid and late 1850s, female antislavery authors hoped that if white men supported the Republican Party, the slave system might be significantly undermined. They insisted that if white male voters managed to get Republican politicians into office, including the White House, the abolitionist cause would greatly benefit. Flying in the face of most Republicans' assertions that they wished to contain rather than abolish slavery, female antislavery authors suggested that to elect a Republican could, in fact, be tantamount to electing an abolitionist.[68] A proslavery character in Hattia M'Keehan's 1858 novel *Liberty or Death; or, Heaven's Infraction of the Fugitive Slave Law*, for instance, asserts darkly that "by agitation they [the

Republicans] git the people down on slavery . . . extendin' it to the new territories. And when they git 'em that fur along, then you see, they'll easy git 'em furder, and dreckly be in for passen laws 'ginst slavery altogether."[69] While most Republican politicians insisted they had no desire to abolish slavery, M'Keehan expressed the hope that Republicans' efforts to prevent the spread of slavery could nonetheless be a vital step in ensuring the institution's ultimate demise. Mattie Griffith made a similar argument in the final chapter of *Madge Vertner,* which completed its serialization in the *National Anti-Slavery Standard* in May 1860, a few short weeks before Abraham Lincoln secured his party's nomination. After summarizing the terrible evils committed by the novel's corrupt, slave-owning male characters, in her very last sentence Griffith urged white male readers to "lessen such unjust power by fighting a good fight and casting a true vote in 1860."[70] These horrors, Griffith indicated, could at the very least be diminished by white male readers voting antislavery Republican politicians into office.

Directly discussing specific political parties and speaking to white male readers about how they ought to vote were notable new developments in women's antislavery literature. Prior to the mid and late 1850s, writers had not addressed male readers, let alone offered them detailed guidance about which candidates they ought to vote for. This shift to addressing male readers is another sign that female authors placed increasingly less faith in white women's abilities to effectively contribute to abolitionism during the late antebellum era. Emphasizing the importance of male political action in determining the future of slavery, authors did all they could to persuade male readers to vote antislavery candidates into positions of political power.

Yet writers' arguments about the necessity of white men voting for Republicans by no means signaled they had abandoned their previous beliefs about white men's innate tendencies toward moral corruption; to the contrary, authors' works were permeated by fears that white men would abuse the political power their race and gender had invested them with. Expressing her frustration with the fickle male voters surrounding her, the formerly enslaved heroine of Griffith's 1856 novel *Autobiography of a Female Slave* affirms that such men continuously showed themselves capable of "vot[ing] for a perpetuation of our captivity. . . . Can we hope for a mitigation of our wrongs when such men are our sovereigns?"[71]

Similarly, just because men ran for office as antislavery candidates did not mean that, once elected, they would actually use their new powers for the benefit of abolitionism. Even a government that included antislavery politicians was likely, female authors worried, to be one dominated by the masculine concerns of personal advancement and money. An abolitionist in Frances Harriet Whipple Green's 1858 novel *Shahmah in Pursuit of Freedom; or, The Branded Hand* declares that male politicians routinely ignore questions of morality and that "Railroads, Land Speculations, Joint Stock Companies, the price of cotton . . . are the engrossing topics."[72] The heroine of Elizabeth Livermore's *Zoë* dismisses politics in equally contemptuous terms, arguing that it is characterized by "diplomacy and pipe-laying, and lobbying and caucusing, and what not they call it, but it is just nothing but cowardice. . . . *Too much man, I say, too much man!*"[73] In "The Kansas Emigrants," Child condemned politicians in comparable terms, noting that the politicians of Washington refused to help the beleaguered antislavery settlers of Kansas because "they were busy with other things that came home to their *business,* not their *bosoms.*"[74]

By making such statements, Green, Livermore, and Child in many ways reinforced dominant notions of gendered separate spheres. Their reflections fit neatly into this ideology's representation of the public, political world of men as a harsh, cutthroat realm of greed and ambition, entirely unlike women's peaceful, moral, domestic world. These authors drew on such rhetoric not to reinforce the justness of separate spheres, however, but rather to represent the dangers of a political world untouched by female morality. The problem with the current American political system was, as Harriet Newell Greene Butts argued in her 1855 novel *Ralph; or, I Wish He Wasn't Black,* that in political circles "tears and lamentations are of no avail; affection, devotion, parental love, and connubial happiness are trampled low in the dust, and made subservient to tyranny, ambition and power."[75] Writers drew clear dividing lines between women and men—between the corrupt, masculine world of politics and the pure, feminine world of feeling and morality. The vicious world of masculine politics clearly needed to be reformed so that it no longer focused on power and money but rather on morality and justice. It was the question of how this transformation could effectively be achieved that antislavery women writers grappled with in their fiction.

Unsure about how white women could best ensure their moral values were represented in government, authors expressed no doubts that white women possessed the moral ideals that at least, *deserved* to predominate in

American society. Writers frequently contrasted women's moral steadfastness, and their ardent desire to work on behalf of the abolitionist cause, with men's strategic political caution, or outright refusal, to act. In *Autobiography of a Female Slave,* Griffith declares, "Woman, when once she interests herself in the great cause of humanity, goes to work with an ability and ardor that put to shame the colder and slower action of man. . . . A woman . . . will achieve with a single effort the mighty deed, for the attainment of which men spend years in idle planning."[76]

Female characters are also represented as immune to the temptations of political corruption in ways male characters are not. Reflecting with exasperation on the morally suspect dealings of male politicians, the heroine of Irving's "Mirth and Melancholy" asserts that, unlike them, she would never compromise her principles or "do evil, that good might come."[77] Unlike the white men who were currently running the government, Griffith's narrator in *Autobiography of a Female Slave* similarly affirms that women are consistently "on the side of right, not might."[78] In "The Kansas Emigrants," after government officials repeatedly, callously dismiss the entreaties of antislavery settlers in the Kansas territories, Kate Bradford also eventually recognizes the fundamental moral corruption of the male-dominated political sphere. "She had such pride in American institutions, she *could* not believe that the government of her country was in league with such abominations and outrages," Child noted, "until the return of messenger after messenger sent to Washington, made the damning proof too strong to be resisted."[79] Likewise mocking male politicians' reluctance to address the slave question, Livermore's Zoë demands, "What are the men *afraid* of? I don't hear of any crack of doom, nor the Union falling to pieces if I cry *freedom* to the very top of my voice."[80] Writers thus created a stark dichotomy between white female characters (who were moral and unafraid of defending their antislavery ideals) and white male ones (who were, at best, morally ambiguous, overcautious, and excessively influenced by worldly considerations.)

One potential solution to the ongoing corruption and immorality of the political sphere was to empower white women with direct political power, as a means of cleaning up this morally dirty realm. Although the possibility of female enfranchisement was certainly present in American culture during the 1850s, antislavery women writers did not fully, directly embrace it in their fiction. A few authors did, however, obliquely express bitterness about women's political invisibility and powerlessness and use suffrage-infused language in their fiction. In *Madge Vertner,* Griffith's narrator notes caustically of one of her many immoral proslavery male characters that he "is a voter—one of the Democratic sovereigns—and his existence cannot be quietly wiped out or overlooked as though he were a woman."[81] In Child's "The Kansas Emigrants," in discussing a longed-for, utopian future of peace and equality in the territory, Kate Bradford's husband tells her, "I, for one, will give you my vote."[82] As Child scholar Carolyn Karcher has argued, this use of voting language can plausibly read as an allusion to the desirability of enfranchising women, as a means of effectively creating a just, egalitarian society.[83]

It is noteworthy that these allusions to female enfranchisement and the injustice of female political marginalization occur in the fiction of two of the most radical antislavery women writers of the 1850s. Child and Griffith were already writing and thinking about women's rights prior to the Civil War, and both became suffrage advocates after it. Their willingness to even indirectly raise the possibility of female enfranchisement was thus likely rooted in their status as women's rights women, already concerned with issues of female political empowerment in American society.

Given their subsequent involvement in the suffrage movement, it is striking that even these radical writers were quite oblique in discussing the possibility of white women voting. One reason for this lack of directness may have been a desire to keep the abolitionist struggle separate from the divisive antebellum women's rights movement. These authors were, after all, publishing their fiction in the wake of the Seneca Falls Convention of 1848, which had scandalized the American public with its demands for women's rights—including, most shockingly, women's right to vote. And it was not just the general American public that found this call for female enfranchisement controversial. At Seneca Falls, the resolution calling for votes for women was the only one not universally agreed on by those in attendance. This resolution inspired even radical abolitionist and feminist Lucretia Mott to worry that by calling for such a thing women's rights activists would make their movement look absurd. The controversy surrounding demands for female political empowerment continued to swirl around the women's rights conventions held during the 1850s. Hostile to virtually all of women's rights activists' demands, detractors of the movement frequently singled out calls for female enfranchisement for particular derision and contempt.[84]

Since women's rights activists' calls for voting rights roused considerable antagonism in the majority of Americans, authors like Child and Griffith may have hoped to avoid directly raising such contentious questions in their fiction. After all, during the 1850s, writers had significant reason to hope their literature might reach a broader reading public than ever before, as the popularity of *Uncle Tom's Cabin* and the rapid rise of the Republican Party signaled that non-abolitionist white northerners were newly willing to grapple with antislavery ideas. Given this more receptive popular climate, female antislavery authors may well have feared they would frighten off more moderate readers if they directly advocated for female enfranchisement.

Another possible reason for writers' oblique allusions to, or outright silence concerning, the possibility of women's political empowerment may also be, of course, that authors did not see giving women the right to vote as the best solution to their dilemma. After all, writers consistently represented politics as a decidedly distasteful, morally corrupt sphere. Authors may, therefore, have believed enfranchising women in the hopes of reforming the innately morally compromised realm of politics would be a fruitless waste of women's time and moral energies. Writers may have hoped the future of slavery might yet be determined elsewhere and that electoral politics would cease to be central in determining the future of abolitionism.

By the time the Civil War broke out in 1861, white female antislavery authors had despaired of emancipation coming about through antislavery women's peaceful moral influence. Disliking and distrusting male-centered forms of activism, such as politics and violence, by the mid- and late 1850s, writers had unhappily conceded that these forms of antislavery activity, not feminine moral suasion, now dominated abolitionism. Faced with an antislavery movement increasingly reliant on white men's political decisions, while not yet fully embracing the idea of white women's political empowerment, authors worried about the disempowerment and marginalization of disenfranchised white women. As the antebellum era came to an end, women's antislavery novels and stories consequently struck a decidedly uneasy note. Convinced gender invested enslaved and free women alike with a powerful moral compass and a steadfast commitment to abolitionism that white men lacked, authors offered no clear forward for their movement or for the women within it. Aware that electoral politics would be vital in determining the future of slavery, female writers remained unsure about how women could best infuse the corrupt political sphere with their antislavery values.

CONCLUSION

"The Duty of Woman in Aiding in Extending This Influence of Letters"

> The pen has become the mighty instrument of reform and rebuke; the press is the teacher and preacher of the world; and it is not only the privilege, but the duty of woman to aiding in extending this influence of letters.
> —MARY E. BRYAN, "How Should Women Write?" (1860)

Discussing Harriet Hamline Bigelow's novel *The Curse Entailed* in the pages of the *Liberator* in 1856, an anonymous reviewer proclaimed the volume would undoubtedly "help swell the tide of virtuous and indignant feeling which is rising in our land to sweep this foul abomination out of existence."[1] By the 1850s, many Americans shared this sense that they might actually see slavery abolished or, at the very least, dramatically undermined in the not-too-distant future. And throughout the antebellum era, antislavery writers and editors shared the perspective that, because of its remarkable emotional power, fiction written by women, specifically, could play a vital role in bringing the peculiar institution to an end.

By examining this female-authored antislavery literature, this study has built on and worked to complicate existing historiography concerning women's roles as authors and readers during the antebellum era. I have argued that antislavery female writers claimed fiction as a gender-appropriate medium to appropriately express their views about slavery, insisting that fiction-writing was a suitably decorous, feminine means to participate in antislavery activism. Their anxiety to assert the private nature of authorship, however, paradoxically indicated awareness that their literary work was indeed deeply public and political and consequently might be perceived as a violation of domestic femininity. However, contended authors, the risk of being viewed as unfeminine was well worth it, given fiction's vital importance for reaching women with the antislavery message. With its highly emotional, distinctly imaginative content, authors and editors maintained fiction would be able to reach female readers as no other kind of appeal could.

My work also enters into the historiography concerning race and ideologies of feminine difference. In some respects, my study builds on the insights of previous scholars, who have noted the ways rhetoric about feminine difference has been (and remains) intensely damaging for, and exclusionary toward, women of color. White abolitionist authors certainly did write fiction that excluded African American women from being fully considered true women. In their novels and stories, white writers expressed fears about enslaved women's capacity for violence and their refusal and, more troubling still, their inability to conform to the norms of white, middle-class femininity. Yet I maintain that white antislavery women writers' use of the rhetoric of feminine difference also contained significant potential to include, as well as exclude, African American women—to undermine, as well as uphold, antebellum hierarchies of race. Antislavery women's fiction insisted that enslaved women shared the same gender-specific virtues as white women, possessing an innate, gender-based ability to think and act morally that was fundamentally denied to men. As such, women's antislavery fiction defined gender as a category that was in many ways more significant than race, throwing into question white male dominance of American institutions and households.

Finally, I enter the extensive scholarship on debates about antebellum ideologies of domesticity and white, middle-class women's work as activists. In recent years, historians of the public and the private have reflected on the complex ways white, middle-class women negotiated conceptions of the public and the private in their daily lives. Scholars have noted that, contrary to previous assumptions, ideologies of the public and the private did not operate in women's lives purely as straitjackets that rigidly confined them to the domestic sphere. My study turns its attention primarily to considering not how ideologies of the public and the private affected antislavery women's lives but rather how writers grappled with these ideologies. Authors depicted both women's fiction and antislavery activism as private, insisting that neither their work as writers nor their characters' abolitionist advocacy transgressed the boundaries of proper domestic femininity. Despite the fundamentally political nature of their activist and literary work, writers defined both as emphatically distinct from the public world of men.

Similarly, female antislavery authors contended that the most desirable way for women to make their voices heard was to morally influence family and friends in the private sphere of the home. Demonstrating evolving beliefs about the viability of this mode of activism, authors remained convinced that if American society were ever to be saved from the national sin of slavery, female morality would need to reign in the public world of men. The question of how, exactly, these private values could be effectively infused into the public world, without compromising women's proper roles, was one with which authors vigorously grappled—and to which they did not offer any definitive, clear answers.

These debates writers engaged in about the nature of women's appropriate place in American society and the importance of race in access to citizenship and public power, continued both during and long after the Civil War. In the wake of that transformative conflict and the subsequent liberation of enslaved people, Americans entered a new phase of defining freedom and considering the rights of newly emancipated African Americans. Debates about women's roles also took on a new intensity in the wake of the war. Women's rights activists, who had deliberately shelved their gender-specific concerns to focus on the war effort, resumed their feminist activism as soon as the war ended.[2] Living in a world where an institution as firmly entrenched and fiercely defended as slavery could be abolished, women's rights advocates felt a new optimism that all kinds of radical social change were possible. Seeing the American government grappling with weighty questions about the legal and political rights of freedpeople, postbellum feminists saw a unique opportunity to raise issues about the rights of Americans of all races and genders. Caught up in an unprecedented moment of social transformation, women's rights activists hoped that all women and all African Americans might be given full rights as citizens and as voters.

Debates about African Americans, white women, and political power quickly became divisive, however. While many women's rights activists also supported abolition and civil rights, discussions about enfranchisement revealed that for some white postbellum feminists, commitment to the political empowerment of African Americans was by no means as strong or consistent as their commitment to white women's rights. During the late 1860s, the women's rights movement was rocked by contentious discussions about whether to focus attention first on fighting for the political enfranchisement of African American men or for all African Americans and white women. These debates soon focused on who was the worthiest of receiving the right to vote, with white feminists such as Elizabeth Cady Stanton voicing anger at the idea of freedmen receiving the vote before middle-class white women. White women would make much better use of the franchise than freedmen, some white feminists argued, not only because they had been raised with the privileges of freedom and education denied to formerly enslaved African American men but also because of innate racial differences.[3] These debates soon became focused on the rights of African American men versus those of white women, a binary that, African American feminists such as Sojourner Truth and Frances E. Watkins Harper noted, left African American women and their needs out of the discussion altogether.[4]

Discussions about the desirability of white women having direct access to political power, and white unease about how freedpeople would use their freedom, were anticipated by conversations that took place in the pages of women's antebellum antislavery literature. Although female abolitionist authors did not, of course, foresee either the Civil War or its aftermath, as early as the 1820s, they were imagining what a post-emancipation world might look like and contemplating what roles white and African American women ought to play in politics and the public sphere. These visions at once included African American women in and excluded them from being considered true women and having access to full American citizenship—tensions and ambiguities that would continue to haunt discussions of female enfranchisement and civil rights for many years.[5]

The debates these authors engaged in about reading, writing, and gender have also remained significant long after the antebellum era. Nearly two centuries after antislavery writers and editors insisted that fiction was a uniquely feminine medium, the genre remains closely associated with female readers and authors. The majority of novel readers in the early twenty-first century are female, and participating in fiction-oriented book clubs is often regarded as a feminine pursuit. Much as was the case in the nineteenth century, specific genres of texts are persistently denigrated as "chick lit" and consequently assumed to lack both intellectual and artistic merit. And, much like sentimental texts were mocked as "silly novels by lady novelists" during the antebellum era, works of "women's fiction" such as romance novels are still widely denigrated as frivolous and shallow in the twenty-first century.[6] However, scholars of women's reading practices and popular fiction have noted that such texts often provide female readers with a sense of community and new ways of understanding themselves and their lives.[7] Thus, although often dismissed as trivial, women's fiction remains an important social space for female readers and writers alike.

Antislavery women's fiction raises several other issues that continue to be vigorously debated by scholars and activists today, about whether women are, indeed, innately different from men, what these differences might be, and how or if rhetoric about feminine difference can successfully be deployed to create meaningful social change. During the second wave of feminism, which emerged in the 1960s and 1970s, many activists reacted against essentialist notions of gender that defined women as inherently inferior to men in their physical and intellectual capabilities. Many feminists of this era insisted on the importance of the social construction of gender, which shaped and naturalized ideas about which qualities were inherently "masculine" or "feminine" and accordingly assigned women and men rigid places in a strict, hierarchical gender binary.[8] In subsequent decades, feminist theorists such as Judith Butler destabilized the notion of a unified category of "woman," arguing that such definitions created deceptively, damagingly dualistic visions of what was in reality a rich, complex spectrum of many different sexes and genders.[9]

On the other side of these debates were cultural feminists, who insisted that the binary categories of "woman" and "man" were, indeed, useful and relevant, that women and men were inherently different from one another, and that these differences were largely rooted in cisgender women's biological potential to bear children. Cultural feminists maintained that because of the close connections between women and mothering, women are innately more nurturing, connected to nature, and committed to fostering peace and cooperation than men.[10] Antislavery female authors articulated very similar ideas, arguing that women made better abolitionists than men precisely because of their innate, maternal capacity for empathy.

An inescapable question that arises in discussions of feminine difference is whether gender essentialist ideas can ever be usefully, non-damagingly deployed in struggles for social change. Feminists who have resisted essentialist ideas have done so in large part because of their belief that gender essentialism is inherently antithetical to gender progress. If one of the primary goals of feminism is to break away from gender binaries and limiting stereotypes concerning women's proper place in the world, then essentialist ideas seem emphatically counterproductive. Linking women to their traditional roles as the caregivers of children and arguing that there is a separate "women's culture" centered on childrearing and homemaking might restore much needed value to these activities, but it also risks suggesting that women are suited by nature to be domestic caregivers. Critics also raise the question of who the "woman" at the heart of essentialist rhetoric is. A significant amount of cultural feminist discourse has been written by and centered on white, middle-class, heterosexual, cisgender women and their experiences, infusing this supposedly universal category with definite racist, classist, heterosexist, and cissexist dimensions.[11]

When women have successfully deployed essentialist ideas in the service of activist causes, typically women who possessed exactly these types of privilege have been able to do so effectively. From rhetoric about motherhood in the late nineteenth-century suffrage movement to organizations such as Women Strike for Peace and Mothers Against Drunk Driving in the twentieth, white, middle-class female activists have insisted that their roles as mothers and their innately more nurturing natures authorized them to agitate for social change. Despite this approach's effectiveness for these specific, privileged groups of women, critics nonetheless contend that gender essentialism remains a limiting, limited way for women to participate in activism, since such approaches are typically bound up in these forms of privilege and tie even privileged women's authority to the possession of a narrow range of ostensibly feminine emotions and characteristics.[12]

In their fiction, antislavery female authors demonstrated no hesitation about drawing on arguments about feminine difference to advocate for female involvement in abolitionism. While they did not perceive any troubling aspects to basing their claims for female activism in feminine difference, authors nonetheless constructed a problematic version of difference feminism in their literary works. These writers focused their conceptions of womanhood on white, middle-class women and did not question definitions of "woman" and "femininity" that closely tied these concepts to domesticity and emotionality. Although their arguments possessed significant rhetorical and persuasive power, authors failed to challenge dominant cultural ideas that insisted women were innately more emotional than rational—more intuitive than intellectual—more likely to act through feeling than through reason. The questions these authors raised—about who women were, what capabilities they possessed, and what roles they ought to play in American politics and activism—continue to rage on centuries after they took those first, daring steps and put pen to paper, hoping to build a better world with their words.

Notes

Introduction

1. Theodore Parker, "A Sermon on the Public Function of Woman," in *Woman's Rights Tracts*, ed. Lucy Stone (Rochester, N.Y., Steam Press of Curtis Butts, 1854), 22.

2. My study considers the literary work of a few African American female fiction writers, but those numbers are relatively small, given the numerous structural barriers that made it difficult for African American women to publish their fiction in white-edited periodicals and white-run presses during the antebellum era.

3. I refer to activists who opposed slavery and wished to see the institution ended as both "antislavery" and "abolitionist." Though these words often could and did have different meanings for antebellum activists—with antislavery advocates typically endorsing more gradual emancipation and abolitionists seeking the immediate end to slavery—the distinctions between these two camps and terms was not always uniform or consistent. Therefore, unless an author herself disavowed the term "abolitionist," I will use both terms for writers.

4. In her ground-breaking monograph *Women and the Work of Benevolence: Morality, Politics, and Class in the Nineteenth-Century United States* (New Haven: Yale Univ. Press, 1990), Lori Ginzberg makes the case for a shift from reform movements centered on gender to those centered on class.

5. See Thomas Gossett, Uncle Tom's Cabin *and American Culture* (Dallas: Southern Methodist Univ. Press, 1985); and Carolyn L. Karcher, *The First Woman in the Republic: A Cultural Biography of Lydia Maria Child* (Durham, N.C.: Duke Univ. Press, 1994).

6. Eve Allegra Raimon, *The 'Tragic Mulatta' Revisited: Race and Nationalism in Nineteenth Century Antislavery Fiction* (New Brunswick, N.J.: Rutgers Univ. Press, 2004); Karen Sánchez-Eppler, *Touching Liberty: Abolition, Feminism, and the Politics of the Body* (Berkeley: Univ. of California Press, 1993); Deborah C. DeRosa, *Domestic Abolitionism and Juvenile Literature* (Albany: State Univ. of New York Press, 2003); and Sarah N. Roth, *Gender and Race in Antebellum Popular Culture* (New York: Cambridge Univ. Press, 2014).

7. Ann Douglas, *The Feminization of American Culture* (New York: Knopf, 1977); Nina Baym, *Woman's Fiction: A Guide to Novels by and about Women in America, 1820-1870* (Ithaca, N.Y.: Cornell Univ. Press, 1978); and Cathy N. Davidson, *Revolution and the Word: The Rise of the Novel in America* (New York: Oxford Univ. Press, 1986).

8. Susan Coultrap-McQuin, *Doing Literary Business: American Women Writers in the Nineteenth Century* (Chapel Hill: Univ. of North Carolina Press, 1990); and Mary Kelley, *Private Woman, Public Stage: Literary Domesticity in Nineteenth-Century America* (New York: Oxford Univ. Press, 1984).

9. Martha Cutter, *Unruly Tongue: Identity and Voice in American Women's Writing, 1850-1930* (Jackson: Univ. Press of Mississippi, 1999); Melissa Homestead, *American Women Authors and Literary Property, 1822-1869* (Cambridge: Cambridge Univ. Press, 2005); Lora Romero, *Home Fronts: Domesticity and Its Critics in the Antebellum United States* (Durham, N.C.: Duke Univ. Press, 1997); and Elizabeth Young, *Disarming the Nation: Women's Writing and the American Civil War* (Chicago: Univ. of Chicago Press, 1999).

10. Christine Stansell, *City of Women: Sex and Class in New York, 1789-1860* (New York: Knopf, 1986); Daniel S. Wright, *"The First Causes of Our Sex": The Female Moral Reform Movement in the Antebellum Northeast, 1834-1848* (New York: Routledge, 2006); and Peggy Pascoe, *Relations of Rescue: The Search for Female Moral Authority in the American West, 1874-1939* (New York: Oxford Univ. Press, 1991). For additional scholarship concerning the perilous aspects of white, middle-class women drawing on rhetoric of feminine distinctiveness, see Nancy F. Cott, *The Grounding of Modern Feminism* (New Haven: Yale Univ. Press, 1987); Alice Echols, *Daring to Be Bad: Radical Feminism in America, 1967-1975* (Minneapolis: Univ. of Minnesota Press, 1989); and Leigh Ann Wheeler, *Against Obscenity: Reform and the Politics of Womanhood in America, 1873-1935* (Baltimore: Johns Hopkins Univ. Press, 2004).

11. Barbara Welter, "The Cult of True Womanhood, 1820-1860," *American Quarterly* 18 (Summer 1966): 151-74; Nancy F. Cott, *The Bonds of Womanhood: "Woman's Sphere" in New England, 1780-1835* (New Haven: Yale Univ. Press, 1977); and Mary Ryan, *The Empire of the Mother: American Writing about Domesticity, 1830 to 1860* (New York: Haworth, 1982).

12. Cathy Davidson and Jessamyn Hatcher, eds., *No More Separate Spheres! A Next Wave American Studies Reader* (Durham: Duke Univ. Press, 2002); Monika M. Elbert, ed., *Separate Spheres No More: Gender Convergence in American Literature, 1830-1930* (Tuscaloosa: Univ. of Alabama, 2000); Alison Piepmeier, *Out in Public: Configurations of Women's Bodies in Nineteenth-Century America* (Chapel Hill: Univ. of North Carolina, 2004); and Joan W. Scott and Debra Keates, eds., *Going Public: Feminism and the Shifting Boundaries of the Private Sphere* (Urbana: Univ. of Illinois Press, 2004).

13. Catherine Allgor, *Parlor Politics: In Which the Ladies of Washington Help Build a City and a Government* (Charlottesville: Univ. Press of Virginia, 2000); Susan Branson, *These Fiery, Frenchified Dames: Women and Political Culture in Early National Philadelphia* (Philadelphia: Univ. of Pennsylvania Press, 2001); Catherine Kelly, *In the New England Fashion: Reshaping Women's Lives in the Nineteenth Century* (Ithaca,

N.Y.: Cornell Univ. Press, 1999); and Cynthia Kierner, *Beyond the Household: Women's Place in the Early South, 1700-1835* (Ithaca, N.Y.: Cornell Univ. Press, 1998). See also Elizabeth Varon, *We Mean to Be Counted: White Women and Politics in Antebellum Virginia* (Chapel Hill: Univ. of North Carolina Press, 1998).

14. Debra Gold Hansen, *Strained Sisterhood: Gender and Class in the Boston Female Anti-Slavery Society* (Amherst: Univ. of Massachusetts Press, 1993); Julie Roy Jeffrey, *The Great Silent Army of Abolitionism: Ordinary Women in the Antislavery Movement* (Chapel Hill: Univ. of North Carolina, 1998); Michael D. Pierson, *Free Hearts and Free Homes: Gender and American Antislavery Politics* (Chapel Hill: Univ. of North Carolina Press, 2003); Alisse Portnoy, *Their Right to Speak: Women's Activism in the Indian and Slave Debates* (Cambridge, Mass.: Harvard Univ. Press, 2005); Beth Salerno, *Sister Societies: Women's Antislavery Organizations in Antebellum America* (DeKalb: Northern Illinois Univ. Press, 2005); Deborah Bingham Van Broekhaven, *The Devotion of These Women: Rhode Island in the Antislavery Network* (Amherst: Univ. of Massachusetts Press, 2002); and Susan Zaeske, *Signatures of Citizenship: Petitioning, Antislavery, and Women's Political Identity* (Chapel Hill: Univ. of North Carolina, 2003).

15. For more on the controversies surrounding antislavery orators Maria W. Stewart, Angelina Grimké, and Sarah Grimké and their careers, see Stephen H. Browne, *Angelina Grimké: Rhetoric, Identity, and the Radical Imagination* (East Lansing: Michigan State Univ. Press, 1999); and *Maria W. Stewart: America's First Black Woman Political Writer,* ed. Marilyn Richardson (Bloomington: Indiana Univ. Press, 1987).

16. For more on the difficulties of gathering data about readers in the antebellum era, see Donald E. Liedel, "The Antislavery Novel, 1838-1861" (PhD diss., Univ. of Michigan, 1961), 8; W. Sherman Savage, *The Controversy over the Distribution of Abolitionist Literature, 1830-1860* (1938; repr., New York: Negro Universities Press, 1968); and Ronald Zboray, *A Fictive People: Antebellum Economic Development and the American Reading Public* (New York: Oxford Univ. Press, 1993).

17. Jacqueline Bacon, Freedom's Journal: *The First African-American Newspaper* (Lanham, Md.: Lexington, 2007); and Elizabeth McHenry, *Forgotten Readers: Recovering the Lost History of African American Literary Societies* (Durham, N.C.: Duke Univ. Press, 2002).

18. Peter P. Hinks, *To Awaken My Afflicted Brethren: David Walker and the Problem of Antebellum Slave Resistance* (University Park: Pennsylvania State Univ. Press, 1997); and Stephanie M. H. Camp, *Closer to Freedom: Enslaved Women and Everyday Resistance in the Plantation South* (Chapel Hill: Univ. of North Carolina Press, 2004).

19. See Davidson, *Revolution and the Word,* 185-232.

20. Providing an estimate of how many antislavery stories were published per year from 1821 to 1861 is difficult, as these rates varied considerably depending on the specific periodical and its circumstances during any given year or decade. For example, when the *Liberator* included both a Ladies' and a Juvenile Department during the 1830s, the newspaper printed an average of three or four stories per week. In contrast, after it eliminated these departments, fiction might appear in the periodical's pages on a monthly rather than a weekly basis.

1. "Her Heart Was Touched with the Wrongs of the Injured Ones"

1. E M C [Elizabeth Margaret Chandler], "Tears of Woman: An Allegory," *Genius of Universal Emancipation*, Nov. 1832, 14-15. (Archives of *Genius of Universal Emancipation* and the *Liberator*, *Child's Friend*, *National Era*, *Independent*, *National Anti-Slavery Standard* and the *North American Review*, as well as *The Liberty Bell*, *Liberty Chimes*, and the *Liberty Cap* gift book annuals are available online at ProQuest Historical Newspapers database [http://www.proquest.com/products-services/pq-hist-news.html]). "Tears of Woman" was, notably, reprinted twice in the *Genius*, once in the *Liberator*, and in all posthumous editions of Chandler's literary work.

2. See *The Power of Her Sympathy: The Autobiography and Journal of Catharine Maria Sedgwick*, ed. Mary C. Kelley (Boston: Massachusetts Historical Society, 2005); Amanda Emerson, "History, Memory, and the Echoes of Equivalence in Catharine Maria Sedgwick's *Hope Leslie*," *Legacy* 24, no. 1 (2007): 24-46; and Quentin Miller, "'A Tyrannical Democratic Force': The Symbolic and Cultural Function of Clothing Symbolism in Catharine Maria Sedgwick's *Hope Leslie*," *Legacy* 19, no. 2 (2002): 121-36. For examinations of Sedgwick's antislavery fiction, see Lucinda L. Damon-Bach, "To 'Act' and 'Transact': *Redwood*'s Revisionary Heroines," and Karen Woods Weierman, "'A Slave Story I Began and Abandoned': Sedgwick's Antislavery Manuscript," both in *Catharine Maria Sedgwick: Critical Perspectives*, ed. Lucinda L. Damon-Bach and Victoria Clements (Boston: Northeastern Univ. Press, 2003), 56-74, 122-40.

3. Scholarship on Chandler's literary work has focused on her poetry and literature intended for children. See Janet Sinclair Gray's *Race and Time: American Women's Poetics from Antislavery to Racial Minority* (Iowa City: Univ. of Iowa Press, 2004); and Deborah C. DeRosa's edited collection *Into the Mouths of Babes: An Anthology of Children's Abolitionist Literature* (Westport, Conn.: Praeger, 2005). Considerations of Chandler's abolitionism have focused on the free produce movement and her construction of an abolitionist community in Michigan. See Carol Faulkner, "The Root of the Evil: Free Produce and Radical Antislavery, 1820-1860," *Journal of the Early Republic* 27 (Fall 2007): 377-405; and John W. Quist, "'The Great Majority of Our Subscribers are Farmers': The Michigan Abolitionist Constituency of the 1840s," *Journal of the Early Republic* 14 (Autumn 1994): 325-58.

4. See Christopher Cameron, *To Plead Our Own Cause: African Americans in Massachusetts and the Making of the Antislavery Movement* (Kent, Ohio: Kent State Univ. Press, 2014); Bruce Dorsey, *Reforming Men and Women: Gender in the Antebellum City* (Ithaca, N.Y.: Cornell Univ. Press, 2002); and Alisse Portnoy, *Their Right to Speak: Women's Activism in the Indian and Slave Debates* (Cambridge, Mass: Harvard Univ. Press, 2005).

5. See Jacqueline Bacon, Freedom's Journal: *The First African-American Newspaper* (Lanham, Md.: Lexington, 2007); and Sarah N. Roth, *Gender and Race in Antebellum Popular Culture* (New York: Cambridge Univ. Press, 2014).

6. Beginning at sixteen, Chandler began to publish her antislavery poetry in several Philadelphia-based periodicals, including the *Atlantic Souvenir* and the *Pearl*. For more information on Chandler's early literary career, see Marcia J. Heringa Mason, introduction to *Remember the Distance That Divides Us: The Family Letters of*

Philadelphia Quaker Abolitionist and Michigan Pioneer, Elizabeth Margaret Chandler, ed. Marcia J. Heringa Mason (East Lansing: Michigan State Univ. Press, 2004), xv-lviii.

7. Benjamin Lundy, "Proposals, for Publishing in MountPleasant [sic], Ohio, A Periodical Work, to Be Entitled *The Genius of Universal Emancipation,* by Benjamin Lundy," c. 1820-21, Massachusetts Historical Society.

8. For more on Lundy's antislavery ideology, see Merton Dillon, *Benjamin Lundy and the Struggle for Negro Freedom* (Urbana: Univ. of Illinois Press, 1966).

9. Although circulation figures for early periodicals are difficult to find, Deborah C. DeRosa estimates that by 1827, the *Genius* had a circulation of approximately a thousand subscribers. This figure likely does not reflect the periodical's readership, as newspapers, a scarce, expensive item, would have been shared among numerous readers. See DeRosa, *Domestic Abolitionism and Juvenile Literature, 1830-1865* (Albany: State Univ. of New York Press, 2003), 20.

10. Eliza Lee Follen to Catharine Maria Sedgwick, Apr. 2, 1834, folder 2, box 4, Catharine Maria Sedgwick Papers, 1798-1908, III, Massachusetts Historical Society.

11. Catharine Maria Sedgwick to Eliza Lee Follen, Apr. 15, 1834, folder 2, box 8, Catharine Maria Sedgwick Papers, 1798-1908, I, Massachusetts Historical Society.

12. Louisa Minot to Catharine Maria Sedgwick, July 16, 1824, folder 3, box 3, Catharine Maria Sedgwick Papers, 1798-1908, III. Massachusetts Historical Society.

13. Catharine Maria Sedgwick, "Untitled: Antislavery Novel," 10, reel 6, folder 8, box 6, Catharine Maria Sedgwick Papers, 1798-1908 Massachusetts Historical Society.

14. Benjamin Lundy, *The Poetical Works of Elizabeth Margaret Chandler: With a Memoir of Her Life and Character by Benjamin Lundy.* Philadelphia: Published by T. E. Chapman. New York: Baker, Crane & Day. 1845: 25.

15. See Nina Baym, *Novels, Readers, and Reviewers: Responses to Fiction in Antebellum America* (Ithaca, N.Y.: Cornell Univ. Press, 1984); and Cathy N. Davidson, *Reading in America: Literature and Social History* (Baltimore: Johns Hopkins Univ. Press, 1989).

16. See Nina Baym, *A Guide to Novels by and about Women in America, 1820-1870* (Ithaca, N.Y.: Cornell Univ. Press, 1978); Cathy N. Davidson, *Revolution and the Word: The Rise of the Novel in America* (New York: Oxford Univ. Press, 1986); and Kelley, *Private Woman, Public Stage: Literary Domesticity in Nineteenth-Century America.*

17. [Benjamin Lundy], "Temple of Muses and Ladies' Literary Cabinet," *Genius of Universal Emancipation,* July 1821, 4.

18. [Elizabeth Margaret Chandler], "To the Ladies of Baltimore," *Genius of Universal Emancipation,* Feb. 5, 1830, 172.

19. [Lundy], "Temple of Muses and Ladies' Literary Cabinet," 4.

20. [Benjamin Lundy], "Sorrows of Flora," *Genius of Universal Emancipation,* May 1822, 179.

21. Benjamin Lundy, preface to *The Poetical Works of Elizabeth Margaret Chandler: With a Memoir of Her Life and Character by Benjamin Lundy* (Philadelphia: Published by T. E. Chapman; New York: Baker, Crane & Day, 1845), 12.

22. See Lori Merish, *Sentimental Materialism: Gender, Commodity Culture, and Nineteenth-Century American Literature* (Durham, N.C.: Duke Univ. Press, 2000);

Laura Mielke, *Moving Encounters: Sympathy and the Indian Question in Antebellum Literature* (Amherst: Univ. of Massachusetts Press, 2008); and Stephanie A. Shields, *Speaking from the Heart: Gender and the Social Meaning of Emotion* (New York: Cambridge Univ. Press, 2002).

23. See Glenna Matthews, *The Rise of the Public Woman: Woman's Power and Woman's Place in the United States, 1630-1970* (New York: Oxford Univ. Press, 1992); Mary Ryan, *Women in Public: Between Banners and Ballots, 1825-1880* (Baltimore: Johns Hopkins Univ. Press, 1990); and Susan Zaeske, *Signatures of Citizenship: Petitioning, Antislavery, and Women's Political Identity* (Chapel Hill: Univ. of North Carolina, 2003).

24. See Barbara Bardes and Suzanne Gossett, *Declarations of Independence: Women and Political Power in Nineteenth-Century American Fiction* (New Brunswick, N.J.: Rutgers Univ. Press, 1990); and Caroline Levander, *Voices of the Nation: Women and Public Speech in Nineteenth-Century American Literature and Culture* (New York: Cambridge Univ. Press, 1998).

25. Lundy, preface to Chandler, *Poetical Works*, 25.

26. [Elizabeth Margaret Chandler], "Opinions," *Genius of Universal Emancipation*, Dec. 11, 1829, 108.

27. See Linda K. Kerber, "Separate Spheres, Female Worlds, Woman's Place: The Rhetoric of Women's History," *Journal of American History* 75 (June 1988): 9-39; Carol Lasser, "Beyond Separate Spheres: The Power of Public Opinion," *Journal of the Early Republic* 21 (Spring 2001): 115-23; and Eyal Rabinovitch, "Gender and the Public Sphere: Alternative Forms of Integration in Nineteenth-Century America," *Sociological Theory* 19 (Nov. 2001): 344-70.

28. See John Lofton, *Denmark Vesey's Revolt: The Slave Plot That Lit a Fuse to Fort Sumter* (Kent, Ohio: Kent State Univ. Press, 2013); David Robertson, *Denmark Vesey: The Buried History of America's Largest Slave Rebellion and The Man Who Led It* (New York: Knopf, 1999); Edward A. Pearson, ed., *Designs against Charleston: The Trial Record of the Denmark Vesey Slave Conspiracy of 1822* (Chapel Hill: Univ. of North Carolina Press, 1999); David Walker, *Appeal to the Coloured Citizens of the World*, ed. Peter P. Hinks (University Park: Pennsylvania State Univ. Press, 2006); and Peter P. Hinks, *To Awaken My Afflicted Brethren: David Walker and the Problem of Antebellum Slave Resistance* (University Park: Pennsylvania State Univ. Press, 1997).

29. Anne M. Boylan, *The Origins of Women's Activism: New York and Boston, 1790-1840* (Chapel Hill: Univ. of North Carolina Press, 2002); Barbara Epstein, *The Politics of Domesticity: Women, Evangelism, and Temperance in Nineteenth-Century America* (Middletown, Conn.: Wesleyan Univ. Press, 1981); and Lori Ginzberg, *Women and the Work of Benevolence: Morality, Politics, and Class in the Nineteenth-Century United States* (New Haven: Yale Univ. Press, 1990).

30. See Faulkner, "Root of the Evil"; and Ruth Ketring Nuermberger, *The Free Produce Movement: A Quaker Protest against Slavery* (New York: AMS Press, 1970).

31. See Margaret Hope Bacon, *Valiant Friend: The Life of Lucretia Mott* (New York: Walker, 1970); and Richard Newman, *Freedom's Prophet: Bishop Richard Allen, the AME Church, and the Black Founding Fathers* (New York: New York Univ. Press, 2008).

32. See Julie L. Holcomb, *Moral Commerce: Quakers and the Transatlantic Boycott of the Slave Labor Economy* (Ithaca, N.Y.: Cornell Univ. Press, 2016); and Charlotte Sussman, *Consuming Anxieties: Consumer Protest, Gender, and British Slavery, 1713-1833* (Palo Alto, Calif.: Stanford Univ. Press, 2000).

33. Elizabeth Heyrick, *Immediate not gradual abolition; or, An inquiry into the shortest, safest, and most effectual means of getting rid of West Indian slavery* (London: Hatchard & Sons, 1824).

34. Amelia Opie, *The Warrior's Return; The Black Man's Lament*, ed. Donald H. Reiman (New York: Garland, 1978); and *The History of Mary Prince, A West Indian Slave, Related by Herself*, ed. Moira Ferguson (London: Pandora, 1987).

35. Ela [Elizabeth Margaret Chandler], "If and But," *Genius of Universal Emancipation*, May 1831, 13.

36. A Lady, "On the Use of Free Produce," *Genius of Universal Emancipation*, Jan. 1832, 131. Gertrude [Elizabeth Margaret Chandler], "The Use of Free Produce," *Genius of Universal Emancipation*, Jan. 1831, 155.

37. Agnes [Elizabeth Margaret Chandler]. "Tea-Table Talk." *Genius of Universal Emancipation*, Nov. 1832, 15.

38. See T. H. Breen, *The Marketplace of Revolution: How Consumer Politics Shaped American Independence* (New York: Oxford Univ. Press, 2005).

39. See Richard Bushman, *The Refinement of America: Persons, Homes, Cities* (New York: Knopf, 1992); and Janet Floyd and Inga Bryden, eds. *Domestic Space: Reading the Nineteenth-Century Interior* (New York: Manchester Univ. Press, 1999).

40. Chandler, preface to Lundy, *Poetical Works*, 19.

41. Agnes [Elizabeth Margaret Chandler], "Letters on Slavery—No. I to Isabel," *Genius of Universal Emancipation*, Oct. 30. 1829, 60; Agnes, "Letters on Slavery—No. VI to Isabel," *Genius of Universal Emancipation*, Dec. 18, 1829, 116.

42. Agnes, "Letters on Slavery—No. VI to Isabel," 116.

43. Although Mary refers to "husbands" and "wives" among the enslaved, part of her sympathy for enslaved women stems from the fact that, as nonpersons under the law, they had no access to legally recognized marriage, which as a free white woman, she enjoyed. Margaret [Elizabeth Margaret Chandler], "The Harmans," *Genius of Universal Emancipation*, Nov. 13, 1829, 77.

44. E M C, "Tears of Woman," 14.

45. See Henrice Althink, *Representations of Slave Women in Discourses of Slavery and Abolition, 1780-1838* (New York: Routledge, 2007); and Deborah Gray White, *Ar'n't I a Woman? Female Slaves in the Plantation South* (New York: Norton, 1999).

46. See Eve Allegra Raimon, *The "Tragic Mulatta" Revisited: Race and Nationalism in Nineteenth Century Antislavery Fiction* (New Brunswick, N.J.: Rutgers Univ. Press, 2004); and Karen Sánchez-Eppler, *Touching Liberty: Abolition, Feminism, and the Politics of the Body* (Berkeley: Univ. of California Press, 1993).

47. See Nancy Isenberg, *Sex and Citizenship in Antebellum America* (Chapel Hill: Univ. of North Carolina Press, 1998); and Shirley Samuels, ed., *The Culture of Sentiment: Race, Gender, and Sentimentality in Nineteenth-Century America* (New York: Oxford Univ. Press, 1992).

48. The Sedgwicks' recollections of Freeman as a kind of second mother to them are, of course, not unproblematic, since Freeman was not a family member but was employed by the Sedgwicks as a domestic worker. We notably do not have recollections from Freeman herself and, as such, do not know how she thought about her relationship to her employers. Sedgwick's insistence that Freeman was a beloved member of the family also uneasily echoes proslavery rhetoric, which often framed enslaved women as cherished, pseudo-maternal figures to their white charges.

49. Catharine Maria Sedgwick, *Redwood; A Tale* (New York: Garrett, 1969), 56.

50. See Sally E. Hadden, "Colonial and Revolutionary Era Slave Patrols in Virginia," *Lethal Imagination: Violence and Brutality in American History,* ed. Michael A. Bellesides (New York: New York Univ. Press, 1999), 69-86.

51. For more on scholars' efforts to accurately date this unfinished novel, see Weierman, "A Slave Story I Began and Abandoned."

52. See Henry Mayer, *All on Fire: William Lloyd Garrison and the Abolition of Slavery* (New York: St. Martin's, 1998); and James Brewer Stewart, *William Lloyd Garrison at Two Hundred: History, Legacy, and Memory* (New Haven: Yale Univ. Press, 2008).

53. See Stephen Oates, *The Fires of Jubilee: Nat Turner's Fierce Rebellion* (New York: Harper & Row, 1975).

54. Lydia Maria Child, *Hobomok and Other Writings on Indians,* ed. Carolyn Karcher (New Brunswick, N.J.: Rutgers Univ. Press, 1986); Lydia Maria Child, *The Frugal Housewife: Dedicated to Those Who Are Not Ashamed of Economy* (Boston: Carter & Hendee, 1829); and Lydia Maria Child, *The Mother's Book* (Boston: Carter & Hendee, 1831).

55. Sedgwick, "Untitled: Antislavery Novel," 10.

56. Catharine Maria Sedgwick, "Untitled: Essay on Mumbet," 20, reel 6, microfilm, Catharine Maria Sedgwick Papers, 1798-1908, I. A version of this essay was subsequently published in *Bentley's Miscellany* in 1853: "Slavery in New England," *Bentley's Miscellany* 34 (1853): 417-18.

57. Ibid., 29, 13.

58. Ibid., 4.

59. See Stephanie M. H. Camp, *Closer to Freedom: Enslaved Women and Everyday Resistance in the Plantation South* (Chapel Hill: Univ. of North Carolina Press, 2004); and Walter Johnson, *Soul by Soul: Life Inside the Antebellum Slave Market* (Cambridge, Mass.: Harvard Univ. Press, 2001).

60. See Darlene Clark Hine and Kathleen Thompson, *A Shining Thread of Hope: The History of Black Women in America* (New York: Broadway, 1998), 65-102.

61. Sedgwick, "Untitled: Antislavery Novel," 19.

62. Ibid., 29.

63. For more on the range of religious, political, and (pseudo-)scientific arguments marshaled to defend slavery in the decades before the Civil War, see Paul Finkelman, ed., *Defending Slavery: Proslavery Thought in the Old South* (New York: Bedford/St. Martin's, 2003).

64. Sedgwick, "Untitled Antislavery Novel," 29.

2. "An Influence Comparatively Silent, but Deep, and Strong, and Irresistible"

1. See Ellen Carol DuBois, *Feminism and Suffrage: The Emergence of an Independent Women's Movement in America, 1848-1869* (Ithaca, N.Y.: Cornell Univ. Press, 1978); Blanche Glassman Hersh, *The Slavery of Sex: Feminist-Abolitionists in America* (Urbana: Univ. of Illinois Press, 1978); and Gerda Lerner, *The Grimké Sisters from South Carolina: Rebels against Slavery* (Boston: Houghton Mifflin, 1967).

2. Julie Roy Jeffrey, *The Great Silent Army of Abolitionism: Ordinary Women in the Antislavery Movement* (Chapel Hill: Univ. of North Carolina, 1998).

3. See Angelina Grimké, *Appeal to the Christian Women of the South* (New York: American Anti-Slavery Society, 1836); Sarah Grimké, *Letters on the Equality of the Sexes and the Condition of Woman, Addressed to Mary E. Parker* (Boston: I. Knapp, 1838); Lucretia Mott, *Discourse on Woman* (Philadelphia: W. Kildare, 1849); and Elizabeth Cady Stanton, "Seneca Falls Declaration of Sentiments (1848)," in *American Protest Literature,* ed. Zoe Trodd (Cambridge, Mass.: Harvard Univ. Press, 2006), 27-31.

4. Susan Zaeske, *Signatures of Citizenship: Petitioning, Antislavery, and Women's Political Identity* (Chapel Hill: Univ. of North Carolina Press, 2003).

5. Alisse Portnoy, *Their Right to Speak: Women's Activism in the Indian and Slave Debates* (Cambridge, Mass: Harvard Univ. Press, 2005).

6. See Beth Salerno, *Sister Societies: Women's Antislavery Organizations in Antebellum America.* (DeKalb: Northern Illinois Univ. Press, 2005); Clare Taylor, *Women of the Anti-Slavery Movement: The Weston Sisters* (New York: St. Martin's, 1995); Deborah Bingham Van Broekhaven, *The Devotion of These Women: Rhode Island in the Antislavery Network* (Amherst: Univ. of Massachusetts Press, 2002).

7. See Ronald Zboray, *A Fictive People: Antebellum Economic Development and the American Reading Public* (New York: Oxford Univ. Press, 1993).

8. Anne Warren Weston, Letter to the Concord Female Anti-Slavery Society, July 22, 1835, Boston Female Anti-Slavery Society Letterbook, Apr. 9, 1834-Jan. 7, 1838, Massachusetts Historical Society.

9. See Peter Kolchin, *American Slavery, 1619-1877* (New York: Hill & Wang, 1994).

10. See Stephen Oates, *The Fires of Jubilee: Nat Turner's Fierce Rebellion* (New York: Harper & Row, 1975).

11. See Paul Simon, *Freedom's Champion: Elijah Lovejoy* (Carbondale: Southern Illinois Univ. Press, 1994).

12. Henry H. Simms, "A Critical Analysis of Abolition Literature, 1830-1840," *Journal of Southern History* 6 (Aug. 1940): 368-82. And see Records of the Pine Street Anti-Slavery Society, Sep.18, 1834, Charles Cushing Barry Papers, Massachusetts Historical Society; "New Books, For Sale by Isaac Knapp, at the A.S. Office, 25, Cornhill," advertisement, Boston, Aug. 19, 1837, and William Lloyd Garrison Jr. to Maria Weston Chapman, undated, Garrison Family Papers, both in Sophia Smith Collection, Smith College, Northampton, Mass.; and L. M. Child, "Communications: Archy Moore," *Liberator,* Mar. 18, 1837, 47.

13. See Julie Winch, *A Gentleman of Color: The Life of James Forten* (New York: Oxford Univ. Press, 2002); and Augusta Rohrbach, *Truth Stranger Than Fiction: Race, Realism, and the U.S. Literary Marketplace* (New York: Palgrave, 2002), 1-28.

14. William Lloyd Garrison, "Untitled," *Liberator*, Jan. 7, 1832, 2.

15. Elizabeth McHenry, *Forgotten Readers: Recovering the Lost History of African American Literary Societies* (Durham, N.C.: Duke Univ. Press, 2002), 64.

16. Deborah C. DeRosa, *Domestic Abolitionism and Juvenile Literature* (Albany: State Univ. of New York Press, 2003).

17. For popular retellings of these stories with which these authors likely would have been familiar, and that they were likely directly evoking in their literary work, see John Marston, *The Wonder of Women; or, The Tragedy of Sophonisba* (1606; repr., New York: Garland, 1979); and Gioacchino Rossini, *Zelmira: A Serious Opera in Two Acts* (London: H. N. Millar, 1822).

18. See Frances Smith Foster, *Written by Herself: Literary Production by African American Women, 1746-1892* (Bloomington: Indiana Univ. Press, 1993); and Carla L. Peterson, *Doers of the Word: African-American Women Speakers and Writers of the North, 1830-1880* (New York: Oxford Univ. Press, 1995).

19. Michelle N. Garfield, "Literary Societies: The Work of Self-Improvement and Racial Uplift," in *Black Women's Intellectual Traditions: Speaking Their Minds*, ed. Kristin Waters and Carol B. Conaway (Burlington: Univ. of Vermont Press, 2007), 113-28; McHenry, *Forgotten Readers*; and Julie Winch, "You Have Talents, Only Cultivate Them," in *The Abolitionist Sisterhood: Women's Political Culture in Antebellum America*, ed. John C. Van Horne and Jean Fagan Yellin (Ithaca, N.Y.: Cornell Univ. Press, 1994), 101-18.

20. During the 1830s, three literary societies—the Female Literary Association, founded in 1831; the Minerva Literary Association, founded in 1834; and the Edgeworth Literary Association, founded in 1837—were established in Philadelphia, and one, the Afric-American Female Intelligence Society (established in 1832), was formed in Boston.

21. "Address to the Female Literary Association of Philadelphia, on Their First Anniversary: By a Member," *Liberator*, Oct. 13, 1832, 162.

22. William Lloyd Garrison to Sarah Mapps Douglass, Mar. 5, 1832. Ms. A.1.1, vol. 1., no. 12, Garrison Papers, Boston Public Library, Boston.

23. Zillah [Sarah Mapps Douglass], "Female Literary Associations," *Liberator*, June 30, 1832, 103. This quotation comes from Garrison's introduction to Douglass's piece.

24. Garrison to Douglass, Garrison Papers.

25. See Harriet Hyman Alonso, *Growing Up Abolitionist: The Story of the Garrison Children* (Amherst: Univ. of Massachusetts Press, 2002); David W. Blight, "William Lloyd Garrison at Two Hundred: His Radicalism and His Legacy for Our Time," in *William Lloyd Garrison at Two Hundred: History, Legacy, and Memory*, ed. James Brewer Stewart (New Haven: Yale Univ. Press, 2008), 1-12; Henry Mayer, *All on Fire: William Lloyd Garrison and the Abolition of Slavery* (New York: St. Martin's, 1998).

26. For examples of this kind of text marking, see Sophonisba [Sarah Mapps Douglass], "Ella: A Sketch." *Liberator,* Aug. 4, 1832, 123; and "Letter," *Liberator,* Mar. 24, 1832, 46-47.

27. "Mental Feasts," *Liberator,* July 21, 1832, 114.

28. A.F.M., "An Address to the Daughters of New England," *Liberator,* Mar. 3, 1832, 34.

29. Zelmire, "Unnatural Distinction," *Liberator,* July 28, 1832, 118.

30. Lady in Worcester County, "Archy Moore," *Liberator,* Mar. 31, 1837, 55.

31. "A Dialogue on Slavery" *Liberator,* July 1832, 82.

32. "Philadelphia," "What Have Ladies to Do with the Subject of Anti-Slavery?" *Liberator,* Mar. 29, 1834, 50.

33. Paulina, "Think of the Slave," *Liberator,* Sept. 1832, 150.

34. Zelmire, "An Evening at Home, No. 1," *Liberator,* Sept. 24, 1831, 155.

35. Sarah Robbins, *Managing Literacy, Mothering America: Women's Narratives on Reading and Writing in the Nineteenth Century* (Pittsburgh: Univ. of Pittsburgh Press, 2006).

36. See Molly Ladd-Taylor and Lauri Umansky's edited collection: *"Bad" Mothers: The Politics of Blame in Twentieth-Century America* (New York: New York Univ. Press, 1998).

37. "Dialogue on Slavery," 82.

38. Ibid.

39. See Stuart Blumin, *The Emergence of the Middle Class: Social Experience in the American City, 1760-1900* (New York: Cambridge Univ. Press, 1989).

40. Zillah [Sarah Mapps Douglass], "A Mother's Love," *Liberator,* July 28, 1832, 118.

41. Ibid.

42. Ibid.

43. Ibid.

44. Y.N., "Family Colloquy," *Liberator,* Aug. 27, 1831, 139.

45. Aunt Margery, "Aunt Margery's Evenings with the Young Folks, Fifth Evening," *Liberator,* Feb. 23, 1833, 30.

46. E M C [Elizabeth Margaret Chandler], "Edward and Mary," *Liberator,* May 21, 1831, 82.

47. H F G [Hannah F. Gould], "The Prisoners Set Free," *Juvenile Miscellany,* May-June 1831, 207. By "Clarkson," Mrs. Elsworth is here alluding to the British abolitionist Thomas Clarkson (1760-1846), one of the founders of the Committee for the Abolition of the Slave Trade, and a noted antislavery lobbyist and speaker.

48. Zillah [Sarah Mapps Douglass], "A Dialogue between a Mother and Her Children," *Liberator,* Sept. 1 1832, 138.

49. Margaret Hope Bacon, *But One Race: The Life of Robert Purvis* (Albany: State Univ. of New York Press, 2007).

50. See *Maria W. Stewart, America's First Black Woman Political Writer: Essays and Speeches,* ed. Marilyn Richardson (Bloomington: Indiana Univ. Press, 1987).

51. See Bera, "Dialogue—No. I," *Liberator,* Aug. 25, 1832; Chandler, "Edward and Mary"; "Slavery," *Liberator,* May 12, 1832, 75; and "Dialogue on Slavery," 82.

52. "Interesting Anecdote," *Philanthropist,* Jan. 8, 1836, 3.

53. Y.N., "Family Colloquy," 139.

54. Aunt Margery, "Aunt Margery's Evening with the Young Folks. First Evening," *Liberator* Apr. 21, 1832, 62.

55. See Sarah N. Roth, "The Mind of a Child: Images of African Americans in Early Juvenile Fiction," *Journal of the Early Republic* 25 (Spring 2005): 79-109.

56. Y.N., "Family Colloquy," 139.

57. "Interesting Anecdote," 3.

58. E. Anthony Rotundo provides a good discussion of nineteenth-century ideals of masculinity in *American Manhood: Transformations in Masculinity from the Revolution to the Modern Era* (New York: Basic Books, 1993).

59. For additional examples of female tears being a potent antislavery force, see chapter 1.

60. "Interesting Anecdote," 3.

61. Zelmire, "An Evening at Home, No. 2," *Liberator,* Oct. 15, 1831, 167.

62. U.I.E., "The Family Circle—No. 8," *Liberator,* June 11, 1831, 94.

63. U.I.E., "The Family Circle, No. V," *Liberator,* Mar. 4, 1831, 39.

64. U.I.E., "The Family Circle, No. VII," *Liberator,* Apr. 23, 1831, 66.

65. See Cristina M. Rodríguez, "Clearing the Smoke-Filled Room: Women Jurors and the Disruption of an Old Boys' Network in Nineteenth-Century America," *Yale Law Journal* 108 (May 1999): 1805-44.

66. "The Coffle Yoke," *The Slave's Friend,* vol. 1 (New York: Published by R. G. Williams for the American Anti-Slavery Society, 1836), 19, 4.

67. N.S., "A Talk by the Fireside: No. III: What Can Children Do for the Slaves?" *Liberator,* Apr. 7, 1837, 59.

68. See Manuela Thurner, "'Better Citizens Without Ballots': American Anti-Suffrage Women and Their Rational during the Progressive Era," in *One Woman, One Vote: Rediscovering the Woman Suffrage Movement,* ed. Marjorie Julian Spruill (Troutdale, Ore.: NewSage Press, 1995), 203-20. See also Janet Saltzman Chafetz and Anthony Gary Dworkin, "In the Face of a Threat: Organized Antifeminism in Comparative Perspective," *Gender and Society* 1 (Mar. 1987): 33-60; and Susan E. Marshall, "Ladies against Women: Mobilization Dilemmas of Antifeminist Movements," *Social Problems* 32 (Apr. 1985): 348-62.

69. See Elizabeth Fox-Genovese, *Within the Plantation Household: Black and White Women of the Old South* (Chapel Hill: Univ. of North Carolina Press, 1988).

70. "Zillah" [Sarah Mapps Douglass], "For the Children Who Read the *Liberator,*" *Liberator,* Aug. 18, 1832, 131.

71. "Zillah" [Sarah Mapps Douglass], "A True Tale for Children," *Liberator,* July 7, 1832, 106.

72. "Zillah" [Sarah Mapps Douglass], "To a Friend," *Liberator,* June 30, 1832, 103.

73. See Gary B. Nash, *Forging Freedom: The Formation of Philadelphia's Black Community, 1720-1840* (Cambridge, Mass.: Harvard Univ. Press, 1988); and Julie Winch, *Philadelphia's Black Elite: Activism, Accommodation, and the Struggle for Autonomy,*

1787-1848 (Philadelphia: Temple Univ. Press, 1988).

74. Peter P. Hinks's *To Awaken My Afflicted Brethren: David Walker and the Problem of Antebellum Slave Resistance* (University Park: Pennsylvania State Univ. Press, 1997), offers a useful analysis of the legacy of Walker's ideas in American society, particularly within African American abolitionist communities. In direct contrast to many of their white colleagues, African American abolitionists frequently turned to Walker's writings in the antebellum era, finding his emphasis on racial pride and his willingness to use violence as a tool in the struggle for the emancipation valuable.

75. A Colored Female of Philadelphia, "Emigration to New Mexico," *Liberator*, Jan. 28, 1832, 14.

76. Jacqueline Bacon argues in her 2002 monograph *The Humblest May Stand Forth: Rhetoric, Empowerment, and Abolition* (Columbia: Univ. of South Carolina Press, 2002) that African American women often built deference to African American men into their antislavery rhetoric, asserting that their primary goal was to ensure that the men of their households had a truly equal voice in American public affairs and the American government.

77. McHenry, *Forgotten Readers*, 62-88.

78. Zillah [Sarah Mapps Douglass], "Untitled," *Liberator*, July 21, 1832, 115.

79. Woodby, "To Zillah," 131.

80. See Wilson Jeremiah Moses, ed., *Classical Black Nationalism from the American Revolution to Marcus Garvey* (New York: New York Univ. Press, 1996).

81. Woodby, "To Zillah," *Liberator*, Aug. 18, 1832, 131.

82. Bera, "Dialogue.—No. II," *Liberator*, Sept. 15, 1832, 146.

3. "They Did Not Relinquish Freedom without a Struggle"

1. Eliza Lee Follen, *The Child's Friend: Designed for Families and Sunday Schools*, vol. 1 of 31 (Boston: Leonard C. Bowles & William Crosby, 1844), 44. "The Courage and Truth of Jesus" was initially published in *Child's Friend*, Nov. 1, 1843, 37-45.

2. See Kristen A. Tegtmeier, "The Ladies of Lawrence Are Arming!: The Gendered Nature of Sectional Violence in Early Kansas," in *Antislavery Violence: Sectional, Racial, and Cultural Conflict in Antebellum America,* ed. John McKivigan and Stanley Harrold (Knoxville: Univ. of Tennessee Press, 1999), 215-35.

3. Stanley Harrold, *The Rise of Aggressive Abolitionism: Addresses to the Slaves* (Lexington: Univ. Press of Kentucky, 2004).

4. Hannah Geffert, with Jean Libby, "Regional Black Involvement in John Brown's Raid on Harpers Ferry," in *Prophets of Protest: Reconsidering the History of American Abolitionism*, ed. Timothy Patrick McCarthy and John Stauffer (New York: New Press, 2006), 165-82.

5. Karen Sánchez-Eppler, *Touching Liberty: Abolition, Feminism, and the Politics of the Body* (Berkeley: Univ. of California Press, 1993); and Jean Fagan Yellin, *Women*

and Sisters: The Antislavery Feminists in American Culture (New Haven: Yale Univ. Press, 1989).

6. Eve Allegra Raimon, *The "Tragic Mulatta" Revisited: Race and Nationalism in Nineteenth Century Antislavery Fiction.* (New Brunswick, N.J.: Rutgers Univ. Press, 2004)

7. Deborah C. DeRosa, ed., *Into the Mouths of Babes: An Anthology of Children's Abolitionist Literature* (Westport, Conn.: Praeger, 2005); Judith Fetterley, ed., *Provisions: A Reader from Nineteenth Century Women* (Bloomington: Indiana Univ. Press, 1985); Janet Gray, ed., *She Wields a Pen: American Women Poets of the Nineteenth Century* (Iowa City: Univ. of Iowa Press, 1997); Lisa Maria Hogeland and Mary Klages, eds., *The Aunt Lute Anthology of U.S. Women Writers* (San Francisco: Aunt Lute Books, 2004); and Clare Taylor, *Women of the Anti-Slavery Movement: The Weston Sisters* (New York: St. Martin's, 1995).

8. Raimon, *"Tragic Mulatta" Revisited,* 40.

9. For selections from Leslie's writings, see Fetterley, *Provisions;* and Hogeland and Klages, *Aunt Lute Anthology of U.S. Women Writers.*

10. See Patricia Okker, *Our Sister Editors: Sarah J. Hale and the Tradition of Nineteenth-Century Women Editors* (Athens: Univ. of Georgia Press, 1995).

11. Lydia Maria Child, "To the Readers of the *Standard,*" *National Anti-Slavery Standard,* May 20, 1841, 198.

12. William Lloyd Garrison to Elizabeth Pease, June 1, 1841, Lydia Maria Child Papers, A.1.1, vol. 3, no. 77, Boston Public Library.

13. Oliver Johnson to Maria Weston Chapman, Sept. 3, 1841, Lydia Maria Child Papers, Ms. A. 9.2, vol. 15, no. 61, Boston Public Library.

14. Carolyn L. Karcher, *The First Woman in the Republic: A Cultural Biography of Lydia Maria Child* (Durham, N.C.: Duke Univ. Press, 1994), 173–219.

15. Gamaliel Bailey, "Introductory," *National Era,* Jan. 7, 1847, 2.

16. For more on Bailey's life and work, see Stanley Harrold, *Gamaliel Bailey and the Antislavery Union* (Kent, Ohio: Kent State Univ. Press, 1986).

17. Bailey, "Introductory," 2.

18. *Annual Report Presented to the Massachusetts Anti-Slavery Society by Its Board of Managers, January 27, 1847, with an Appendix.* (Boston: Printed by Andrews & Prentiss, 1847), 30.

19. For more on Chapman's life and activism, see Taylor, *Women of the Anti-Slavery Movement.*

20. Sánchez-Eppler, *Touching Liberty,* 25.

21. Chapman was the author of numerous fictional and nonfictional tracts about slavery, including *Right and Wrong in Massachusetts* (Boston: Anti-Slavery Press, 1839) and *How Can I Help to Abolish Slavery? or, Counsels to the Newly Converted* (New York: American Anti-Slavery Society, 1855), available online at the *Antislavery Literature Project,* http://antislavery.eserver.org/tracts/chapmancounsels/index_html/.

22. "The Fair and Soiree," *Liberator,* Jan. 1, 1841, 3.

23. "The Liberty Bell." *Liberator,* Nov. 29, 1839, 191.

24. Alison Easton, "Hawthorne and the Question of Women," in *The Cambridge Companion to Nathaniel Hawthorne*, ed. Richard H. Millington (New York: Cambridge Univ. Press, 2004), 79-98.

25. "The Liberty Bell for 1848," *National Anti-Slavery Standard*, Jan. 6, 1847, 127.

26. See chapter 2 for more on children's literature in abolitionism during the 1830s.

27. Deborah C. DeRosa, *Domestic Abolitionism and Juvenile Literature* (Albany: State Univ. of New York Press, 2003).

28. For more on Follen, see DeRosa, *Into the Mouths of Babes;* Gray, *She Wields a Pen;* William Lloyd Garrison to Elizabeth Pease, July 31, 1849, William Lloyd Garrison Papers, Ms. A.1.1, vol. 4, no. 98, Boston Public Library; Catharine Maria Sedgwick Papers, Massachusetts Historical Society; and Mary E. Dewey, *Life and Letters of Catharine M. Sedgwick* (New York: Harper & Brothers, 1872), 173-74.

29. Harriet Wilson, *Our Nig; or, Sketches from the Life of a Free Black, in A Two-Story White House, North: Showing That Slavery's Shadows Fall Even There* (1859; repr., New York: Vintage, 2001).

30. See Ira W. Brown, "Cradle of Feminism: The Philadelphia Female Anti-Slavery Society, 1833-1840," *Pennsylvania Magazine of History and Biography* 102 (Apr. 1978): 143-66; Lisa Shawn Hogan, "A Time for Silence: William Lloyd Garrison and the 'Woman Question' at the 1840 World Anti-Slavery Convention," *Gender Issues* 25, no. 2 (2008): 63-79; and Martha S. Jones, *All Bound Up Together: The Woman Question in African-American Public Culture, 1830-1900* (Chapel Hill: Univ. of North Carolina Press, 2007).

31. Maria Weston Chapman, Lydia Maria Child, Eliza Lee Follen, and the female editors of and contributors to the *Liberty Bell* and the *National Anti-Slavery Standard*, for example, were staunch Garrisonians, while female contributors to the more moderate *National Era*, such as E. D. E. N. Southworth, were more inclined to be sympathetic to the AFASS.

32. Lydia Maria Child, "The Quadroons," *The Liberty Bell: By the Friends of Freedom* (Boston: Andrews & Prentiss, 1842), 120.

33. Caroline W. Healey Dall, "Annie Gray," *The Liberty Bell: By the Friends of Freedom* (Boston: Andrews & Prentiss, 1848), 205.

34. Child, "Quadroons."

35. Caroline W. Healey Dall, "Amy. A Tale," *The Liberty Bell: By the Friends of Freedom* (Boston: Andrews & Prentiss, 1849); Dall, "Annie Gray."

36. Frances H. Green, "The Slave-Wife," *Liberty Chimes* (Providence, R.I.: Ladies Anti-Slavery Society, 1845), 99.

37. See Sánchez-Eppler, *Touching Liberty;* and Yellin, *Women and Sisters*.

38. Child, "Quadroons," 137.

39. E. D. E. N. Southworth, *The Mother-In-Law*, *National Era*, Apr. 18, 1850, 16.

40. It is worth noting that many of these heroines were "tragic mulattas" and that white authors stressed the significant amount of "white blood" they possessed. Their natural modesty and delicacy might, therefore, in the eyes of their authors, come in part from their white heritage.

41. Green, "Slave Wife," 96.

42. Child, "Quadroons," 140-41.

43. For more on popular representations and retellings of the Lucretia myth (in which the virtuous Lucretia kills herself rather than live with the "shame" of her rape) in nineteenth-century American and British culture, see Ian Donaldson, *The Rapes of Lucretia: A Myth and Its Transformations* (Oxford: Clarendon, 1982). It was a common trope throughout American fiction in the eighteenth and nineteenth centuries for a woman to die after rape or to kill herself rather than face what, according to the sexual mores of these eras, was considered sexual dishonor.

44. See Audrey A. Fisch, *American Slaves in Victorian England: Abolitionist Politics in Popular Literature and Culture* (New York: Cambridge Univ. Press, 2000).

45. Green, "Slave Wife," 100, 107.

46. See Nancy F. Cott, "Passionlessness: An Interpretation of Victorian Sexual Ideology, 1790-1850," *Signs* 4 (Winter 1978): 219-36.

47. Child, "Quadroons," 119.

48. Southworth, *The Mother-In-Law, National Era,* Dec. 6, 1849, 193.

49. Southworth, *The Mother-In-Law, National Era,* Apr. 25, 1850, 65.

50. Child, "Quadroons," 132.

51. Child, "Slavery's Pleasant Homes," 155. While marriages between enslaved people were not legally recognized in the slaveowning south and were not respected by slave owners, marriage was nonetheless an important institution within enslaved communities. For more on enslaved people and marriage in the antebellum era, see Frances Smith Foster, *'Til Death or Distance Do Us Part: Love and Marriage in African America* (New York, Oxford Univ. Press, 2010).

52. Green, "Slave Wife," 103.

53. See Barry Hankins, *The Second Great Awakening and the Transcendentalists* (Westport, Conn.: Greenwood, 2004), 109-28.

54. Chapman, *Pinda,* 10.

55. Dall, "Annie Gray," 195-96, 198.

56. See Marcus Wood, *Blind Memory: Visual Representations of Slavery in England and America* (New York: Routledge, 1999).

57. Eliza Leslie, "The Traveling Tinman," *National Anti-Slavery Standard,* June 13, 1844, 8.

58. See Carol Faulkner, *Women's Radical Reconstruction: The Freedmen's Aid Movement* (Philadelphia: Univ. of Pennsylvania Press, 2004).

59. This shift was particularly noteworthy among white abolitionists; for example, well before the 1840s, many African American abolitionists had already been willing to consider fugitive slaves using force to make their escapes and prevent their recapture.

60. Lydia Maria Child, "The Black Saxons," *The Liberty Bell: By the Friends of Freedom* (Boston: Andrews & Prentiss, 1841), 31-32.

61. Karcher also notes that Child creates a clear racial distinction here between "full-blooded" African American characters (pacifist, Christian, and docile), and those who have some white heritage (fierce, independent-minded, and inclined to

use violence to secure their freedom—these qualities being directly linked to their "white blood"). This racialized dichotomy is one many other white authors of the antebellum era (including, most famously, Harriet Beecher Stowe) would draw on in their literary work. See Karcher, *First Woman in the Republic,* 333-35.

62. Child, "Slavery's Pleasant Homes," 159.

63. Karcher, *First Woman in the Republic,* 339-43.

64. Child, "Black Saxons" 43.

65. The idea of the Saxons as noble, oppressed people and the Normans as their tyrannous rulers had been popularized in the United States through bestselling novels written British author Sir Walter Scott such as *Ivanhoe* (1817; repr., New York: Heritage, 1950).

66. Child, "Black Saxons," 31, 35-36.

67. For more on these associations of white ancestry with enslaved revolution, please see Nancy Bentley, "White Slaves: The Mulatto Hero in Antebellum Fiction," *American Literature* 65:3 (Sept. 1993): 501-22; and Marlene L. Daut, "'Sons of White Fathers': Mulatto Vengeance and the Haitian Revolution in Victor Séjour's 'The Mulatto,'" *Nineteenth-Century Literature* 65 (June 2010): 1-37.

68. See Mia Bay, *To Tell the Truth Freely: The Life of Ida B. Wells* (New York: Hill & Wang, 2009); and Paula Giddings, *Ida: A Sword among Lions: Ida B. Wells and the Campaign against Lynching* (New York: Amistad, 2008).

69. Karcher also notes that Child continuously draws parallels between these enslaved rebels and the American rebels of the Revolutionary War, thus clearly writing enslaved people's violent resistance into larger histories of American struggles for liberty. See Karcher, *First Woman in the Republic,* 333-35.

70. Eliza Lee Follen, "Dialogue," in *The Liberty Cap* (Boston: Leonard C. Bowles, 1846), 28.

71. Jane Elizabeth Jones, *The Young Abolitionists; or, Conversations on Slavery* (Boston: Anti-Slavery Office, 1848), 134.

72. See Mark C. Carnes and Clyde Griffen, eds., *Meanings of Manhood: Constructions of Masculinity in Victorian America* (Chicago: Univ. of Chicago Press, 1990).

73. For examples of such tales, "The Wishing Cap," in DeRosa, *Into the Mouths of Babes,* 84; Maria Weston Chapman, *Pinda: A True Tale* (New York: American Anti-Slavery Society, 1840), 9; Green, " Slave Wife," 104; and Charlotte H. L. Coues, "Appeal to Mothers," *The Liberty Bell: By the Friends of Freedom.* (Boston: Andrews & Prentiss, 1845), 5.

74. Jones, *Young Abolitionists,* 112.

75. For more on the importance which white female authors placed on sons as the future public face of abolitionism, see chapter 2.

76. See DeRosa, *Domestic Abolitionism and Juvenile Literature.*

77. Follen, "Dialogue," 28.

78. Jones, *Young Abolitionists,* 136.

79. See C. Bradley Thompson, ed., *Antislavery Political Writings, 1833-1860* (Armonk, N.Y.: M. E. Sharpe, 2004); Frederick Blue, *The Free Soilers: Third Party Politics, 1848-1854* (Urbana: Univ. of Illinois Press, 1973); and Jonathan Halperin Earle,

Jacksonian Antislavery and the Politics of Free Soil, 1848-1854 (Chapel Hill: Univ. of North Carolina Press, 2004).

80. Follen, "Reformatory," 136.

81. Ibid.

82. Lori Ginzberg, *Women and the Work of Benevolence: Morality, Politics, and Class in the Nineteenth-Century United States* (New Haven: Yale Univ. Press, 1990); and James Brewer Stewart, *Holy Warriors: The Abolitionists and American Slavery* (New York: Hill & Wang, 1976). For more on the decline of moral suasion within the abolitionist movement, see chapter 4.

83. See Anne Boylan, "Women and Politics in the Era before Seneca Falls," *Journal of the Early Republic* 10 (Autumn 1990): 363-82; and Lori Ginzberg, *Untidy Origins: A Story of Women's Rights in Antebellum New York* (Chapel Hill: Univ. of North Carolina Press, 2005).

84. See *Mary Chesnut's Diary* (1905; repr., New York: Penguin, 2011); Ella Gertrude Clanton Thomas, *The Secret Eye: The Journal of Ella Clanton Thomas, 1848-1889* (Chapel Hill: Univ. of North Carolina Press, 1990); Drew Gilpin Faust, *Mothers of Invention: Women of the Slaveholding South in the American Civil War* (Chapel Hill: Univ. of North Carolina Press, 1996); and Anya Jabour, *Scarlett's Sisters: Young Women in the Old South* (Chapel Hill: Univ. of North Carolina Press, 2007).

85. Cynthia Kierner, *Beyond the Household: Women's Place in the Early South, 1700-1835* (Ithaca, N.Y.: Cornell Univ. Press, 1998); Elizabeth Varon, *We Mean to Be Counted: White Women and Politics in Antebellum Virginia* (Chapel Hill: Univ. of North Carolina Press, 1998); and Anne Firor Scott, *The Southern Lady: From Pedestal to Politics, 1830-1930* (Chicago: Univ. of Chicago Press, 1970).

86. See Craig Thompson Friend and Lorri Glover, eds., *Southern Manhood: Perspectives on Masculinity in the Old South* (Athens: Univ. of Georgia Press, 2004).

87. See Jabour, *Scarlett's Sisters*.

88. Child, "Slavery's Pleasant Homes," 152.

89. Catherine Clinton, *The Plantation Mistress: Woman's World in the Old South* (New York: Pantheon, 1982); Elizabeth Fox-Genovese, *Within the Plantation Household: Black and White Women of the Old South* (Chapel Hill: Univ. of North Carolina Press, 1988); and Harriet Jacobs, *Incidents in the Life of a Slave Girl* (1861; repr., New York: Oxford Univ. Press, 1988).

90. In her reading of the story, Karcher also underlines the ways Child highlights the vast gap in sexual knowledge and experience that exists between the worldly Frederic and the sheltered Marion, to draw attention to the dramatic sexual double standard of antebellum southern (and overall American) society. Carolyn Sorisio similarly underlines how Child emphasizes that both Marion and Rosa come from New Orleans, a city often associated in antislavery literature (as it was in the real world) with the "fancy trade," or the forced prostitution, of enslaved women, thus emphasizing the parallels (as well as the dramatic differences) between enslaved women being sold into sexual slavery and white women entering an unequal, often transactional marriage market. See Karcher, *First Woman in the Early Republic*, 339-43; and Carolyn Sorisio, "The Spectacle of the Body: Torture in the Antislavery

Writing of Lydia Maria Child and Frances E. Watkins Harper," *Modern Language Studies* 30 (Spring 2000): 45-66.

91. E. D. E. N. Southworth, *The Mother-In-Law. National Era,* Apr. 25, 1850, 65.

92. E. D. E. N. Southworth, *Retribution: A Tale of Passion, National Era,* Apr. 12, 1849, 60.

93. See *Mistress of Herself: Speeches and Letters of Ernestine L. Rose, Early Women's Rights Leader,* ed. Paula Doress-Worters (New York: Feminist Press, 2008).

94. Dall, "Amy," 198.

95. The story ends with Amy committing suicide rather than being sold into the fancy trade, her master dying after becoming an alcoholic, and her mistress's life blighted by grief and regret over her complicity in her husband's moral ruin and Amy's death.

96. Child, "Quadroons," 136.

97. Southworth, *The Mother-in-Law, National Era,* Apr. 25, 1850, 65.

98. See T. Walter Herbert, *Sexual Violence and American Manhood* (Cambridge, Mass.: Harvard Univ. Press, 2002).

99. Southworth, *The Mother-In-Law, National Era,* Dec. 6, 1849, 193.

4. "We Women Will Set All Things Right"

1. "The Anti-Slavery Novels," *Liberator,* Jan. 5, 1855, 2. The first epigraph is taken from Caroline W. Healey Dall, "Pictures of Southern Life, for the Drawing Rooms of American Women," *The Liberty Bell: By the Friends of Freedom (*Boston: Andrews & Prentiss, 1851), 146.

2. Lori Ginzberg, *Women and the Work of Benevolence: Morality, Politics, and Class in the Nineteenth-Century United States* (New Haven: Yale Univ. Press, 1990), 87-88, 98-132; Julie Roy Jeffrey, *The Great Silent Army of Abolitionism: Ordinary Women in the Antislavery Movement* (Chapel Hill: Univ. of North Carolina, 1998), 19-33, 96-133, 171-209; and James Brewer Stewart, *Holy Warriors: The Abolitionists and American Slavery* (New York: Hill & Wang, 1996), 51-125.

3. See Michael D. Pierson, *Free Hearts and Free Homes: Gender and American Antislavery Politics* (Chapel Hill: Univ. of North Carolina Press, 2003), 25-69.

4. Mary Ryan, *Women in Public: Between Banners and Ballots, 1825-1880* (Baltimore: Johns Hopkins Univ. Press, 1990); and Elizabeth Varon, *We Mean to Be Counted: White Women and Politics in Antebellum Virginia (*Chapel Hill: Univ. of North Carolina Press, 1998).

5. See Pierson, *Free Hearts and Free Homes.*

6. "Speech of Wendell Phillips at the Melodeon, Thursday Evening, Jan. 27, 1853," Slavery and Anti-Slavery Collection, Sophia Smith Collection, Smith College, Northampton, Mass.

7. See *Twenty-First Annual Report, Presented to the Massachusetts Anti-Slavery Society, By Its Board of Managers, January 26, 1853, With an Appendix.* (Boston: Prentiss & Sawyer, 1853), 53; "Review of *The Minister's Wooing," National Era,* Nov. 3, 1859,

116; and Theodore Parker to Franklin B. Sanborn, Mar. 23, 1860, Theodore Parker Papers, Massachusetts Historical Society.

8. D.H.W., "Uncle Tom's Cabin," *National Anti-Slavery Standard,* Aug. 26, 1852, 55. For an additional example of such rhetoric, see "Anti-Slavery Novels," 2.

9. Donald Liedel offers a useful overview of the few other antislavery works that achieved some measure of popular success in the wake of *Uncle Tom's Cabin* in "The Puffing of *Ida May:* Publishers Exploit the Antislavery Novel," *Journal of Popular Culture* 3, no. 2 (1969): 287-306.

10. "Review of *Gertrude Lee,*" *National Era,* July 10, 1856, 109; and "Anti-Slavery Literature," *National Era,* Apr. 30, 1857, 70.

11. "Uncle Tom Literature," *Independent,* Sept. 30, 1852, 159.

12. "Review of *The Curse Entailed,*" *National Era,* Nov. 13, 1856, 182.

13. See "Brunswick," *Life and Letters of Harriet Beecher Stowe,* ed. Annie Fields (New York: Houghton, Mifflin, 1897), 150; Anna, "I Wish I Could Do Something," *Independent,* June 10, 1852, 96; Eliza Lee Follen, *To the Mothers in the Free States* (Westport, Conn.: Negro Universities Press, 1970), 2; Harriet Beecher Stowe, *Uncle Sam's Emancipation: Earthly Care, a Heavenly Discipline, and Other Sketches* (Detroit: Negro History Press, 1969), 30; Julia Colman and Matilda G. Thompson, "A Few Words about American Slave Children," in DeRosa, *Into the Mouths of Babes,* 317-18; Lydia Maria Child to Mrs. M. J. C. Mason, Dec. 17, 1859, *Correspondence between Lydia Maria Child and Gov. Wise and Mrs. Mason, of Virginia* (Boston: American Anti-Slavery Society, 1860), 24; Robert W. Audretsch, ed., *The Salem, Ohio Women's Rights Convention Proceedings* (Salem, Ohio: Salem Public Library, 1976); Caroline W. Healey Dall, "Pictures of Southern Life, for the Drawing Rooms of American Women," *Liberty Bell: By the Friends of Freedom* (Boston: Andrews & Prentiss, 1851), 139; "Review of *Old Hepsy,*" *Independent,* Apr. 15, 1858, 2; and Mary Hayden Green Pike, *Ida May; Story of Things Actual and Possible* (Boston: Phillips, Sampson & Company; 1854), iii-iv.

14. As was the case in previous decades, a few authors publishing during the 1850s did so anonymously or under pseudonyms. And while it is impossible to say with absolute certainty who these authors were, or if they were female, the dominance of women within antislavery fiction and the feminized nature of the spaces in which they published make their being female authors very likely.

15. See *A Brighter Coming Day: A Frances Ellen Watkins Harper Reader,* ed. Frances Smith Foster (New York: Feminist Press, 1993); Harriet Jacobs, *Incidents in the Life of a Slave Girl, Written by Herself* (1861; repr., New York: Oxford Univ. Press, 1988); and Harriet Wilson, *Our Nig; or, Sketches from the Life of a Free Black, In a Two-Story White House, North. Showing That Slavery's Shadows Fall Even There* (1859; repr., New York: Vintage, 2002).

16. Please note that I refer to this author as Frances E. Watkins Harper throughout, as that is the professional name under which she is best known, though she did not marry her husband, Fenton Harper until 1860.

17. For additional biographical data on these authors, please see Loretta Cody, *A Mighty Social Force: Phebe Ann Coffin Hanaford, 1829-1921* (Charleston, S.C.: Book-

Spring, 2009); Caroline W. Healey Dall, *Daughter of Boston: The Extraordinary Diary of a Nineteenth-Century Woman,* ed. Helen Deese (Boston: Beacon, 2005); Sarah J. Hale, *Woman's Record; or, Sketches of All Distinguished Women, from the Creation to A.D. 1854. Arranged in Four Eras. With Selections from Female Writers of Every Age* (1855; repr., New York: Source Book, 1970); Edward T. James, Janet Wilson James, and Paul S. Boyer, eds., *Notable American Women, 1607-1950* (Cambridge, Mass.: Harvard Univ. Press, 1971); and Carolyn Karcher, *The First Woman in the Republic: A Cultural Biography of Lydia Maria Child* (Durham, N.C.: Duke Univ. Press, 1994).

18. See Gordon Baker, *This Imperfect Revolution: Anthony Burns and the Landscape of Race in Antebellum America* (Kent, Ohio: Kent State Univ. Press, 2010).

19. See Deborah Gray White, *Ar'n't I a Woman? Female Slaves in the Plantation South* (New York: Norton, 1999); and Patricia Hunt, "The Struggle to Achieve Individual Expression through Clothing and Adornment: African American Women under and after Slavery" and Cynthia Lynn Lyerly, "Religion, Gender, and Identity: Black Methodist Women in a Slave Society, 1770-1810," in *Discovering the Women in Slavery: Emancipating Perspectives on the American Past,* ed. Patricia Morton (Athens: Univ. of Georgia Press, 1996), 202-26, 227-41; and Stephanie M. H. Camp, *Closer to Freedom: Enslaved Women and Everyday Resistance in the Plantation South* (Chapel Hill: Univ. of North Carolina Press, 2004).

20. See Harriet Beecher Stowe, *Uncle Tom's Cabin; or, Life among the Lowly* (1852; repr. New York: Modern Library, 2001), 210-11, 221, 249-50; and Mary Hayden Green Pike, *Ida May* (Boston: Phillips, Sampson & Co., 1854), 40, 76.

21. Pike, *Ida May,* 40.

22. Ibid., 40-41.

23. Mary Irving, "Mirth and Melancholy," *National Era,* Aug. 28, 1856, 85.

24. See Harriet Beecher Stowe, *Dred; A Tale of the Great Dismal Swamp,* vol. 2 of 2 (1856; repr., Grosse Pointe, Mich.: Scholarly Press, 1968), 234, 59. Much as she had done in *Uncle Tom's Cabin,* Stowe maintained that African Americans were innately more inclined toward Christianity because of their inherently docile, pious natures.

25. Ibid., 33.

26. See Joan Hedrick, *Harriet Beecher Stowe: A Life* (New York: Oxford Univ. Press, 1994), 235.

27. For more on debates within the United States about radical religious movements of the antebellum era, see Lawrence Foster, *Religion and Sexuality: The Shakers, the Mormons, and the Oneida Community* (Urbana: Univ. of Illinois Press, 1984). See also Helen Lefkowitz Horowitz, *Rereading Sex: Battles over Sexual Knowledge and Suppression in Nineteenth-Century America* (New York: Knopf, 2002); Joanne Ellen Passet, *Sex Radicals and the Quest for Women's Equality* (Urbana: Univ. of Illinois Press, 2003); Sandra Ellen Schroer, *State of the "Union": Marriage and Free Love in the Late 1800s* (New York: Routledge, 2005); and Stephen Nissenbaum, *Sex, Diet, and Debility in Jacksonian America: Sylvester Graham and Health Reform* (Westport, Conn.: Greenwood, 1980).

28. For examples of these discussions in antislavery women's literature, see Sophia Little, *Thrice through the Furnace: A Tale of the Time of the Iron Hoof* (Pawtucket, R.I.: A. W. Pearce, 1852), 159, 186; and Phebe Ann Coffin Hanaford, *Lucretia, the Quakeress; or, Principle Triumphant* (Boston: J. Buffum, 1853), 113-15.

29. Hanaford, *Lucretia*, 164.

30. Little, *Thrice Through the Furnace*, 167.

31. Nancy F. Cott, "Passionlessness: An Interpretation of Victorian Sexual Ideology, 1790-1850," *Signs* 4 (Winter 1978): 219-36. Clelia Duel Mosher's survey conducted in the late nineteenth century reveals particularly interesting and detailed data on these issues, revealing women's reflections on the pleasures of sex and their desire for more effective birth control. See James MaHood and Kristine Wenburg, ed., *The Mosher Survey: Sexual Attitudes of Forty-Five Victorian Women* (New York: Arno, 1980).

32. Anya Jabour, *Marriage in the Early Republic: Elizabeth and William Wirt and the Companionate Ideal* (Baltimore: Johns Hopkins Univ. Press, 2002).

33. See Karen Lystra, *Searching the Heart: Women, Men, and Romantic Love in Nineteenth-Century America* (New York: Oxford Univ. Press, 1989).

34. Margaret Hope Bacon, *Mothers of Feminism: The Story of Quaker Women in America* (San Francisco: Harper & Row, 1986). For a valuable overview of Quaker women's involvement in their religious communities in the eighteenth and nineteenth centuries, see Elizabeth Potts Brown and Susan Mosher Stuard, *Witnesses for Change: Quaker Women over Three Centuries* (New Brunswick, N.J.: Rutgers Univ. Press, 1989). In her monograph *The Politics of Domesticity: Women, Evangelism, and Temperance in Nineteenth-Century America* (Middletown, Conn.: Wesleyan Univ. Press, 1981), Barbara Leslie Epstein draws a similarly powerful connection between nineteenth-century women's religious convictions and their activism, contending that involvement in evangelical Christianity raised women's gender consciousness and motivated them to create an increasingly feminist-oriented temperance movement.

35. See Jennifer L. Connerley, "Quaker Bonnets and the Erotic Feminine in American Popular Culture," *Material Religion: The Journal of Objects, Art, and Belief* 2, no. 2 (2006): 174-203.

36. See Rebecca Larson, *Daughters of the Light: Quaker Women Preaching and Prophesying in the Colonies and Abroad, 1700-1775* (New York: Knopf, 1999); Catherine A. Brekus, *Strangers and Pilgrims: Female Preaching in America, 1740-1845* (Chapel Hill: Univ. of North Carolina Press, 1998); and Susan Juster, *Disorderly Women: Sexual Politics and Evangelicalism in Revolutionary New England* (Ithaca, N.Y.: Cornell Univ. Press, 1994).

37. One useful example of such literature is abolitionist William Goodell's 1845 pamphlet *Come-outerism: The Duty of Secession from a Corrupt Church* (New York: American Anti-Slavery Society, 1845), which insists that remaining within a church which has not decried slavery is akin to buying goods produced through slavery.

38. Mitchell Snay's *Gospel of Disunion: Religion and Separatism in the Antebellum South* (New York: Cambridge Univ. Press, 1993), offers a useful consideration of the ways these divisions within Protestant Christianity operated in southern congregations.

39. Stowe, *Uncle Tom's Cabin*, 200.

40. Ibid., 198-99.

41. Ibid., 543-51.

42. Little, *Thrice Through the Furnace,* 159, 186.

43. Hanaford, *Lucretia,* 115, 113-14.

44. In Hanaford's *Lucretia,* there is a lengthy discussion between the eponymous heroine and one of her friends, in which the virtuous Lucretia insists, over her friend's objections, that because of their powerful, domestic moral influence women need not covet the right to vote (113-15).

45. Ibid., 135.

46. See Lucy Elizabeth Frank, ed., *Representations of Death in Nineteenth-Century United States Writing and Culture* (Burlington, Vt.: Ashgate, 2007).

47. See Elizabeth Ammons, "Heroines in *Uncle Tom's Cabin,*" *American Literature* 49 (May 1977): 161-79. See also John Frick, "*Uncle Tom's Cabin* in the Antebellum Stage," *Uncle Tom's Cabin and American Culture,* 2007, http://utc.iath.virginia.edu/interpret/exhibits/frick/frick.html. David Pierce offers a valuable discussion of the centrality of the figure of Eva in twentieth-century films in "'Carl Laemmle's Outstanding Achievement': Harry Pollard and the Struggle to Film *Uncle Tom's Cabin,*" *Film History* 10, no. 4 (1998): 459-76.

48. E. D. E. N. Southworth, *India: The Pearl of Pearl River* (Philadelphia: T. B. Peterson & Brothers, 1857), 383. Southworth serialized her novel in 1853 under the title *Mark Sutherland* in the antislavery newspaper the *National Era.*

49. See Julie Stern, "The Politics of Tears: Death in the Early American Novel," in *Mortal Remains: Death in Early America,* ed. Andrew Burstein and Nancy Isenberg (Philadelphia: Univ. of Pennsylvania Press, 2003), 108-22.

50. Stowe, *Uncle Tom's Cabin,* 84, 618.

51. Southworth, *India,* 383. See Elizabeth Reis, "Immortal Messengers: Angels, Gender, and Power in Early America," in Burstein and Isenberg, *Mortal Remains,* 163-75.

52. See Rebecca Edwards, *Angels in the Machinery: Gender in American Party Politics from the Civil War to the Progressive Era* (New York: Oxford Univ. Press, 1997); and Judith Ann Giesberg, *Civil War Sisterhood: The United States Strategy Commission and Women's Politics in Transition* (Boston: Northeastern Univ. Press, 2000).

53. Mrs. W. H. Corning, *Western Border Life; or, What Fanny Hunter Saw and Heard in Kanzas [sic] and Missouri.* (New York: Derby & Jackson, 1856), 301.

54. Mrs. Hadden, *National Era,* July 24, 1856, 117.

55. See Stowe, *Dred,* 76-77, 144-45, 168-87; Harriet Hamline Bigelow, *The Curse Entailed* (Boston: Wentworth & Company, 1857), 116; Mary A. Denison, *Old Hepsy* (New York: A. B. Burdick, 1858), 268.

56. *Woman's Faith: A Tale of Southern Life* (New York: Derby & Jackson, 1856), 65.

57. Bigelow, *Curse Entailed,* 116.

58. See Elliott Gorn, "'Gouge and Bite, Pull Hair and Scratch': The Social Significance of Fighting in the Southern Backcountry," *American Historical Review* 90 (Feb. 1985): 18-43; Walter Johnson, *Soul by Soul: Life inside the Antebellum Slave Market* (Cambridge, Mass.: Harvard Univ. Press, 2001); and Bertram Wyatt-Brown, *Honor and Violence in the Old South* (New York: Oxford Univ. Press, 1986).

59. See Sylvia D. Hoffert, *When Hens Crow: The Women's Rights Movement in Antebellum America* (Bloomington: Indiana Univ. Press, 1995).

60. See Daniel S. Wright, *"First Causes of Our Sex": The Female Moral Reform Movement in the Antebellum Northeast, 1834-1848* (New York: Routledge, 2006).

61. Lydia Maria Child, *Autumnal Leaves: Tales and Sketches in Prose and Rhyme* (New York: C. S. Francis & Co., 1857), 316, 361.

62. Stowe, *Dred,* 246.

63. Mattie Griffith, *Madge Vertner* (1859-60; repr., Hastings, Neb.: Hastings College Press, 2015), 321.

64. See Jean H. Baker, *James Buchanan* (New York: Times Books, 2004); and Larry Gara, *The Presidency of Franklin Pierce* (Lawrence: Univ. Press of Kansas, 1991).

65. See Don E. Fehrenbacher, *The Dred Scott Case: Its Significance in American Law and Politics* (New York: Oxford Univ. Press, 1978).

66. Elizabeth A. Roe, *Aunt Leanna; or, Early Scenes in Kentucky* (Chicago: Published for the Author, 1855), 44.

67. See William E. Gienapp, *The Origins of the Republican Party, 1852-1856* (New York: Oxford Univ. Press, 1987); and Hinton Rowan Helper, *The Impending Crisis of the South: How to Meet It* (New York: Burdick Brothers, 1857).

68. See Eric Foner, *Free Soil, Free Labor, Free Men: The Ideology of the Republican Party before the Civil War* (New York: Oxford Univ. Press, 1970); and Michael F. Holt, "Making and Mobilizing the Republican Party, 1854-1860," in *The Birth of the Grand Old Party: The Republicans' First Generation,* ed. Robert F. Engs and Randall M. Miller (Philadelphia: Univ. of Pennsylvania Press, 2002), 29-59.

69. Hattia M'Keehan, *Liberty or Death; or, Heaven's Infraction of the Fugitive Slave Law* (Cincinnati: Author, 1858), 64.

70. Griffith, *Madge Vertner,* 321.

71. Mattie Griffith, *Autobiography of a Female Slave* (1856; repr., Jackson: Univ. of Mississippi, 1998), 187.

72. Frances Harriet Whipple Green, *Shahmah in Pursuit of Freedom; or, The Branded Hand, Translated from the Original Showiah and Edited by an American Citizen* (New York: Thatcher & Hutchinson, 1858), 76-77.

73. Elizabeth D. Livermore, *Zoë; or The Quadroon's Triumph,* 2 vols. (Cincinnati: Truman & Spofford, 1855), 2:183.

74. Lydia Maria Child, "The Kansas Emigrants," *Autumnal Leaves: Tales and Sketches in Prose and Rhyme* (New York.: C. S. Francis & Co., 1857), 358.

75. Hannah Newell Greene Butts, "*Ralph; or, I Wish He Wasn't Black,*" in DeRosa, *Into the Mouths of Babes,* 256-57.

76. Griffith, *Autobiography of a Female Slave,* 196-97.

77. Irving, "Mirth and Melancholy," 137.

78. Griffith, *Autobiography of a Female Slave,* 129.

79. Child, "Kansas Emigrants," 356.

80. Livermore, *Zoë,* 186.

81. Griffith, *Madge Vertner,* 67.

82. Child, "Kansas Emigrants," 316.

83. Karcher, *First Woman of the Republic*, 384-416.

84. See Sally Gregory McMullen, *Seneca Falls and The Origins of the Women's Rights Movement* (New York: Oxford Univ. Press, 1998), 71-103; and Judith Wellman, *The Road to Seneca Falls: Elizabeth Cady Stanton and the First Women's Rights Convention* (Chicago: Univ. of Illinois Press, 2004), 183-209.

Conclusion

1. Review of *The Curse Entailed, Liberator*, Sept. 19, 1856, 154. This epigraph is from Mary E. Bryan, "How Should Women Write?" in *Hidden Hands: An Anthology of American Women Writers, 1790-1870*, ed. Lucy M. Freibert and Barbara A. White (New Brunswick, NJ: Rutgers Univ. Press, 1985), 369.

2. See Faye Dudden, "New York Strategy: The New York Woman's Movement and the Civil War," in *Votes for Women: The Struggle for Suffrage Revisited*, ed. Jean H. Baker (New York: Oxford Univ. Press, 2002), 56-76.

3. Ann D. Gordon offers an insightful consideration of racist and nativist attitudes in Cady Stanton's suffrage rhetoric in "Stanton and the Right to Vote: An Account of Race or Sex," in *Elizabeth Cady Stanton, Feminist as Thinker: A Reader in Documents and Essays*, ed. Ellen Carol DuBois and Richard Candida Smith (New York: New York Univ. Press, 2007), 111-27.

4. See Nell Irvin Painter, "Voices of Suffrage: Sojourner Truth, Frances Watkins Harper, and the Struggle for Woman Suffrage," in Baker, *Votes for Women;* and Sojourner Truth, "Two Speeches," in *The Essential Feminist Reader*, ed. Estelle B. Freedmen (New York: Modern Library, 2007), 63-67.

5. See Ann D. Gordon and Bettye Collier-Thomas, eds., *African-American Women and the Vote, 1837-1965* (Amherst: Univ. of Massachusetts Press, 1997); and Glenda Elizabeth Gilmore, *Gender and Jim Crow: Women and the Politics of White Supremacy in North Carolina, 1896-1920* (Chapel Hill: Univ. of North Carolina Press, 1996).

6. George Eliot, "Silly Novels by Lady Novelists," *Westminster Review* 66 (Oct. 1856): 442-44.

7. See Janice Radway, *A Feeling for Books: The Book of the Month Club, Literary Taste, and Middle-Class Desire* (Chapel Hill: Univ. of North Carolina Press, 1997); and *Reading the Romance: Women, Patriarchy, and Popular Literature* (Chapel Hill: Univ. of North Carolina Press, 1984); Cecilia Koncharr Farr, *Reading Oprah: How Oprah's Book Club Changed the Way America Reads* (Albany: State Univ. of New York Press, 2005); and Suzanne Ferriss and Mallory Young, eds., *Chick Lit: The New Women's Fiction* (New York: Routledge, 2006).

8. For more on the theory and history of essentialism in American feminism, see Norma Alarcon, "'What Has Happened Here': The Politics of Difference in Women's History and Feminist Politics," and Luce Irigaray, "The Questions of Essentialism," both in *The Second Wave: A Reader in Feminist Theory*, ed. Linda J. Nicholson (New York: Routledge, 1997), 272-87, 317-22.

9. One of Judith Butler's first full-length works of feminist theory, *Gender Trouble:*

Feminism and the Subversion of Identity (New York: Routledge, 1990), remains a key articulation of the problematic aspects of claiming a unified category of "woman" in feminist rhetoric.

10. See Alice Echols, *Daring to Be Bad: Radical Feminism in America, 1967-1975* (Minneapolis: Univ. of Minnesota Press, 1989), 243-86.

11. For an important deconstruction of the class and race biases endemic within much mainstream American feminism, see Aida Hurtado, *The Color of Privilege: Three Blasphemies on Race and Feminism* (Ann Arbor: Univ. of Michigan Press, 1996).

12. See Sara Hunter Graham, "The Suffrage Renaissance: A New Image for a New Century, 1896-1910," in *One Woman, One Vote: Rediscovering the Women's Suffrage Movement,* ed. Marjorie Julian Spruill (Troutdale, Ore.: NewSage Press, 1995), 157-78; Amy Swerdlow, "Ladies' Day at the Capitol: Women Strike for Peace versus HUAC," *Feminist Studies* 8 (Autumn 1982): 493-520; and Craig Reinarmer, "The Social Construction of an Alcohol Problem: The Case of Mothers Against Drunk Driving and Social Control in the 1980s," *Theory and Society* 17 (Jan. 1985): 91-120.

Bibliography

Primary Sources

MANUSCRIPT COLLECTIONS
Boston Public Library, Boston, Massachusetts
    Anti-Slavery Manuscripts
    Lydia Maria Child Papers
    William Lloyd Garrison Papers
    Weston/Chapman Papers
Massachusetts Historical Society, Boston
    Charles Cushing Barry Papers, 1834-1906
    Boston Female Anti-Slavery Society Letterbook, 1834-38
    Caroline Wells Healey Dall Papers, 1811-1917
    Charles Follen Papers II, 1815-60
    William Lloyd Garrison Papers
    Juvenile Anti-Slavery Society Records, 1837-38
    Horace Mann Papers
    Theodore Parker Papers
    John Parkman Papers, 1839-75
    Quincy, Wendall, Holmes, and Upham Family Papers
    Robie-Sewall Family Papers, 1611-1905
    Sedgwick Family Papers, 1717-1846
    Catharine Maria Sedgwick Papers, 1798-1908
    Stevens Family Papers, 1770-1911
    Swan Family Papers, 1816-1929
    William Hickling Prescott Letters, 1783-1874

Ohio Historical Society, Columbus
   Bates-Harrison Family Papers
   Elizabeth Margaret Chandler Papers
   Benjamin Lundy Papers
   Charles Osborn Papers
   Alice McMillan Papers
Sophia Smith Collection, Smith College, Northampton, Massachusetts
   Fanny Fern and Ethel Parton Papers
   Garrison Family Papers
   Slavery/Anti-Slavery Collection

NEWSPAPERS AND PERIODICALS

Emancipator (Nashville, Tennessee), 1820.
Emancipator (New York), 1835-41.
Genius of Universal Emancipation, 1821-39.
Independent, 1848-1921.
Knapp's Liberator, 1842.
Liberator, 1831-65.
National Anti-Slavery Standard, 1840-70.
National Era, 1847-70.
Non-Slaveholder, 1846-54.
Philanthropist, 1836-43.
Radical Abolitionist, 1854-58.
Slave's Friend, 1836-38.

PUBLISHED PRIMARY SOURCES—BOOKS AND ARTICLES

Annual Report Presented to the Massachusetts Anti-Slavery Society By Its Board of Managers, January 27, 1847, With an Appendix. Boston: Printed by Andrews & Prentiss, 1847.
Audretsch, Robert W., ed. *Salem, Ohio 1850 Women's Rights Convention Proceedings.* Salem, Ohio: Salem Area Bicentennial Committee and the Salem Public Library, 1976.
Bigelow, Harriet Hamline. *The Curse Entailed.* Boston: Wentworth & Company, 1857.
Chapman, Maria Weston. *"How Could I Help to Abolish Slavery?" or, Counsels to the Newly Converted.* New York: American Anti-Slavery Society, 1855.
———, ed. *Liberty Bell.* Boston: American Anti-Slavery Society, 1839-58.
———. *Pinda; A True Tale.* New York: American Anti-Slavery Society, 1840.
———. *Right and Wrong in Massachusetts.* Boston: Anti-Slavery Press, 1839.
Chandler, Elizabeth Margaret. *The Poetical Works of Elizabeth Margaret Chandler: With a Memoir of Her Life and Character by Benjamin Lundy.* Edited by Benjamin Lundy. Philadelphia: Published by T. E. Chapman; New York: Baker, Crane & Day, 1845.
———. *Remember the Distance That Divides Us: The Family Letters of Philadelphia Quaker Abolitionist and Michigan Pioneer Elizabeth Margaret Chandler, 1830-1842.* Edited by Marcia J. Heringa Mason. East Lansing, Mich.: Michigan State University, 2004.
Chesnut, Mary Boykin. *Mary Chesnut's Diary.* 1905. Reprint, New York: Penguin, 2011.

———. *Mary Chesnut's Civil War*. Edited by C. Vann Woodward. New Haven: Yale University Press, 1981.

Child, Lydia Maria. *An Appeal in Favor of That Class of Americans Called Africans*. 1833. Reprint, Amherst: University of Massachusetts Press, 1996.

———. *Autumnal Leaves: Tales and Sketches in Prose and Rhyme*. New York: C. S. Francis & Co., 1857.

———. *Correspondence between Lydia Maria Child and Gov. Wise and Mrs. Mason, of Virginia*. Boston: American Anti-Slavery Society, 1860.

———. *The Frugal Housewife: Dedicated to Those Who Are Not Ashamed of Economy*. Boston: Carter & Hendee, 1829.

———. *Hobomok and Other Writings on Indians*. Edited by Carolyn L. Karcher. New Brunswick, New Jersey: Rutgers University Press, 1986.

Child, Lydia Maria. *A Lydia Maria Child Reader*. Edited by Carolyn L. Karcher. Durham, North Carolina: Duke University Press, 1997.

———. *The Mother's Book*. Boston: Carter & Hendee, 1831.

———, ed. *The Oasis*. Boston: Benjamin C. Bacon, 1834.

Corning, W. H., *Western Border Life; or What Fanny Hunter Saw and Heard in Kanzas and Missouri*. New York: Derby & Jackson, 1856.

Dall, Caroline W. Healey. *Daughter of Boston: The Extraordinary Diary of a Nineteenth-Century Woman*. Edited by Helen Deese. Boston: Beacon, 2005.

Denison, Mary A. *Old Hepsy*. New York: A. B. Burdick, 1858.

DeRosa, Deborah C. *Into the Mouths of Babes: An Anthology of Children's Abolitionist Literature*. Westport, Conn.: Praeger, 2005.

Eliot, George. "Silly Novels by Lady Novelists." *Westminster Review* 66 (October 1856): 442-44.

Fetterley, Judith, ed. *Provisions: A Reader from Nineteenth Century Women*. Bloomington: Indiana University Press, 1985.

Finkelman, Paul, ed. *Defending Slavery: Proslavery Thought in the Old South*. Boston: Bedford / St. Martin's, 2003.

Follen, Eliza Lee. *The Child's Friend; Designed for Families and Sunday Schools*. 31 vols. Boston: Leonard C. Bowles & William Crosby, 1843-58.

———. *The Liberty Cap*. Boston: Leonard C. Bowles, 1846.

———. *To the Mothers in the Free States*. Westport, Connecticut: Negro Universities Press, 1970.

Freedmen, Estelle B., ed. *The Essential Feminist Reader*. New York: Modern Library, 2007.

Freibert, Lucy M., and Barbara A. White, eds. *Hidden Hands: An Anthology of American Women Writers, 1790-1870*. New Brunswick, New Jersey: Rutgers University Press, 1985.

Goodell, William. *Come-outerism: The Duty of Secession from a Corrupt Church*. New York: American Anti-Slavery Society, 1845.

Green, Frances Harriet Whipple. *Shahmah in Pursuit of Freedom; or, The Branded Hand, Translated from the Original Showiah and Edited by an American Citizen*. New York: Thatcher & Hutchinson, 1858.

Griffith, Mattie. *Autobiography of a Female Slave.* 1856. Reprint, Jackson: University Press of Mississippi, 1998.

———. *Madge Vertner.* 1859–60. Reprint, Hastings, Nebraska: Hastings College Press, 2015.

Grimké, Angelina. *Appeal to the Christian Women of the South.* New York: American Anti-Slavery Society, 1836.

Grimké, Sarah. *Letters on the Equality of the Sexes and the Condition of Woman, Addressed to Mary E. Parker.* Boston: I. Knapp, 1838.

Hale, Sarah J. *Woman's Record; or, Sketches of All Distinguished Women, from the Creation to A.D. 1854. Arranged in Four Eras. With Selections from Female Writers of Every Age.* 1855. Reprint, New York: Source Book, 1970.

Hanaford, Phebe Ann Coffin. *Lucretia, the Quakeress; or, Principle Triumphant.* Boston: J. Buffum, 1853.

Harper, Frances Ellen Watkins. *A Brighter Coming Day: A Frances Ellen Watkins Harper Reader.* Edited by Frances Smith Foster. New York: Feminist Press, 1990.

Helper, Hinton Rowan. *The Impending Crisis of the South: How to Meet It.* New York: Burdick Brothers, 1857.

Heyrick, Elizabeth. *Immediate, not gradual abolition; or, An inquiry into the shortest, safest, and most effectual means of getting rid of West Indian slavery.* London: Hatchard & Sons, 1824.

Hogeland, Lisa Maria, and Mary Klages, eds. *The Aunt Lute Anthology of U.S. Women Writers.* San Francisco: Aunt Lute Books, 2004.

Jacobs, Harriet. *Incidents in the Life of a Slave Girl.* 1861. Reprint, New York: Oxford University Press, 1988.

Jones, Jane Elizabeth. *The Young Abolitionists; or, Conversations on Slavery.* Boston: Anti-Slavery Office, 1848.

Little, Sophia. *Thrice through the Furnace: A Tale of the Time of the Iron Hoof.* Pawtucket, Rhode Island: A. W. Pearce, 1852.

Livermore, Elizabeth D. *Zoë; or, The Quadroon's Triumph.* Cincinnati: Truman & Spofford, 1855.

Lundy, Benjamin. Preface to Chandler, *The Poetical Works of Elizabeth Margaret Chandler.*

———. "Proposals, for Publishing in MountPleasant [sic], Ohio, A Periodical Work, To Be Entitled *The Genius of Universal Emancipation,* by Benjamin Lundy." Mount Pleasant, Ohio, c. 1820.

Marston, John. *The Wonder of Women, or The Tragedy of Sophonisba.* 1606. Reprint, New York: Garland, 1979.

M'Keehan, Hattia. *Liberty or Death; or, Heaven's Infraction of the Fugitive Slave Law.* Cincinnati: Author, 1858.

Moses, Wilson Jeremiah. *Classical Black Nationalism from the American Revolution to Marcus Garvey.* New York: New York University Press, 1996.

Mott, Lucretia. *Discourse on Woman.* Philadelphia: W. Kildare, 1849.

Nicholson, Linda J., ed. *The Second Wave: A Reader in Feminist Theory.* New York: Routledge, 1997.

Opie, Amelia. *The Warrior's Return; The Black Man's Lament*. Edited by Donald H. Reiman New York: Garland, 1978.

Pearson, Edward A., ed. *Designs against Charleston: The Trial Record of the Denmark Vesey Slave Conspiracy of 1822*. Chapel Hill: Univ. of North Carolina Press, 1999.

Pike, Mary Hayden Green. *Ida May: Story of Things Actual and Possible*. Boston: Phillips, Sampson & Company, 1854.

Prince, Mary. *The History of Mary Prince, A West Indian Slave, Related by Herself*. Edited by Moira Ferguson. London: Pandora, 1987.

Roe, Elizabeth A. *Aunt Leanna; or, Early Scenes in Kentucky*. Chicago: Published for the Author, 1855.

Rose, Ernestine L. *Mistress of Herself: Speeches and Letters of Ernestine L. Rose, Early Women's Rights Leader*. Edited by Paula Doress-Worterss. New York: Feminist Press, 2008.

Rossini, Gioacchino. *Zelmira: A Serious Opera in Two Acts*. London: H. N. Millar, 1822.

Scott, Walter. *Ivanhoe*. 1817. Reprint, New York: Heritage Press, 1950.

Sedgwick, Catharine M. *Life and Letters of Catherine M. Sedgwick*. Edited by Mary E. Dewey, New York: Harper & Brothers, 1872.

———. *The Power of Her Sympathy: The Autobiography and Journal of Catharine Maria Sedgwick*. Edited by Mary C. Kelley. Boston: Massachusetts Historical Society, 2005.

———. *Redwood; A Tale*. New York: Garrett, 1969.

Southworth, E. D. E. N. *India: The Pearl of Pearl River*. Philadelphia: T. B. Peterson and Brothers, 1857.

Stanton, Elizabeth Cady. *Elizabeth Cady Stanton, Feminist as Thinker: A Reader in Documents and Essays*. Edited by Ellen Carol DuBois and Richard Candida Smith. New York: New York University Press, 2007.

Star of Emancipation. Boston: Massachusetts Female Emancipation Society, 1841.

Stewart, Maria W. *Maria W. Stewart: America's First Black Woman Political Writer*. Edited by Marilyn Richardson. Bloomington: Indiana University Press, 1987.

Stone, Lucy, ed. *Woman's Rights Tracts, No. 1-5*. Rochester, New York: Steam Press of Curtis, Butts, 1854.

Stowe, Harriet Beecher. *Dred; A Tale of the Great Dismal Swamp*. 2 vols. 1856. Reprint, Grosse Pointe, Michigan: Scholarly Press, 1968.

———. *Life and Letters of Harriet Beecher Stowe*. Edited by Annie Fields. New York: Houghton, Mifflin, 1897.

———. *Uncle Tom's Cabin; or, Life among the Lowly*. 1852. Reprint, New York: Modern Library, 2001.

———. *Uncle Sam's Emancipation; Earthly Care, a Heavenly Discipline, and Other Sketches*. Detroit: Negro History Press, 1969.

Thomas, Ella Gertrude Clanton. *The Secret Eye: The Journal of Ella Clanton Thomas, 1848-1889*. Chapel Hill: University of North Carolina Press, 1990.

Thompson, C. Bradley, ed. *Antislavery Political Writings, 1833-1860*. Armonk, New York: M. E. Sharpe, 2004.

Trodd, Zoe, ed. *American Protest Literature*. Cambridge, Massachusetts: Harvard University Press, 2006.

Twenty-First Annual Report, Presented to the Massachusetts Anti-Slavery Society, By Its Board of Managers, January 26, 1853, With an Appendix. Boston: Prentiss & Sawyer, 1853.

Walker, David. *Appeal to the Coloured Citizens of the World.* Edited by Peter P. Hinks. University Park: Pennsylvania State University Press, 2006.

Wilson, Harriet E. *Our Nig; or, Sketches from the Life of a Free Black, In a Two-Story White House, North. Showing That Slavery's Shadows Fall Even There.* 1859. Reprint, New York: Vintage, 2001.

Woman's Faith. A Tale of Southern Life. Cincinnati: H. W. Derby, 1856.

Secondary Sources

BOOKS

Allgor, Catherine. *Parlor Politics: In Which the Ladies of Washington Help Build a City and a Government.* Charlottesville: University Press of Virginia, 2000.

Alonso, Harriet Hyman. *Growing Up Abolitionist: The Story of the Garrison Children.* Amherst: University of Massachusetts Press, 2002.

Althink, Henrice. *Representations of Slave Women in Discourses of Slavery and Abolition, 1780-1838.* New York: Routledge, 2007.

Bacon, Jacqueline. Freedom's Journal: *The First African-American Newspaper.* Lanham, Maryland: Lexington, 2007.

———. *The Humblest May Stand Forth: Rhetoric, Empowerment, and Abolition.* Columbia: University of South Carolina Press, 2002.

Bacon, Margaret Hope. *But One Race: The Life of Robert Purvis.* Albany: State University of New York Press, 2007.

———. *Mothers of Feminism: The Story of Quaker Women in America.* San Francisco: Harper & Row, 1986.

———. *Valiant Friend: The Life of Lucretia Mott.* New York: Walker, 1970.

Baker, Gordon. *This Imperfect Revolution: Anthony Burns and the Landscape of Race in Antebellum America.* Kent, Ohio: Kent State University Press, 2010.

Baker, Jean H. *James Buchanan.* New York: Times Books, 2004.

———, ed. *Votes for Women: The Struggle for Suffrage Revisited.* New York: Oxford University Press, 2002.

Bardes, Barbara, and Suzanne Gossett. *Declarations of Independence: Women and Political Power in Nineteenth-Century American Fiction.* New Brunswick, New Jersey: Rutgers University Press, 1990.

Bay, Mia. *To Tell the Truth Freely: The Life of Ida B. Wells.* New York: Hill & Wang, 2009.

Baym, Nina. *Novels, Readers, and Reviewers: Responses to Fiction in Antebellum America.* Ithaca, New York: Cornell University Press, 1984.

———. *Woman's Fiction: A Guide to Novels by and about Women in America, 1820-1870.* Ithaca, New York: Cornell University Press, 1978.

Bellesides, Michael A., ed. *Lethal Imagination: Violence and Brutality in American History.* New York: New York University Press, 1999.

Blue, Frederick. *The Free Soilers: Third Party Politics, 1848-1854*. Urbana: University of Illinois Press, 1973.

Blumin, Stuart. *The Emergence of the Middle-Class: Social Experience in the American City, 1760-1900*. New York: Cambridge University Press, 1989.

Boylan, Anne M. *The Origins of Women's Activism: New York and Boston, 1790-1840*. Chapel Hill: University of North Carolina Press, 2002.

Branson, Susan. *These Fiery, Frenchified Dames: Women and Political Culture in Early National Philadelphia*. Philadelphia: University of Pennsylvania Press, 2001.

Breen, T. H. *The Marketplace Revolution: How Consumer Politics Shaped American Independence*. New York: Oxford University Press, 2004.

Brekus, Catherine A. *Strangers and Pilgrims: Female Preaching in America, 1740-1845*. Chapel Hill: University of North Carolina Press, 1998.

Brown, Elizabeth Potts, and Susan Mosher Stuard, eds. *Witnesses for Change: Quaker Women over Three Centuries*. New Brunswick, New Jersey: Rutgers University Press, 1989.

Browne, Stephen H. *Angelina Grimké: Rhetoric, Identity, and the Radical Imagination*. East Lansing: Michigan State University Press, 1999.

Burstein, Andrew, and Nancy Isenberg, eds. *Mortal Remains: Death in Early America*. Philadelphia: University of Pennsylvania Press, 2003.

Bushman, Richard. *The Refinement of America: Persons, Homes, Cities*. New York: Knopf, 1992.

Butler, Judith. *Gender Trouble: Feminism and the Subversion of Identity*. New York: Routledge, 1990.

Cameron, Christopher. *To Plead Our Own Cause: African Americans in Massachusetts and the Making of the Antislavery Movement*. Kent, Ohio: Kent State University Press, 2014.

Camp, Stephanie M. H. *Closer to Freedom: Enslaved Women and Everyday Resistance in the Plantation South*. Chapel Hill: University of North Carolina Press, 2004.

Carnes, Mark C., and Clyde Griffen, eds. *Meanings for Manhood: Constructions of Masculinity in Victorian America*. Chicago: University of Chicago Press, 1990.

Clinton, Catherine. *The Plantation Mistress: Woman's World in the Old South*. New York: Pantheon, 1982.

Cody, Loretta. *A Mighty Social Force: Phebe Ann Coffin Hanaford, 1829-1921*. Charleston, South Carolina: BookSpring, 2009.

Cott, Nancy F. *The Bonds of Womanhood: "Woman's Sphere" in New England, 1780-1835*. New Haven: Yale University Press, 1977.

———. *The Grounding of Modern Feminism*. New Haven: Yale University Press, 1987.

———. *Public Vows: A History of Marriage and the Nation*. Cambridge, Massachusetts: Harvard University Press, 2000.

Coultrap-McQuin, Susan. *Doing Literary Business: American Women Writers in the Nineteenth Century*. Chapel Hill: University of North Carolina Press, 1990.

Cutter, Martha. *Unruly Tongue: Identity and Voice in American Women's Writing, 1850-1930*. Jackson: University Press of Mississippi, 1999.

Damon-Bach, Lucinda L., and Victoria Clements, eds. *Catharine Maria Sedgwick: Critical Perspectives.* Boston: Northeastern University Press, 2003.

Davidson, Cathy N. *Reading in America: Literature and Social History.* Baltimore: Johns Hopkins University Press, 1989.

———. *Revolution and the Word: The Rise of the Novel in America.* New York: Oxford University Press, 1986.

Davidson, Cathy, and Jessamyn Hatcher, eds. *No More Separate Spheres! A Next Wave American Studies Reader.* Durham, North Carolina: Duke University Press, 2002.

DeRosa, Deborah C. *Domestic Abolitionism and Juvenile Literature.* Albany: State University of New York Press, 2003.

Dillon, Merton. *Benjamin Lundy and the Struggle for Negro Freedom.* Urbana: University of Illinois Press, 1966.

Donaldson, Ian. *The Rapes of Lucretia: A Myth and Its Transformations.* Oxford: Clarendon, 1982.

Dorsey, Bruce. *Reforming Men and Women: Gender in the Antebellum City.* Ithaca, New York: Cornell University Press, 2002.

Douglas, Ann. *The Feminization of American Culture.* New York: Knopf, 1977.

DuBois, Ellen Carol. *Feminism and Suffrage: The Emergence of an Independent Women's Movement in America, 1848-1869.* Ithaca, New York: Cornell University Press, 1978.

Earle, Jonathan Halperin. *Jacksonian Antislavery and the Politics of Free Soil, 1824-1854.* Chapel Hill: University of North Carolina Press, 2004.

Echols, Alice. *Daring to Be Bad: Radical Feminism in America, 1967-1975.* Minneapolis: University of Minnesota Press, 1989.

Edwards, Rebecca. *Angels in the Machinery: Gender in American Party Politics from the Civil War to the Progressive Era.* New York: Oxford University Press, 1997.

Elbert, Monika M., ed. *Separate Spheres No More: Gender Convergence in American Literature, 1830-1930.* Tuscaloosa: University of Alabama Press, 2000.

Engs, Robert F., and Randall M. Miller, eds. *The Birth of the Grand Old Party: The Republicans' First Generation.* Philadelphia: University of Pennsylvania Press, 2002.

Epstein, Barbara. *The Politics of Domesticity: Women, Evangelism, and Temperance in Nineteenth-Century America.* Middletown, Connecticut: Wesleyan University Press, 1981.

Farr, Cecilia Koncharr. *Reading Oprah: How Oprah's Book Club Changed the Way America Reads.* Albany: State University of New York Press, 2005.

Faust, Drew Gilpin. *Mothers of Invention: Women of the Slaveholding South in the American Civil War.* Chapel Hill: University of North Carolina Press, 1996.

Faulkner, Carol. *Women's Radical Reconstruction: The Freedmen's Aid Movement.* Philadelphia: University of Pennsylvania Press, 2004.

Fehrenbacher, Don E. *The Dred Scott Case: Its Significance in American Law and Politics.* New York: Oxford University Press, 1978.

Ferriss, Suzanne, and Mallory Young, eds. *Chick Lit: The New Women's Fiction.* New York: Routledge, 2006.

Fisch, Audrey. *American Slaves in Victorian England.* Cambridge: Cambridge University Press, 2000.

Floyd, Janet, and Inga Bryden, eds. *Domestic Space: Reading the Nineteenth-Century Interior.* New York: Manchester University Press, 1999.

Foner, Eric. *Free Soil, Free Labor, Free Men: The Ideology of the Republican Party Before the Civil War.* New York: Oxford University Press, 1970.

Foster, Frances Smith. *'Til Death or Distance Do Us Part: Love and Marriage in African America.* New York: Oxford University Press, 2010.

———. *Written by Herself: Literary Production by African American Women, 1746-1892.* Bloomington: Indiana University Press, 1993.

Foster, Lawrence. *Religion and Sexuality: The Shakers, the Mormons, and the Oneida Community.* Urbana: University of Illinois Press, 1984.

Fox-Genovese, Elizabeth. *Within the Plantation Household: Black and White Women of the Old South.* Chapel Hill: University of North Carolina Press, 1988.

Frank, Lucy Elizabeth, ed. *Representations of Death in Nineteenth-Century United States Writing and Culture.* Burlington, Vermont: Ashgate, 2007.

Friend, Craig Thompson, and Lorri Glover, eds. *Southern Manhood: Perspectives on Masculinity in the Old South.* Athens: University of Georgia Press, 2004.

Gara, Larry. *The Presidency of Franklin Pierce.* Lawrence: University of Kansas Press, 1991.

Giddings, Paula. *Ida: A Sword among Lions, Ida B. Wells and the Campaign against Lynching.* New York: Amistad, 2008.

Gienapp, William E. *The Origins of the Republican Party, 1852-1856.* New York: Oxford University Press, 1987.

Giesberg, Judith Ann. *Civil War Sisterhood: The United States Strategy Commission and Women's Politics in Transition.* Boston: Northeastern University Press, 2000.

Gilmore, Glenda Elizabeth. *Gender and Jim Crow: Women and the Politics of White Supremacy in North Carolina, 1896-1920.* Chapel Hill: University of North Carolina Press, 1996.

Ginzberg, Lori. *Untidy Origins: A Story of Women's Rights in Antebellum New York.* Chapel Hill: University of North Carolina Press, 2005.

———. *Women and the Work of Benevolence: Morality, Politics, and Class in the Nineteenth-Century United States.* New Haven: Yale University Press, 1990.

Gordon, Ann D., and Bettye Collier-Thomas, eds. *African-American Women and the Vote, 1837-1965.* Amherst: University of Massachusetts Press, 1997.

Gossett, Thomas. Uncle Tom's Cabin *and American Culture.* Dallas: Southern Methodist University Press, 1985.

Gray, Janet Sinclair. *Race and Time: American Women's Poetics from Racial Modernity.* Iowa City: University of Iowa Press, 2004.

———. *She Wields a Pen: American Women Poets of the Nineteenth Century.* Iowa City: University of Iowa Press, 1997.

Hankins, Barry. *The Second Great Awakening and the Transcendentalists.* Westport, Connecticut: Greenwood, 2004.

Hansen, Debra Gold. *Strained Sisterhood: Gender and Class in the Boston Female Anti-Slavery Society.* Amherst: University of Massachusetts Press, 1993.

Harrold, Stanley. *Gamaliel Bailey and Antislavery Union.* Kent, Ohio: Kent State University Press, 1986.

———. *The Rise of Aggressive Abolitionism: Addresses to the Slave*. Lexington: University Press of Kentucky, 2004.

Hedrick, Joan. *Harriet Beecher Stowe: A Life*. New York: Oxford University Press, 1994.

Herbert, T. Walter. *Sexual Violence and American Manhood*. Cambridge, Massachusetts: Harvard University Press, 2002.

Hersh, Blanche Grassman. *The Slavery of Sex: Feminist-Abolitionists in America*. Urbana: University of Illinois Press, 1978.

Hine, Darlene Clark, and Kathleen Thompson. *A Shining Thread of Hope: The History of Black Women in America*. New York: Broadway, 1998.

Hinks, Peter P. *To Awaken My Afflicted Brethren: David Walker and the Problem of Antebellum Slave Resistance*. University Park: Pennsylvania State University Press, 1997.

Hoffert, Sylvia D. *When Hens Crow: The Women's Rights Movement in Antebellum America*. Bloomington: Indiana University Press, 1995.

Holcomb, Julie L. *Moral Commerce: Quakers and the Transatlantic Boycott of the Slave Labor Economy*. Ithaca, New York: Cornell University Press, 2016.

Homestead, Melissa. *American Women Authors and Literary Property, 1822-1869*. New York: Cambridge University Press, 2005.

Horowitz, Helen Lefkowitz. *Rereading Sex: Battles over Sexual Knowledge and Suppression in Nineteenth-Century America*. New York: Knopf, 2002.

Hurtado, Aida. *The Color of Privilege: Three Blasphemies on Race and Feminism*. Ann Arbor: University of Michigan Press, 1996.

Isenberg, Nancy. *Sex and Citizenship in Antebellum America*. Chapel Hill: University of North Carolina Press, 1998.

Jabour, Anya. *Marriage in the Early Republic: Elizabeth and William Wirt and the Companionate Ideal*. Baltimore: Johns Hopkins University Press, 1998.

———. *Scarlett's Sisters: Young Women in the Old South*. Chapel Hill: University of North Carolina Press, 2007.

James, Edward T., Janet Wilson James, and Paul S. Boyer, eds. *Notable American Women, 1607-1950*. Cambridge, Massachusetts: Harvard University Press, 1971.

Jeffrey, Julie Roy. *The Great Silent Army of Abolitionism: Ordinary Women in the Antislavery Movement*. Chapel Hill: University of North Carolina Press, 1998.

Johnson, Walter. *Soul by Soul: Life inside the Antebellum Slave Market*. Cambridge, Mass.: Harvard University Press, 2001.

Jones, Martha S. *All Bound Up Together: The Woman Question in African-American Public Culture, 1830-1900*. Chapel Hill: University of North Carolina Press, 2007.

Juster, Susan. *Disorderly Women: Sexual Politics and Evangelicalism in Revolutionary New England*. Ithaca, New York: Cornell University Press, 1994.

Karcher, Carolyn L. *The First Woman in the Republic: A Cultural Biography of Lydia Maria Child*. Durham, North Carolina: Duke University Press, 1994.

Kelley, Mary. *Learning to Stand and Speak: Women, Education, and Public Life in America's Republic*. Chapel Hill: University of North Carolina Press, 2006.

———. *Private Woman, Public Stage: Literary Domesticity in Nineteenth-Century America*. New York: Oxford University Press, 1984.

Kelly, Catherine. *In the New England Fashion: Reshaping Women's Lives in the Nineteenth Century.* Ithaca, New York: Cornell University Press, 1999.

Kierner, Cynthia. *Beyond the Household: Women's Place in the Early South, 1700-1835.* Ithaca, New York: Cornell University Press, 1998.

Kolchin, Peter. *American Slavery, 1619-1877.* New York: Hill & Wang, 1994.

Ladd-Taylor, Molly, and Lauri Umansky, eds. *"Bad" Mothers: The Politics of Blame in Twentieth-Century America.* New York: New York University Press, 1998.

Larson, Rebecca. *Daughters of the Light: Quaker Women Preaching, and Prophesying in the Colonies and Abroad, 1700-1775.* New York: Knopf, 1999.

Lerner, Gerda. *The Grimké Sisters from South Carolina: Rebels against Slavery.* Boston: Houghton Mifflin, 1967.

Levander, Caroline. *Voices of the Nation: Women and Public Speech in Nineteenth-Century American Literature and Culture.* New York: Cambridge University Press, 1998.

Lofton, John. *Denmark Vesey's Revolt: The Slave Plot That Lit a Fuse to Fort Sumter.* Kent, Ohio: Kent State University Press, 2013.

Lystra, Karen. *Searching the Heart: Women, Men, and Romantic Love in Nineteenth-Century America.* New York: Oxford University Press, 1989.

MaHood, James, and Kristine Wenburg, ed. *The Mosher Survey: Sexual Attitudes of Forty-five Victorian Women.* New York: Arno, 1980.

Matthews, Glenna. *The Rise of the Public Woman: Woman's Power and Woman's Place in the United States, 1630-1970.* New York: Oxford University Press, 1992.

Mayer, Henry. *All on Fire: William Lloyd Garrison and the Abolition of Slavery.* New York: St. Martin's, 1998.

McCarthy, Timothy Patrick, and John Stauffer, eds. *Prophets of Protest: Reconsidering the History of American Abolitionism.* New York: New Press, 2006.

McHenry, Elizabeth. *Forgotten Readers: Recovering the Lost History of African American Literary Societies.* Durham, North Carolina: Duke University Press, 2002.

McKivigan, John R, ed. *Abolitionism and Issues of Race and Gender.* New York: Garland, 1999.

McKivigan, John R., and Stanley Harrold, eds. *Antislavery Violence: Sectional, Racial, and Cultural Conflict in Antebellum America.* Knoxville: University of Tennessee Press, 1999.

McMullen, Sally Gregory. *Seneca Falls and the Origins of the Women's Rights Movement.* New York: Oxford University Press, 1998.

Merish, Lori. *Sentimental Materialism: Gender, Commodity Culture, and Nineteenth-Century American Literature.* Durham, North Carolina: Duke University Press, 2000.

Mielke, Laura. *Moving Encounters: Sympathy and the Indian Question in Antebellum Literature.* Amherst: University of Massachusetts Press, 2008.

Millington, Richard H., ed. *The Cambridge Companion to Nathaniel Hawthorne.* New York: Cambridge University Press, 2004.

Morton, Patricia, ed. *Discovering the Women in Slavery: Emancipating Perspectives on the American Past.* Athens: University of Georgia Press, 1996.

Nash, Gary B. *Forging Freedom: The Formation of Philadelphia's Black Community, 1720-1840.* Cambridge, Massachusetts: Harvard University Press, 1988.

Newman, Richard S. *Freedom's Prophet: Bishop Richard Allen, the AME Church, and the Black Founding Fathers*. New York: New York University Press, 2008.

Nissenbaum, Stephen. *Sex, Diet, and Debility in Jacksonian America: Sylvester Graham and Health Reform*. Westport, Connecticut: Greenwood, 1980.

Nuermberger, Ruth Ketring. *The Free Produce Movement: A Quaker Protest against Slavery*. New York: AMS Press, 1970.

Oates, Stephen. *The Fires of Jubilee: Nat Turner's Fierce Rebellion*. New York: Harper & Row, 1975.

Okker, Patricia. *Our Sister Editors: Sarah J. Hale and the Tradition of Nineteenth-Century American Women Editors*. Athens: University of Georgia Press, 1995.

Pascoe, Peggy. *Relations of Rescue: The Search for Female Moral Authority in the American West, 1874-1939*. New York: Oxford University Press, 1991.

Passet, Joanne Ellen. *Sex Radicals and the Quest for Women's Equality*. Urbana: University of Illinois Press, 2003.

Peterson, Carla L. *Doers of the Word: African-American Women Speakers and Writers of the North, 1830-1880*. New York: Oxford University Press, 1995.

Piepmeier, Alison. *Out in Public: Configurations of Women's Bodies in Nineteenth-Century America*. Chapel Hill: University of North Carolina, 2004.

Pierson, Michael D. *Free Hearts and Free Homes: Gender and American Antislavery Politics*. Chapel Hill: University of North Carolina Press, 2003.

Portnoy, Alisse. *Their Right to Speak: Women's Activism in the Indian and Slave Debates*. Cambridge, Massachusetts: Harvard University Press, 2005.

Radway, Janice. *A Feeling for Books: The Book-of-the-Month Club, Literary Taste, and Middle-Class Desire*. Chapel Hill: University of North Carolina Press, 1997.

———. *Reading the Romance: Women, Patriarchy, and Popular Literature*. Chapel Hill: University of North Carolina Press, 1984.

Raimon, Eve Allegra. *The "Tragic Mulatta" Revisited: Race and Nationalism in Nineteenth Century Antislavery Fiction*. New Brunswick, New Jersey: Rutgers University Press, 2004.

Robertson, David. *Denmark Vesey: The Buried History of America's Largest Slave Rebellion and the Man Who Led It*. New York: Knopf, 1999.

Robbins, Sarah. *Managing Literacy, Mothering America: Women's Narratives on Reading and Writing in the Nineteenth Century*. Pittsburgh: University of Pittsburgh Press, 2006.

Rohrbach, Augusta. *Truth Stranger Than Fiction: Race, Realism, and the U.S. Literary Marketplace*. New York: Palgrave, 2002.

Romero, Lora. *Home Fronts: Domesticity and Its Critics in the Antebellum United States*. Durham, North Carolina: Duke University Press, 1997.

Roth, Sarah N. *Gender and Race in Antebellum Popular Culture*. New York: Cambridge University Press, 2014.

Rotundo, E. Anthony. *American Manhood: Transformations in Masculinity from the Revolution to the Modern Era*. New York: Basic Books, 1993.

Ryan, Mary. *The Empire of the Mother: American Writing about Domesticity, 1830 to 1860*. New York: Haworth, 1982.

———. *Women in Public: Between Banners and Ballots, 1825–1880*. Baltimore: Johns Hopkins University Press, 1990.

Salerno, Beth. *Sister Societies: Women's Antislavery Organizations in Antebellum America*. DeKalb: Northern Illinois University Press, 2005.

Samuels, Shirley, ed. *The Culture of Sentiment: Race, Gender, and Sentimentality in Nineteenth-Century America*. New York: Oxford University Press, 1992.

Sánchez-Eppler, Karen. *Dependent States: The Child's Part in Nineteenth-Century American Culture*. Chicago: University of Chicago Press, 2005.

———. *Touching Liberty: Abolition, Feminism, and the Politics of the Body*. Berkeley: University of California Press, 1993.

Savage, W. Sherman. *The Controversy over the Distribution of Abolitionist Literature, 1830–1860*. 1938. Reprint, New York: Negro Universities Press, 1968.

Schroer, Sandra Ellen. *State of the "Union": Marriage and Free Love in the Late 1800s*. New York: Routledge, 2005.

Scott, Anne Firor. *The Southern Lady: From Pedestal to Politics, 1830–1930*. Chicago: University of Chicago Press, 1970.

Scott, Joan W., and Debra Keates, eds. *Going Public: Feminism and the Shifting Boundaries of the Private Sphere*. Urbana: University of Illinois Press, 2004.

Shields, Stephanie A. *Speaking from the Heart: Gender and the Social Meaning of Emotion*. New York: Cambridge University Press, 2002.

Simon, Paul. *Freedom's Champion: Elijah Lovejoy*. Carbondale: Southern Illinois University Press, 1994.

Snay, Mitchell. *Gospel of Disunion: Religion and Separatism in the Antebellum South*. New York: Cambridge University Press, 1993.

Spruill, Marjorie Julian, ed. *One Woman, One Vote: Rediscovering the Woman Suffrage Movement*. Troutdale, Oregon: NewSage Press, 1995.

Stansell, Christine. *City of Women: Sex and Class in New York, 1789–1860*. New York: Knopf, 1986.

Stewart, James Brewer. *Holy Warriors: The Abolitionists and American Slavery*. New York: Hill & Wang, 1976.

———, ed. *William Lloyd Garrison at Two Hundred: History, Legacy, and Memory*. New Haven: Yale University Press, 2008.

Sussman, Charlotte. *Consuming Anxieties: Consumer Protest, Gender, and British Slavery, 1713–1833*. Palo Alto, California: Stanford University Press, 2000.

Taylor, Clare. *Women of the Anti-Slavery Movement: The Weston Sisters*. New York: St. Martin's, 1995.

Van Broekhaven, Deborah Bingham. *The Devotion of These Women: Rhode Island in the Antislavery Network*. Amherst: University of Massachusetts Press, 2002.

Varon, Elizabeth. *We Mean to Be Counted: White Women and Politics in Antebellum Virginia*. Chapel Hill: University of North Carolina Press, 1998.

Waters, Kristin, and Carol B. Conaway, eds. *Black Women's Intellectual Traditions: Speaking Their Minds*. Burlington: University of Vermont Press, 2007.

Wellman, Judith. *The Road to Seneca Falls: Elizabeth Cady Stanton and the First Women's Rights Convention*. Chicago: University of Illinois Press, 2004.

Wheeler, Leigh Ann. *Against Obscenity: Reform and the Politics of Womanhood in America, 1873-1935.* Baltimore: Johns Hopkins University Press, 2004.
White, Deborah Gray. *Ar'n't I a Woman? Female Slaves in the Plantation South.* New York: Norton, 1999.
Winch, Julie. *A Gentleman of Color: The Life of James Forten.* New York: Oxford University Press, 2002.
Wood, Marcus. *Blind Memory: Visual Representations of Slavery in England and America.* New York: Routledge, 1999.
Wright, Daniel S. *"The First Causes of Our Sex": The Female Moral Reform Movement in the Antebellum Northeast, 1834-1848.* New York: Routledge, 2006.
Wyatt-Brown, Bertram. *Honor and Violence in the Old South.* New York: Oxford University Press, 1986.
Yellin, Jean Fagan. *Women and Sisters: The Antislavery Feminists in American Culture.* New Haven: Yale University Press, 1989.
Yellin, Jean Fagan, and John C. Van Horne, eds. *The Abolitionist Sisterhood: Women's Political Culture in Antebellum America.* Ithaca, New York: Cornell University Press, 1994.
Young, Elizabeth. *Disarming the Nation: Women's Writing and the American Civil War.* Chicago: University of Chicago Press, 1999.
Zaeske, Susan. *Signatures of Citizenship: Petitioning, Antislavery, and Women's Political Identity.* Chapel Hill: University of North Carolina, 2003.
Zboray, Ronald. *A Fictive People: Antebellum Economic Development and the American Reading Public.* New York: Oxford University Press, 1993.

JOURNAL ARTICLES

Ammons, Elizabeth. "Heroines in *Uncle Tom's Cabin.*" *American Literature* 49 (May 1977): 161-79.
Bentley, Nancy. "White Slaves: The Mulatto Hero in Antebellum Fiction." *American Literature* 65 (September 1993): 501-22.
Boylan, Anne M. "Women and Politics in the Era Before Seneca Falls." *Journal of the Early Republic* 10 (Autumn 1990): 363-82.
Brown, Ira W. "Cradle of Feminism: The Philadelphia Female Anti-Slavery Society, 1833-1840." *Pennsylvania Magazine of History and Biography* 102 (April 1978): 143-66.
Chafetz, Janet Saltzman, and Anthony Gary Dworkin, "In the Face of a Threat: Organized Antifeminism in Comparative Perspective." *Gender and Society* 1 (March 1987): 33-60.
Connerley, Jennifer L. "Quaker Bonnets and the Erotic Feminine in American Popular Culture." *Material Religion: The Journal of Objects, Art, and Belief* 2, no. 2 (2006): 174-203.
Cott, Nancy F. "Passionlessness: An Interpretation of Victorian Sexual Ideology, 1790-1850." *Signs* 4 (Winter 1978): 219-36.
Daut, Marlene L. "'Sons of White Fathers': Mulatto Vengeance and the Haitian Revolution in Victor Séjour's 'The Mulatto.'" *Nineteenth-Century Literature* 65 (June 2010): 1-37.

Emerson, Amanda. "History, Memory, and the Echoes of Equivalence in Catharine Maria Sedgwick's *Hope Leslie*." *Legacy* 24, no. 1 (2007): 24-46.

Faulkner, Carol. "The Root of the Evil: Free Produce and Radical Antislavery, 1820-1860." *Journal of the Early Republic* 27 (Fall 2007): 377-405.

Frick, John. "*Uncle Tom's Cabin* in the Antebellum Stage." *Uncle Tom's Cabin and American Culture.* 2007. http://utc.iath.virginia.edu/interpret/exhibits/frick/frick.html.

Gorn, Elliott. "'Gouge and Bite, Pull Hair and Scratch': The Social Significance of Fighting in the Southern Backcountry." *American Historical Review* 90 (February 1985): 18-43.

Hogan, Lisa Shawn. "A Time for Silence: William Lloyd Garrison and the 'Woman Question' at the 1840 World Anti-Slavery Convention." *Gender Issues* 25, no. 2 (2008): 63-79.

Kerber, Linda K. "Separate Spheres, Female Worlds, Woman's Place: The Rhetoric of Women's History." *Journal of American History* 75 (June 1988): 9-39.

Lasser, Carol. "Beyond Separate Spheres: The Power of Public Opinion." *Journal of the Early Republic* 21 (Spring 2001): 115-23.

Liedel, Donald E. "The Puffing of *Ida May*: Publishers Exploit the Antislavery Novel." *Journal of Popular Culture* 3, no. 2 (1969): 287-306.

Marshall, Susan E. "Ladies against Women: Mobilization Dilemmas of Antifeminist Movements." *Social Problems* 32 (April 1985): 348-62.

Miller, Quentin. "'A Tyrannical Democratic Force': The Symbolic and Cultural Function of Clothing Symbolism in Catharine Maria Sedgwick's *Hope Leslie*." *Legacy* 19, no. 2 (2002): 121-36.

Pierce, David. "'Carl Laemmle's Outstanding Achievement': Harry Pollard and the Struggle to Film *Uncle Tom's Cabin*." *Film History* 10, no. 4 (1998): 459-76.

Quist, John W. "'The Great Majority of Our Subscribers are Farmers': The Michigan Abolitionist Constituency of the 1840s." *Journal of the Early Republic* 14 (Autumn 1994): 325-58.

Rabinovitch, Eyal. "Gender and the Public Sphere: Alternative Forms of Integration in Nineteenth-Century America." *Sociological Theory* 19 (November 2001): 344-70.

Reinarmer, Craig. "The Social Construction of an Alcohol Problem: The Case of Mothers Against Drunk Driving and Social Control in the 1980s." *Theory and Society* 17 (January 1985): 91-120.

Rodríguez, Cristina M. "Clearing the Smoke-Filled Room: Women Jurors and the Disruption of an Old Boys' Network in Nineteenth-Century America." *Yale Law Journal* 108 (May 1999): 1805-44.

Roth, Sarah N. "The Mind of a Child: Images of African Americans in Early Juvenile Fiction." *Journal of the Early Republic* 25 (Spring 2005): 79-109.

Simms, Henry H. "A Critical Analysis of Abolition Literature, 1830-1840." *Journal of Southern History* 6 (August 1940): 368-82.

Sorisio, Carolyn. "The Spectacle of the Body: Torture in the Antislavery Writing of Lydia Maria Child and Frances E. Watkins Harper." *Modern Language Studies* 30 (Spring 2000): 45-66.

Swerdlow, Amy. "Ladies' Day at the Capitol: Women Strike for Peace versus HUAC." *Feminist Studies* 8 (Autumn 1982): 493-520.
Welter, Barbara. "The Cult of True Womanhood, 1820-1860." *American Quarterly* 18 (Summer 1966): 151-74.

DISSERTATION

Liedel, Donald E. "The Antislavery Novel, 1838-1861." PhD diss., University of Michigan, 1961.

Index

abolitionist fiction and literature. *See* antislavery fiction; antislavery literature
abolitionist movement: 1840s developments in, 76-77; debates on women's roles in, 15, 42, 86-87; dying in service of, 133-35; setbacks in, 120-21, 139; studies on early, 18-19; studies on feminism and, 43; studies on women in, 7-8; women at heart of, 12. *See also* antislavery activism; enslaved women: resistance to slavery; resistance to slavery, violent
"Address to the Daughters of New England, An" ("A.F.M."), 53
African American female authors: 1850s publications by, 117-18; on civil rights, 69-72; on colonization, 61-62, 71-73; decline in publications of, 84-85, 117; on free African Americans' involvement in abolitionism, 61-62, 73-74; literary societies of, 10, 51-53; missing perspectives of, 118-19; white women's works *vs.* works of, 13-14, 45-46; William Lloyd Garrison's promotion of, 52-53; writing under pseudonyms, 50-51
African Americans: colonization movement and, 19-20; involvement of free women in abolitionism, 61-62, 73-74; voting rights of, 149-50. *See also* African American female authors; enslaved men; enslaved women
Aliened American, 117
American Anti-Slavery Society (AASS), 47, 82, 86
American Colonization Society, 19-20
American and Foreign Anti-Slavery Society (AFASS), 86
"Amy, A True Tale" (Dall), 89, 110
Anglo-African Magazine, 86, 118
"Annie Gray" (Dall), 88, 89, 94
antislavery activism: enslaved women's *vs.* white women's, 35-39; feminine respectability of, 13; free produce movement and, 26-28; gentility and, 13, 25; studies on white women's, 6; of white women, 24-31. *See also* enslaved women: resistance to slavery; resistance to slavery, violent
antislavery fiction: differences between African Americans' and white women's, 13-14, 45-46; dissemination of, in South, 46-47; increased number of venues for, 47; juvenile, 4, 42, 47, 49-50, 84; subversive potential of, 2-3
antislavery literature: 1840s expansion of, 76; efforts to popularize, 79-81; gift book as, 10, 81-82, 85 (see also

antislavery literature (cont.) *Liberty Bell; Liberty Chimes*); limited audience of, 9; loss of African American perspectives in, 118-19; motivation for women writing in 1850s, 117; studies on, 3-4; studies on circulation of, 9-10; *Uncle Tom's Cabin*'s influence on rise of, 116

antislavery movement. *See* abolitionist movement

Appeal in Favor of That Class of Americans Called Africans, An (Child), 34

Appeal to the Coloured Citizens of the World (Walker), 10, 25, 46-47, 71

Aunt Leanna (Roe), 140

"Aunt Margery," 60, 63

"Aunt Margery's Evenings with the Young Folks" ("Aunt Margery"), 60

authors, female. *See* African American female authors; white female authors

authorship, studies on, 5

Autobiography of a Female Slave (Griffith), 141, 143

Bailey, Gamaliel, 81

Bera ("Dialogues" series), 73-74

Bigelow, Harriet Hamline, 119, 136, 147

black female authors. *See* African American female authors

"Black Man's Lament, the; or, How to Make Sugar" (Opie), 26

"Black Saxons, The" (Child), 97, 98-99

Boston Female Anti-Slavery Society (BFASS), 11, 82, 83

boycotts of slave-produced goods, 26-28

boys, 59-62, 64-65

British antislavery boycotts, 26

Browning, Elizabeth Barrett, 82

Buchanan, James, 139

Burns, Anthony, 121

Butts, Harriet Newell, 119, 142

Catholic immigrants, 129

Chandler, Elizabeth Margaret, 11, 12-13, 17, 21, 48-49, 50, 80; antislavery activism and gentility, 25; Benjamin Lundy on emotional appeals of, 22-23; career of, 19; "Edward and Mary," 60; *Genius of Universal Emancipation*'s Ladies' Department and, 18; emotion as positive change agent, 31; empathy's transformative impact, 29; enslaved women in fiction of, 30, 31; free produce movement and, 26, 27-28; "The Harmans," 29; "Letters on Slavery, to Isabel," 29; on suitability of fiction for abolitionist cause, 22, 24; "Tears of Woman," 17, 18, 29-30; "Tea-Table Talk," 27-28; white women's activism in fiction of, 24-31

Chapman, Maria Weston, 79, 81; editorship of *Liberty Bell*, 82-84; *Pinda*, 82, 93-94, 94-95

Chestnut, Mary, 106

Child, Lydia Maria, 3, 11, 50, 79, 117, 119, 145; "The Black Saxons," 97, 98-99; editorship of the *National Anti-Slavery Standard*, 80-81; "The Kansas Emigrants," 138-39, 142, 143, 144; maternal feelings of enslaved women, 88; "The Quadroons," 88-89, 90, 92, 93, 110; sexual violence against enslaved women, 88-89; "Slavery's Pleasant Homes," 89, 93, 98, 107-8; writing career of, 33-34

children: fiction for spreading abolitionism to, 55-56; literature for, 4, 42, 47, 49-50, 84; raising abolitionist, 42-43, 101-2

Child's Friend, 79-80

Christianity, evangelical, 129

civil rights, African American female authors on, 69-74

"Coffle Yoke, The," 67-68

colonizationist movement, 19-20, 71-73

Colored American, 85

"Colored Female, A" (pseudonym), 71-72

consumerism, negative attitudes toward frivolous, 28

Corning, W. H., 119, 136

"Courage and Truth of Jesus, The" (Follen), 75-76

cultural feminists, 151

Curse Entailed, The (Bigelow), 136, 147

Dall, Caroline W. Healey, 11, 79, 89, 117, 119; "Amy, A True Tale," 89, 110; "Annie Gray," 88, 89, 94

daughters, 62-69
death, in service of abolitionism, 133-35, 138-39
Democratic Party, 140
"Dialogue" (Follen), 100, 102
"Dialogue between a Mother and Her Children, A" (Douglass), 61, 64-65
"Dialogue on Slavery, A," 56-58
"Dialogues" series (Bera), 73-74
difference feminism/gender essentialism, 3, 6, 44, 151-53
Douglass, Frederick, 85, 97
Douglass, Sarah Mapps ("Zillah"), 51; "A Dialogue between a Mother and Her Children," 61; "A Mother's Love," 58-59; "A True Tale for Children," 70; "For the Children Who Read the *Liberator*," 70; "To a Friend," 70-71; on U.S. as rightful home, 72-73; William Lloyd Garrison on, 53
Dred: A Tale of the Great Dismal Swamp (Stowe), 124-25, 139
Dred Scott v. Sanford, 139

"Edward and Mary" (Chandler), 60, 64-65
"Eliza Harris" (Harper), 117-18
Emerson, Ralph Waldo, 82
emotion: appeal to, 22-23; fiction as means of connecting with, 13; as positive agent of change, 31, 55
empathy, 28-29
enfranchisement. *See* voting rights
enslaved men: in Catharine Maria Sedgwick's fiction, 31-33; violent resistance of, 96-101
enslaved women: attitudes of white Southern women toward, 106; blame for sexual violence against, 108; in Catharine Maria Sedgwick's fiction, 31-32, 33, 34-39; Christlike, 92-93; commonalities and differences between white women and, 30; dependence on whites for freedom, 93-95; early 1800s visions of, 12; emphasis on victimization of, 87; ideals of sexual respectability of, 90-91; maternal feelings of, 87-88; moral guidance by white women, 12, 38; passivity of, 24-25, 30, 87, 92, 94; resistance to slavery, 95-96, 120-25; resistance to slavery, violent, 38-39, 59, 122-24; sexualized assessment of, 90; sexual violence against, 87, 88-89, 91-92, 136-37; studies on representations of, 78; white female authors' depictions, overview, 14-15, 15-16; white women's activism *vs.* activism of, 35-39
"Evening at Home, An" ("Zelmire"), 55, 65

"Family Circle" stories ("U.I.E."), 65-67
"Family Colloquy" ("Y.N."), 60, 63
female authors. *See* African American female authors; white female authors
feminine difference/gender essentialism, 3, 6, 44, 151-53
femininity, ideals of: antislavery activism and, 13, 25; free produce movement and, 28; Southern, 107
feminism: second-wave, 151; studies on abolitionism and, 43
fiction: anxiety over moral dangers of, 21; as feminized medium, 8-9, 12, 150-51; as means of spreading abolitionism, 2, 10-11, 22-24, 113; for spreading abolitionism to children, 55-56; studies on women's, 3-5; Theodore Parker on women's reform-oriented, 1-2; value of, for abolitionist cause, 21, 22, 55. *See also* antislavery fiction
Follen, Eliza Lee, 11, 20, 47, 50, 84; "The Courage and Truth of Jesus," 75-76; "Dialogue," 100, 102; distrust of politics, 102-3; "Reformatory," 103-4
Forten, James, 48
Forten, Sarah, 50-51
"For the Children Who Read the *Liberator*" (Douglass), 70
Frederick Douglass' Paper, 85, 117
Freedom's Journal, 9-10, 20, 85
Freeman, Elizabeth, 31-32, 35
free produce movement, 26-28
Free Soil Party, 76, 103, 115, 140
Frémont, John C., 140
Fugitive Slave Law, 120-21

Garner, Margaret, 118, 122
Garrison, William Lloyd, 11, 13, 33, 48, 51, 86; attack on, 47; controversy stirred up by, 41-42; on Lydia Maria Child's editorship of the *National Anti-Slavery Standard*, 80-81; problematic presentation of African American writings by, 53-54; promotion of African American female authors by, 52-53. See also *Liberator*
gender, social construction of, 151
gender essentialism/feminine difference, 3, 6, 44, 151-53
Genius of Universal Emancipation, 13, 17, 22, 29; Ladies' Department of, 18, 19, 22, 25, 48
gentility. See femininity, ideals of
gift book, 10, 81-82, 85. See also *Liberty Bell; Liberty Chimes*
girls, 62-69
Gould, Hannah F., 47, 50; "The Prisoners Set Free," 60
Green, Frances H., 79; *Shahmah in Pursuit of Freedom*, 142; "The Slave Wife," 89, 91-92, 93
Griffith, Mattie, 145; *Autobiography of a Female Slave*, 141, 143; *Madge Vertner*, 139, 144
Grimké, Angelina, 42, 44, 128
Grimké, Sarah, 42, 44, 128

Hanaford, Phebe Ann Coffin, 119; *Lucretia, a Quakeress*, 126, 131-32
Harlan, Mary, 119
"Harmans, The" (Chandler), 29
Harper, Frances E. Watkins, 86, 150; "Eliza Harris," 117-18; "The Two Offers," 86, 118
Hawthorne, Nathaniel, 83
Heyrick, Elizabeth, 26, 27
History of Mary Prince, The (Prince), 27
Hobomok (Child), 33, 34
Hope Leslie (Sedgwick), 18, 34, 50
Hugo, Victor, 82
husbands. See white men

Ida May (Pike), 122, 123-24
imagination, 8, 22, 55

Immediate, Not Gradual Abolition (Heyrick), 26
"Interesting Anecdote," 64
Irving, Mary, 119; "Mirth and Melancholy," 124, 143

Jacobs, Harriet, 108
Johnson, Oliver, 81
Jones, Jane Elizabeth, 79; distrust of politics, 102-3; "The Young Abolitionists," 100, 101-2
juvenile antislavery literature, 4, 42; in 1840s, 84; beginnings of, 47; as socially acceptable venue, 49-50
Juvenile Anti-Slavery Society of Boston, 11
juvenile departments, 49, 63-64, 84-85
Juvenile Miscellany, 34, 47

"Kansas Emigrants, The" (Child), 138-39, 142, 143, 144
Kelley, Abby, 86

ladies' departments, 18, 48-49, 84-85; of *Genius of Universal Emancipation*, 18, 19, 22, 25, 48
"Lady in Worcester County," 55
Leslie, Eliza, 79, 80; "The Traveling Tinman," 95-96
"Letters on Slavery, to Isabel" (Chandler), 29
Liberator, 13, 33, 81, 117; founding and early years of, 47-48; Juvenile Department of, 63-64, 84-85; Ladies' Department of, 48-49, 84-85. See also Garrison, William Lloyd
Liberty Bell, 79-80, 82-84, 85
Liberty Cap, 79
Liberty Chimes, 79, 82
Liberty or Death (M'Keehan), 140-41
Liberty Party, 76, 103, 140
literary societies, female: African American, 10, 51-53; exchange of views in, 72
literature, antislavery. See antislavery fiction; antislavery literature
Little, Sophia, 119; *Thrice through the Furnace*, 126-27, 131
Livermore, Elizabeth D., 119, 142, 143
Logan Female Anti-Slavery Society, 19

Longfellow, Henry Wadsworth, 82
love: maternal, 58-59, 87-88; romantic, 127-28
Lovejoy, Elijah, 47, 118
Lucretia, a Quakeress (Hanaford), 126, 131-32
Lundy, Benjamin, 11, 19, 20, 48; on Elizabeth Margaret Chandler and fiction's appeal, 21, 22-23, 24

Madge Vertner (Griffith), 139, 144
"Magawisca," 50
magazines. *See* periodicals
Mark Sutherland (Southworth), 133, 134
marriage: implicit criticism of, 109-10; interracial, 71; moral suasion and companionate, 127-28; powerlessness of women in, 78
married women's property rights, 109
Martineau, Harriet, 82
Massachusetts Anti-Slavery Society, 82
Massachusetts Female Emancipation Society gift book, 82
maternal love, 58-59, 87-88. *See also* motherhood, republican; mothers, abolitionist
men. *See* African Americans; white men
Mexican-American War, 76, 100, 103
"Mirth and Melancholy" (Irving), 124, 143
M'Keehan, Hattia, 119, 140-41
moral suasion, 77, 79, 149; in *Dred*, 124-25; failure of, 136-37; in "Mirth and Melancholy," 124; romantic love and, 127-28; shift to political activism from, 14, 76, 114-15, 125-26, 135-36; white Southern women and, 105-12; white women and, 101-5
Mormons, 129
motherhood, republican, 61-62. *See also* maternal love
Mother-in-Law, The (Southworth), 90, 92, 108, 110, 111
mothers, abolitionist, 56-59; education of children over husbands' objections, 101-2; mothers raising daughters, 62-69; mothers raising sons, 59-62, 64-65

Mothers Against Drunk Driving, 152
"Mother's Love, A" (Douglass), 58-59
Mott, Lucretia, 44, 128, 144
Mrs. Hadden, 136
"mulatta, tragic," 78

Narrative of the Life of Frederick Douglass (Douglass), 97
National Anti-Slavery Standard, 79, 80, 82, 85, 105; Lydia Maria Child's editorship of, 80-81; on *Uncle Tom's Cabin*, 116
National Era, 79-80, 81, 85, 105, 115; on antislavery literature, 116
Newsom, Celia, 122
Newsom, Robert, 122
newspapers, African American, 85-86; *Freedom's Journal*, 9-10, 20, 85. *See also* periodicals
North Star, 85
"N.S.," 68

Oasis, The (Child), 47
Oneida Community, 129
Opie, Amelia, 26, 27
Our Nig (Wilson), 117

pacifism, 97
Parker, Theodore, 1-2
passionlessness, 127
"Paulina," 55
Pease, Elizabeth, 80
pen names, women writing under, 50-51
periodicals: 1830s fiction in, 54-56; 1840s rise of, 76; African American-edited, 85-86; decline of African American works in, 85; efforts to popularize, 79-81
persuasion. *See* moral suasion
petitioning, 44
Philanthropist, 47
Phillips, Wendell, 116
Pierce, Franklin, 139
Pike, Mary Hayden Green, 119; *Ida May*, 122, 123-24
Pinda: A True Tale (Chapman), 82, 93-94, 94-95
Poems on Miscellaneous Subjects (Harper), 117
political parties, antislavery, 76

politics: corruption in men *vs.* women, 143; female engagement in, 15, 23, 44-45, 145-46; impetus for engaging in, 139-40; male engagement in, 140-42; shift from moral suasion to, 14, 76, 114-15, 125-26, 135-36; women's suffrage, 119-20, 143-44, 145
Prince, Mary, 26-27
print culture, 1830s, 42, 46-50
"Prisoners Set Free, The" (Gould), 60
Prosser, Gabriel, 32
Protestants, 129, 130
"Public Function of Woman, The" (Parker), 1-2
public *vs.* private spheres, 6-7, 148-49

"Quadroons, The" (Child), 88-89, 90, 92, 93, 110
Quaker women, 128-33

racial prejudice, African American writers on, 69-74, 117
Ralph; or, I Wish He Wasn't Black (Butts), 142
rebellions, slave. *See* slave rebellions
Redwood (Sedgwick), 18, 20, 32-33
"Reformatory" (Follen), 103-4
religious movements, 126. *See also* Quaker women
republican motherhood, 61-62
Republican Party, 115, 140-41, 145
resistance to slavery, violent: 1840s receptiveness to, 96-97; abolitionists' views on, 77; by enslaved men, 96-101; by enslaved women, 38-39, 59, 122-24; masculinity and, 78, 97; studies on, 77-78; white women's perspectives on, 77, 78
Retribution (Southworth), 108
Right and Wrong in Massachusetts (Chapman), 82
Roe, Elizabeth, 140
romantic love, 127-28
Russwurm, John, 20

Scott, Dred, 121
Scott, Harriet, 121
Second Great Awakening, 129
Sedgwick, Catharine Maria, 11, 17, 18; antislavery appeals of enslaved women *vs.* white women, 36-37; Elizabeth Freeman and, 31-32; enslaved males in fiction of, 32-33; enslaved women and violent resistance, 38-39; enslaved women and white women in fiction of, 31-39; enslaved women's *vs.* white women's activism, 35-39; futility of enslaved women's antislavery appeals, 37-38; initial reluctance to embrace abolitionism, 20; *Redwood*, 18, 20, 32; unpublished novel by, 33, 34-39; on value of fiction for abolitionism, 21
Sedgwick, Henry, 20
Sedgwick, Theodore, 35
Seneca Falls Convention, 105, 144
sentimentalism, 23. *See also* emotion; empathy
sexuality: efforts to legislate male, 137-38; and ideals of respectability of enslaved women, 90-91; of male slaveholders, corrupted, 110, 136-37; moral suasion and white female passionlessness, 126-27
sexual violence: against enslaved women, 87, 88-89, 91-92; inability of white women to stop, 136-37
Shahmah in Pursuit of Freedom (Green), 142
Shakers, 129
slaveholders, sexual corruption of male, 110, 136-37
slave rebellions: anxieties about, 32; led by Nat Turner, 10, 33, 46, 97-98
slavery, failure of legal challenges to, 120-21
"Slavery's Pleasant Homes" (Child), 89, 93, 98, 107-8
slaves. *See* enslaved men; enslaved women
Slave's Friend, The, 47
"Slave Wife, The" (Green), 89, 91-92, 93
sons, 59-62, 64-65
"Sophonisba," 51
Southworth, E. D. E. N., 79; Christlike enslaved women, 92; *Mark Sutherland,* 133, 134; *The Mother-in-Law,* 90, 92, 108, 110, 111; *Retribution,* 108-9
Stanton, Elizabeth Cady, 150
Star of Emancipation, 82

Stewart, Maria W., 42, 62
Stowe, Harriet Beecher, 3, 119; *Dred,* 124-25, 139. See also *Uncle Tom's Cabin* (Stowe)
suffrage. *See* voting rights
sugar boycott, 26-27

"Talk by the Fireside" ("N.S."), 68
"Tears of Woman: An Allegory" (Chandler), 17, 18, 29-30
"Tea-Table Talk" (Chandler), 27-28
Thomas, Ella Gertrude Clanton, 106
Thrice through the Furnace (Little), 126-27, 131
"To a Friend" (Douglass), 70-71
Tocqueville, Alexis de, 82
tracts, antislavery, 46
"tragic mulatta," 78
"Traveling Tinman, The," 95-96
"True Tale for Children, A" (Douglass), 70
Truth, Sojourner, 150
Turner, Nat, 10, 32, 33, 46, 97-98
"Two Offers, The" (Harper), 86, 118

"U.I.E.," 65-67
Uncle Tom's Cabin (Stowe), 9, 15, 113-14, 123, 125, 145; death in service of abolitionism, 133, 134; Quaker women, 130-31; success and influence, 115-17; violent resistance of slaves, 122-23
"Unnatural Distinction" ("Zelmire"), 54
utopian movements, 126

Vesey, Denmark, 25, 32
violence, sexual. *See* sexual violence
voting, as antislavery action, 140-41
voting rights: debate over women's *vs.* African Americans', 149-50; women's, 119-20, 143-44, 145

Walker, David, 10, 25, 46, 71
Western Border Life (Corning), 136
Weston, Anne Warren, 46
"What Have the Ladies to Do with Anti-Slavery?," 55
white female authors: African American authors' works *vs.* works of, 13-14; depictions of enslaved women, overview, 14-15, 15-16; enslaved women's resistance and, 120-25; female suffrage and, 119-20; regions of, 119; studies on authorship and, 5
white men: efforts to legislate sexuality of, 137-38; engagement in politics by, 102-4, 140-42; as impediments to abolition, 101; sexual corruption of slaveholding, 110, 136-37; as upholders of slavery, 102-3
white women: attitudes toward enslaved women by Southern, 106; commonalities and differences between enslaved women and, 30; criticism of reformers, 25; dying in service of abolitionism, 133-35, 138-39; enslaved women's activism *vs.* activism of, 35-39; feminine ideal of Southern, 107; involvement in abolitionism, 12; moral power of sexual virtue of, 126-27; moral steadfastness of, 142-43; moral suasion and, 101-5; moral suasion and Southern, 105-12; moral suasion through romantic love, 127-28; politically corrupt men *vs.*, 143; Quakers, 128-33; Southern, as potential abolitionists, 106-7; Southern, inability to free slaves, 109-10; Southern, ineffectual as abolitionists, 111-12; Southern, sympathy for slaves, 107-8; Southern single, 108-9; studies on activism of, 6; tears of, as force for antislavery change, 29-30; on violent abolitionism, 77, 78
Wilson, Harriet, 117
woman question, 42, 86-87
Woman's Faith, 136
women: African American women in antislavery movement, 61-62, 73-74; antislavery fiction to reach, 11, 22; appeal to middle-class, 56-58; politics and, 15, 23, 44-45, 145-46; property rights of married, 109; republican motherhood, 61-62. *See also* African American female authors; enslaved women; mothers, abolitionist; white female authors
women's rights: 1840s debates on, 105; antislavery activism and, 44-45; to property, 109; suffrage, 119-20, 143-44, 145

Women Strike for Peace, 152
"Woodby" (pseudonym), 72–73
writers, female. *See* African American female authors; white female authors

"Y.N.," 60, 63
"Young Abolitionists, The" (Jones), 100, 101–2

"Zelmire," 51, 54, 55
"Zillah." *See* Douglass, Sarah Mapps ("Zillah")
Zoë (Livermore), 142, 143